LISTENING TO THE SPIRITS

ALSO BY NICHOLAS E. BRINK, PH.D.

Grendel and His Mother
The Power of Ecstatic Trance
Baldr's Magic
Beowulf's Ecstatic Trance Magic
Trance Journeys of the Hunter-Gatherers
Ecstatic Soul Retrieval
Applying the Constructivist Approach to Cognitive Therapy
Loki's Children

Listening to the Spirits

SURVIVING THE COMING APOCALYPSE
WITH ECSTATIC TRANCE

Nicholas E. Brink, Ph.D.

Foreword by Barbara Hand Clow

Red Elixir
Rhinebeck, New York

Listening to the Spirits: Surviving the Coming Apocalypse with Ecstatic Trance
© 2022 by Nicholas E. Brink, Ph.D.

All rights reserved. No part of this book may be used or reproduced in any manner without the consent of the publisher except in critical articles or reviews. Contact the publisher for information.

Paperback ISBN 978-1-954744-57-8
eBook ISBN 978-1-954744-58-5

Library of Congress Control Number: 2022932870

Book and cover design by Colin Rolfe

Red Elixir is an imprint of Monkfish Book Publishing Company

Red Elixir
22 East Market Street, Suite 304
Rhinebeck, NY 12572
(845) 876-4861
monkfishpublishing.com

Contents

Acknowledgments	vii
Foreword by Barbara Hand Clow	ix
1. The Spirits	1
2. Ecstatic Trance	19
3. Living in Peace with the Goddess: The Ynglings of Sweden	35
4. Bridging the Two Worlds: The Skjǫldung of Denmark	72
5. Learning the Ways of the Chumash Shaman of California	95
6. Learning the Way of the Huchiun Hunter of California	121
7. Venerating the De Danaan's Circle of Light, Ireland	146
8. Learning the Esopus Way of Oneness with the Earth, New York	171
9. Living in Oneness with the Sami Reindeer, Finland	196
10. Seeking Peace of the Community Garden Terraces, Peru	220
11. Learning the Power of Ecstatic Trance, New Mexico	246
12. Epilogue	266
Appendix: The Ecstatic Postures	269
Notes	277
Glossary	281
Bibliography	289

Acknowledgments

I would like to acknowledge the Cuyamungue Institute founded by Felicitas Goodman in 1978. The Institute, on the Pojoaque Pueblo north of Santa Fe, NM, continues to promote Dr. Goodman's research and findings in the use of ecstatic trance and the ecstatic postures, shamanic postures from antiquity that provide direction to the trance experiences. Dr. Goodman's procedure of ecstatic trance induction, known today as the Cuyamungue Method, focuses on the use of ancient sacred practices and postures of the hunting and gathering cultures that provide experiences of expanded reality. These ecstatic experiences provide healing, communing with ancestral spirits and the spirits of the Earth, and direction in what we need to do to survive into the New Age, as I have written about in my previous eight books, and now in *Listening to the Spirits*. Dr. Goodman's research and findings are described in her book, *Where the Spirits Ride the Wind*. I became a certified instructor of ecstatic trance with my training in the history and use of the Cuyamungue Method at the Cuyamungue Institute.

To learn more about Dr. Goodman's original work in ecstatic trance and her development and use of the Cuyamungue Method, visit the Cuyamungue Institute's website, www.cuyamungueinstitute.com. I offer two ecstatic trance workshops a week on Zoom, free of charge. If you are interested in experiencing the power of ecstatic trance, contact me at brinknick9@gmail.com and I will send you the Zoom link.

The Book Cover Image

The figure on the cover of the book is the Priestess of Malta, a 5,000-year-old figurine that was found in the Hypogeum on the Island of Malta. The Hypogeum is a series of underground limestone chambers believed to have been a temple to the Goddess. This figurine's posture, an ecstatic posture, leads us on spirit journeys, past and present, in the middle world, a posture frequently used in this book.

Foreword
BY BARBARA HAND CLOW

Nicholas Brink's investigation of hunter-gathering and horticultural cultures in *Listening to the Spirits* explores ways our ancestors lived sustainably on Earth for many thousands of years. Because our relationship with Earth is in a profound crisis, an ever-increasing number of people know we must return to balance and be in harmony with all forms of life. *Listening to the Spirits* offers a unique approach.

I am deeply aligned with Nick in our research and writings, so I felt honored when he asked me to write this foreword. We are both teachers of Ecstatic Trance for the Cuyamungue Institute, Santa Fe, New Mexico, and we are experienced time-travelers. I explored my own past lives during over 100 past-life regression sessions under hypnosis from 1982 through 1992, work that was published in a trilogy, *The Mind Chronicles*, which is very dear to me because it has linked me with Earth's beating heart. When I journeyed into the past, my consciousness was almost always centered at sacred sites, such as at Avebury, the Great Pyramid, Delphi, and Mayan temples. Some might say this perspective shows that I was imagining things I'd read about, but I don't think so because I recovered a full sense of entire cultures centered at sacred sites. I think we all have a personal story of a time that we detect when we travel to special places. Many have forgotten we once interacted with sacred sites using ritual and geomancy, which long ago connected us profoundly with Earth. Nick offers some great examples of finding these connections and resources.

Under hypnosis, I brought back experiences at sacred sites as far back as 30,000 years ago, and then later I traveled to these places with students to awaken and share these feelings with them. Nick goes to sacred sites and uses postures while in trance to access the wisdom they hold, knowledge that reverential humans have shared over many thousands of years. For me, *Listening to the Spirits,* is an exciting contribution to sacred sites research. Our ancestors believed their psychic and personal enrichment at these sites kept them in communication with our planet, places where they breathed with Earth. Our ancestors lived in harmony with Earth for thousands of years, so we think this approach is a way back to balance.

We truly are at a crisis point with our planetary ecology that challenges human intelligence and calls forth compassion. Nick admires a writer I also admire very much—Jean Gebser, the author of *The Ever-Present Origin.* Gebser names four stages of the mutation of human consciousness—Archaic, Magical, Mythical, and Rational—and then the fifth we are moving into now, *Time-Free Transparency,* a spherical form of consciousness that is holistic and embraces our ancient past and future potential by learning to live fully in the present moment. I resonate deeply with Gebser's ideas because I have been activating time-free transparency for many years with my past-life research and in *Catastrophobia* (2001), which became *Awakening the Planetary Mind* in 2011.

I've searched for ways people can tune into the long cycles of time and the planetary intelligence available at planetary sacred sites. In 1993, I studied Ecstatic Trance with Dr. Felicitas Goodman to find more ways to access archaic and magical consciousness, and then I incorporated trance work into my journeys with students at sacred sites around the world. I used the ecstatic postures in Egypt, Greece, Mexico, and England, and these few experiences were mind-bending for the students and me. This book encourages us to continue to enjoy trance work at sacred sites. I am especially intrigued by Nick's trances at New Grange in the Boyne Valley, Ireland, because I think this site holds much deeply secretive information about potent occult techniques that are triggered by the light of the winter solstice Sun and Venus rising, rites that may have been used to regenerate human genetics, another critical issue of our times.

Considering advanced research on sacred sites by Jean Richer, author of *Sacred Geography of the Ancient Greeks*, and John Michell and Christine Rhone, authors of *Twelve-Tribe Nations*, we can see that before the emergence of Christianity, our whole planet was mapped out in *sacred districts* where people celebrated seasonal and sexual rituals. Michell and Rhone globally explore landscapes divided into zodiacal wheels of twelve, and Richer maps the same wheels centered at Delos, Delphi, and Sardis. According to Michell and Rhone, within these astrological zones, celebrants enacted mystery plays to activate the qualities of the astrological signs. In those days, the landscape was *enchanted*—activated by specific sounds and chanting that helped celebrants remain in harmony with Earth throughout the year. I believe we can recover these ancient ways, the ways of being in relationship with all-that-is, but the question always is, how?

Nick notes that spirits outside of time inhabit sacred sites to guard and express their knowledge. I agree with him because I also contact them as *gatekeepers* when I go to a sacred site. They protect the rich records in these places, and I ask them if I may enter. I am psychic because I kept my consciousness open when I was a child by my Cherokee grandfather and Celtic grandmother, so I talk with them like a child, which makes them palpable. I've noticed some earnest students have difficulty feeling and hearing these spirits, so sometimes I transmitted messages from the spirits. Sometimes we could find spirits and other dimensions together when we were at sacred sites. Well, with sacred postures, *anybody* can open these doorways because the postures open other times and dimensions, a process that is thoroughly described in this wonderful and timely book.

Now that we have discovered the quantum with its mysterious principles of non-locality and ever-renewing probabilities, multidimensional skills are awakening in people even though they are very distracted by digitalization. Studying long cycles and sacred sites is very complex. However, using ecstatic trance is very simple and direct, the magical process for which it may strongly attract the younger generations once they get bored with social media and shopping. Anybody can go into a light trance, relax, and feel other worlds and dimensions. *Listening to the Spirits* is a great guide, so enjoy!

Barbara Hand Clow, author of *The Mayan Code; The Mind Chronicles: Awakening the Planetary Mind,* and a recent novel trilogy, *Revelations of the Ruby Crystal, Revelations of the Aquarian Age,* and *Revelations from the Source.*

CHAPTER 1
The Spirits

Introduction

I first began experimenting with ecstatic trance in 2006 and eventually became a certified instructor of ecstatic trance through the Cuyamungue Institute in New Mexico. I have since offered many workshops around the country, regular workshops in Central Pennsylvania, and then, upon moving, in the Hudson Valley of New York. I now offer two workshops a week on Zoom because of the pandemic. From the participants in these workshops, I have collected well over 3,000 ecstatic experiences, experiences that have led people to access the world of spirits, the spirits of past lives, of their ancestors, and spirits of the land. On my second trip to Sweden and Denmark in 2006, I began using ecstatic trance twice a day to commune with the spirits of the land, the spirits of where I was at the moment. Since this beginning, I have visited the spirits of Ireland, Finland, Estonia, Latvia, Germany, Peru, here at home in the Hudson Valley of New York, and in both the East Bay across from San Francisco and along the coast of Santa Barbara in California, as well as the spirits I met in the Kiva at the Cuyamungue Institute in New Mexico.

In calling upon the spirits of the land, I connect at a much deeper level with the land in which I am traveling, with the spirits of both its ancient and contemporary life and the features of the Earth. The spirits of these places become much more integrated within me, such that when I return home, I can easily revisit them, spirits that bring me new meaning to where I have been. At home, the ecstatic journeys to these places become more coherent, coming from the most spiritual places I visited. When traveling, we seldom spend more than a day in one location, but from home, I can repeatedly return to the special spiritual places I visited. In Pennsylvania, this ecstatic journeying took place on our sauna deck, in New York from the treehouse built by our son-in-law, in California from the Cesar Chavez Park in Berkeley or a cliff in Santa Barbara overlooking the Pacific, and in New Mexico, from the kiva at the Cuyamungue Institute. These experiences often draw me to read more about where I have been, which often gives me the language and names used in describing my experiences.

While calling upon the spirits, I am often full of questions, sometimes stated but often unstated, questions for which the spirits have given me answers. Some questions have dominated my life over the last few years, questions concerning the global climate catastrophe, and how we can survive the impending demise of our way of life, the impending doom of our species. I am not surprised that the spirits that come to me are those of the ancient hunting and gathering cultures of the lands I have visited, of those people who lived sustainably with the Earth for many thousand years before the development of agriculture and the domestication of animals. I have learned much from these hunter-gatherers. They lived a much more harmonious life in venerating their great nurturing and compassionate Earth Mother, the Earth Mother that provides everything needed to sustain a healthy life. The people of this earliest era often lived longer lives than those of the following era when humans began striving to control the Earth through agriculture and the domestication of animals. They lived in oneness with the Earth and all life on Earth. They did not feel superior to other life but saw other life as their ancestors from whom there was much to learn. In this

Garden of Eden, they showed reverence for all life, a life that sustained them in health. Only when we turned to believing we had dominion over the Earth in our greedy and destructive ways did we lose our place in this beautiful garden. We lost our way when we began taking from rather than giving to her. A world of giving is a world of nurturance and compassion. Visiting these spirits shows us what life was like and what it could be again if we would change our ways.

This connection with the hunter-gatherers is still available to us through ecstatic trance. There are many hunter-gatherers who live on Earth today on all continents, in Africa, South America, Asia, in Australia with their aborigines, in North America among the Indians and the Eskimo of the far north, and even in Europe with the Sami of Scandinavia. We still have available to us how they live, an enlightened way that protects our Mother Earth upon which we depend. After centuries of oppression, many of these people are now speaking up eloquently, telling us how important it is to protect the Earth to save civilization as we know it.

Visiting the more recent spirits, spirits of the Middle Ages, and spirits of the present day shows us where we went wrong. These spirits show us how people struggled to survive. Some people, the kings and chieftains of the time sought to control and have power over others, and to become dependent upon others for sustenance, thus making life much more difficult for those whose lives depended upon growing their own food and raising their own animals, tasks for which weather, illness, and other phenomena of life interfered. Before, when the people knew every nook and cranny of where they lived and knew where they needed to move each season of the year to find what they needed to survive, when they were truly part of nature, life was considerably easier. When people worked together in cooperation and gave their energy and what they hunted and gathered to the community, life was peaceful and nurturing. When we lost these ways, when we begin to believe that we could take better care of ourselves rather than depend upon all life around us, we found ourselves in a world of suffering and lived shorter lives.

I find myself repeatedly drawn by the spirits of nature, of where and how we can live this healthier way of life. When I visit some city, though the spirits still come to me, I feel they draw me out of the city and into the world of nature. In the city, I find them in a quiet park or garden or along the water's edge, such as a fountain or a river that runs through the city. It is difficult to find the spirits of the Earth in a city.

Before visiting the spirits I have met in my journeys on three continents, I will explain to you how you, too, can call upon the spirits, and, in fact, open yourself to the spirits that you experience each day. In our world of rationality, we have learned that the spirits are superstitious or not real when, in fact, the spirit world around us is full of life and things to learn. Opening ourselves to this other world beyond our five senses opens us to living a more complete and vibrant life.

Spirits and the Nature of Consciousness

The blessing I offer the readers is, *May the spirits of the Earth become alive to you as they were to your ancestors*. With this blessing, you may ask: What are these spirits? The spirits were and are ever-present, alive, and meaningful to those people who lived and continue to live the life of hunting and gathering in both ancient and current times.

Considering the writing of Jean Gebser,[1] we are currently moving into the fifth era of consciousness, the era of time-free transparency, the New Age. The first era was the era of the hunter and gatherer that began around 160,000 years ago, of a people who lived in a dream-state of consciousness. Sometime within these 160,000 years, the human consciousness mutated into what Gebser calls the magical age of consciousness, an age when people found ways of coping with life and the environment through the magic found in being one with the Earth. In the words of Christian DeQuincey, this was the "time when our ancestors moved with the animals and sang with the wild symphony of the natural world—the swoop of a hawk, the roar of a waterfall, the whisper of evening breezes, the kiss of moonlight. We lived *in* the world, responded to its *felt* and subtle messages, understood its deeper meanings. We not only communed with nature, we were in open communication with all its great variety of sounds and rhythms. In short, we understood and spoke the *language* of nature."[2]

During these first two eras, the spirits were very much alive, first within their dream state of life and then when they experienced the oneness of all life and all that is of the Earth. Humans did not see themselves as superior to other life. They saw other life as being their ancestors, and they were part of and continually learned from this life. They called upon the spirits of their ancestors to show them how to live, often calling upon their earliest ancestors of different species, the animals they lived with and knew well.

Then came what Gebser calls the mythic era, the era when answers to the questions of life were found in the mythic stories. This era began around 10,000 years ago, the beginning of recorded history, the beginning of the era of agriculture and domestication of animals. These stories, explaining the phenomena of life and the Earth, came from the dreams and trance experiences of these people. As they shared these dreams and experiences, stories also experienced by others of the time, the stories developed to a level of coherency of the creation and other mythic stories that we listen to even today. During these eras, spirits were very much alive, valued, and meaningful to the people of the time, spirits that came from their nighttime dreams and other trance states of consciousness.

Then came the fourth era of consciousness, the rational era, an era that considered anything not perceived through the five senses, the senses of sight, hearing, smell, taste, and touch, as superstitious and untrue. Those of the rational era gave a thumbs-down and rejected the experiences of dreams and other altered states of consciousness. We lost the magical power provided us in communing with the spirits. With this loss, we believed we were superior to all other life on Earth. We believed we had dominion over the Earth and could use it for our greedy profit without consideration for the rest of life on Earth. This loss has brought us to the edge of destroying our own species and much of the Earth. We sometimes talk of a sixth sense, a sense of intuition, intuition that is brought to us by the spirits, but that, too, is now ignored. Gebser believes that this rational era began approximately 2,500 years ago and peaked at about the time of Leonardo da Vinci, but it is now waning as we begin a journey of mutation into the era of time-free transparency.[3]

Gebser wrote his book, *The Ever-present Origin*[4], in 1949 and since then it has become increasingly clear that this journey into the new age of time-free transparency is happening. As classical physics crumbles in the face of modern physics, a state of the science that even Einstein[5] called *spooky*, things do not happen in the mechanical and linear ways of classical physics. New discoveries are rapidly developing. One such scientific development is the theory of nonlocal coherence, that with the splitting of the atomic particle, something that happens to one part of the split particle that exists in one particular location and time, the same thing instantaneously happens to the other portion of the particle that now exists at some distant location.

When a particle splits, a portion of the particle may sometimes go backward in time. This adds to and expands the meaning of the relativity of time. Such discoveries of which there have been many are indeed spooky and open the door to a new era of consciousness, the era of time-free transparency, the new age. In this new age, these beliefs and ideas are becoming more and more reputable. Other writers, including Sheldrake,[6] Laszlo,[7] and Braden,[8] propose an energy field called by such names as the morphic field, the akashic field, or the divine matrix, a concept parallel to the gravitational field or the electromagnetic field. Since the composition of living cells is of atoms and molecules with their individual electromagnetic fields, how can we discount Sheldrake's belief that the cell and organs composed of these atoms and molecules have their own field, a field that he has named the morphic field? Laszlo believes that this field that he calls the Akashic field contains all information of everything that has happened since the beginning of time, information that is available to us through a sixth sense, through dreams, and other altered states of consciousness. Laszlo proposes that the sensory receptor for this in-formation field is the cytoskeletal structure[9] of our brain that is composed of 10^{18} microtubules, the structure that gives our brain its shape. Just as seeing something takes paying attention to that something, and hearing something also takes paying attention, paying attention to what is coming to us through this cytoskeletal structure is best perceived by paying attention while in an altered state of consciousness. The altered state of consciousness suppresses what we consciously perceive through the other five senses, thus clearing our minds to attend to what comes to us through the cytoskeletal structure. It is through this mechanism that we can perceive and commune with the spirits of our past lives, our ancestors, and of the Earth.

Accessing These Spirits

The spirits come from beyond our five senses, from beyond what we experience through our senses of sight, sound, smell, taste, and touch, the senses that limit our rational consciousness. Most everyone experiences some of these spirits in our dreams while we sleep. There are those who would say that dreams are the random and meaningless firing of the neurons in our brains, but from my work with dreams, that belief is the farthest from the truth. As a psychologist, I have often said that dreams come from and represent what is in our unconscious mind, and they can lead us to experience life in a much fuller way. I am a member and have been on the board of the International Association for the Study of Dreams, and at our annual conferences, we examine ways to find greater meaning in our dreams. What we experience in our dreams is from beyond our five senses and from the spirit world. We may dream of someone we know, yet in the dream, that person differs from the person we know through our five senses. How we see the person has something important to say to us. We may dream of an animal, but the animal may take on human characteristics, or we may dream of a river. Walking down a path or flowing down a river opens us to the spirit of the river or the path and likely tells us something about how we experience the course of life.

I used to believe that the content of all dreams came from our unconscious mind and that the dream content points to some life conflict or the solution to some life conflict. But more recently I have recognized that the dream may come from someplace beyond us, beyond even our unconscious mind, from what I call the universal mind but what others have called the akashic field, the morphic field, the divine matrix, or the collective unconscious. Barbara Hand Clow in her book *The Pleiadian Agenda* calls it the Galactic Mind. Robert Waggoner, in his book on lucid dreaming, tells the story that while within a lucid dream he has asked of the dream, "What is behind the dream or where does the dream come from?" What he has received as an answer in the dream experience is seeing a blue light, a blue light that I see coming from the divine matrix or universal mind.[10]

Dreaming is an altered state of consciousness, but there are other altered states. Hypnotic and ecstatic trance are two other altered states important to me that bring us into communion with the spirits. Whereas a dream happens spontaneously at night, though something that happened during the day or some thought we carry with us as we fall asleep may trigger the dream, the altered states of consciousness of hypnosis and ecstatic trance occur in response to some ritual of induction that can give some direction to the trance experience, i.e. by asking questions while in trance or by taking a particular posture that nonverbally provides some direction to the experience. I will describe the nature of these ecstatic postures in the next chapter. The experiences that come from these two forms of trance are more readily recalled upon coming out of the trance state, but since the language of the experience is metaphoric, finding meaning in these trance experiences, as with dreams, may take some time, but many techniques are available to help interpret the meaning of these experiences.

These forms of trance are similar in that they bring us to communion with the spirits, but they are different in their energy and rituals for induction. The energy of the hypnotic trance is slow, quiet, and letting go of thoughts. The energy of ecstatic trance is stronger, more directed, and intentional. The induction of hypnotic trance is through words with a rate of speech to match a person's rate of breathing, while the induction of ecstatic trance is with rapid stimulation to the nervous system, stimulation from the rapid beating of a drum or shaking of a rattle at around 210 beats per minute. While in hypnotic trance, the heart rate slows down, and the body responds with relaxation, a response of the parasympathetic nervous system. In ecstatic trance, the sympathetic nervous system takes over with a rapid heartbeat and the flow of adrenalin. Yet, with the rapid heartbeat, a drop in blood pressure occurs, a parasympathetic response. This response to the rapid neural stimulation is similar to a near-death experience. Carlos Castaneda has written about the two ways of gaining access to the other world, i.e. dreaming and stalking.[11] I believe that dreaming is like hypnotic trance, of letting go, of relaxing and waiting to see what happens, while ecstatic trance is like stalking, i.e. directed with intent. Castaneda likens stalking to the way of a warrior.

Another altered state of consciousness that brings us into communion with the spirits are times of deep thought, lost in reading a book, watching a movie, or immersed in one's own imagination. These are common everyday trance experiences that can be equally valuable in communing with and learning from the spirits.

I need to mention three other altered states of consciousness that I have experienced and value that do not seem to bring me into communion with the spirits. First is transcendental meditation, where the goal of the experience is to go into an alpha state, a state of no thought or a blank mind. The other two are Zen meditation and tai chi, where I am in the moment, focusing on my abdomen rising and falling as I breathe or focusing on the flow of motion of my body as in tai chi. I believe that in these two states, I am primarily sensing what is happening through my kinesthetic sense, and I am not going beyond into the extrasensory world.

Whether with dreaming, hypnotic trance, or ecstatic trance, by paying attention to these altered states of consciousness, valuing these states, and appreciating the spirits that these states bring us, the spirits will again come alive and occasionally show themselves spontaneously as they did for our ancient ancestors, even when we have not gone intentionally into an altered state of consciousness.

Kinds of Spirits

Past Life Spirits

For some people, a very common spirit that comes to them in trance is a past life spirit. Barbara Hand Clow, in her book *Mind Chronicles*, experiences these spirits as spirits of her past lives. As a psychologist, I have had several clients in hypnotic trance go to a past life, trance experiences that are very significant and important to their present lives. I have had only one person in my ecstatic trance groups describe his ecstatic experience as of a past life:

"I went to a past life in Alaska, a treed area. I was ten or eleven and found myself alone. A group of fourteen people were hunting bears, and I was communicating with them from the other side of the hill. They found two brown bears, treed, and killed one of them. We used the bear for food and fat and hide to make things. At fourteen years of age, I was killed on a bear hunt. Lois was my mother. Joe was my brother. My father in Alaska was my father from my current lifetime. I died in 1849."

Lois, in his current lifetime, is his wife, and Joe is a close friend.

Past life experiences are quite in vogue in the New Age and offer us powerful spirit guides for personal growth and for gaining new spiritual insights, but more central to the hunting and gathering cultures is the veneration of ancestors and communing with and finding direction from these ancestors.

Ancestral Spirits

Communing with ancestral spirits has become a very common experience for me. My first ancestral experience came on January 17, 2010, while in an ecstatic trance:

I found myself in a much earlier time, probably around 5000 BC near what is currently Baden-Württemberg, Germany, likely one of my ancestral places of origin. I am in a thatched hall, long and narrow, that sits near the entrance of a cave. A man wearing a bearskin is with me, not the leader, but the second or third in command of the other men. He tells me that the group is preparing to go on a hunt in the morning. Some men are drawing pictures of animals in the dirt and drawing spears stuck in them. Others are carving, sharpening the ends of their spears. He then tells me that since I am from the future, I must have some wisdom or knowledge that would help in the hunt. I shake my head no, but he is insistent that I am to lead them in the morning's hunt. We sleep on the dirt floor around the fire, and in the morning I take the group in what feels to me like a random direction, though we come to several deer. I motion for the men, about a dozen of them, to spread out, and we herd the deer over a cliff. The men all seem overjoyed and appreciative, though I still feel as if I had done nothing of significance or had no special knowledge.

This first ancestral experience led to a long series of such experiences that are told in the first half of my book, *Baldr's Magic: The Power of Norse Shamanism and Ecstatic Trance*.

Earth Spirits

Personally, what feels most common to me is what I would call Earth Spirits or Spirits of the Earth. My fourth book, *Beowulf's Ecstatic Trance Magic: Accessing the Archaic Powers of the Universal Mind*, is of ecstatic trance experiences I consider as communing with the spirits of the Earth. This story takes place at the southern tip of Sweden near Trelleborg and at Gammel Lejre, Denmark. Gammel Lejre is the place of the remains of a great and ancient hall, possibly King Hrothgar's hall from the old English poem of Beowulf.[12] I have made two trips to these two places where I have spent some time. As I go into ecstatic trance in these places and afterward, while at home, the spirits of these places come alive in me, yet I consider them neither past life nor ancestral spirits but spirits of the place or spirits of the land.

Though the spirits of the land are everywhere, the spirits become most alive in the place where I am at the moment and in highly spiritual places. In my travels to three continents, I have made it a point to go into ecstatic trance to bring alive the places I visit. This has made my traveling experiences much deeper and more alive. Once I have communed with the spirits of a particular place, when I return home, these spirits continue to be quite accessible, take me to the especially powerful and spiritual places I have visited, and continue to deepen my experience of these places. This book is about the spirits of the places I have visited, spirits that are both ancient and current to the place. The ancient spirits bring to me the history of the place while the current spirits bring to me the present life of the place. When visiting a place, I try to use ecstatic trance twice a day, both morning and evening, though when I am in a place that feels especially spiritual, I will seek to go into trance there too.

Fairies and Angels

Though I have had little personal experience with fairies and angels, they have been spirit guides for several individuals in the trance groups I have led. Fairies often exhibit a blue glow and arise in gardens and places in nature, bringing to the person a sense of playfulness and innocence. Angels generally wear white, have wings, and come from above, bringing some spiritual insight or epiphany to the recipient.

A couple of days after I wrote this last paragraph, I had my first fairy experience:

While standing in the Shawabty initiation posture, I hear the rattle sending up sparkles that become fairies flitting around the room, looking for a way to get out. They soon fly out through the window and into the garden where they celebrate, going from flower to flower carrying their sparkles or pollen between the flowers. This brings the flowers alive in full bloom. Gradually, the flowers swell into full fruit. Everything in the garden is joyous and playful in the new dawn of spring.

It is April first, April Fool's Day, and I wonder about the history of this day. I find myself in the king's cold castle court with fools, jesters, or tricksters working hard to bring laughter and joy into the cold court of the Middle Ages, an artificial joy unlike the genuine joy of the spring garden. With this, I quickly return to the celebration and joy of the spring garden.

Regarding angels, in another recent experience, Juliana, who is in our regular monthly group, had an epiphany that she called angelic while using the Tanum Underworld Posture:

"I feel like I had a spiritual insight soon after the drumming started, but it's rather hard to explain. It is of the akashic records or the universal mind and how it unites all minds now and throughout history, making the myths of long ago still relevant to the modern psyche. While humanity has been under the spell of time throughout the ages, we collectively have only ever been living in 'the now,' which is why it has always been the same repeated history and the same myths. The sagas and dramas with which the ancient people coped and struggled are really no different from today. We are all just experiencing our lives on different holodecks of the same 'now.'

"So, in trance, I have this realization as an archangel steps to my right side and places his hand on my right shoulder. He then appears in front of me. Though fully illuminated with light, the archangel does not look particularly male or female. The sky is very blue, and he is flapping his wings slowly to emit more light from his body. Then I see his beating sacred heart as the drumming ends."

Thus fairies and angels arise as special forms of the spirits, spirit guides that bring us new insights and understanding of the world around us. Many of our spirit guides come to us as animals, birds, and sea life, and other earthly features such as mountains, rivers, or paths, each with unique characteristics but each with important messages for us.

All these spirits we might call spirits of the Earth, but some come to us much more readily than others. The spirits that come to us most easily seem to be those of our past lives and of our ancestors. Others that come easily are from the place/location that we are in at the moment. Once the channels to those Earth spirits are open, they are relatively easy to access from other locations. Animal spirits seem relatively easy for me to access, while fairies and angels seem to come to other people with ease. Again, with practice in calling the spirits through ecstatic trance, the channels to the spirits seem to open and become much easier to access.

What the Spirits Offer Us

These guiding spirits bring to us messages of importance for our personal and spiritual growth. They bring us answers to questions that we may have in life. Though we may not have formally asked a question, the spirits know our mind, know what we need and seek at the moment. The spirits provide us with direction in life.

We may not immediately understand the messages the spirits bring. The messages are likely to be in images or pictures rather than words and are in the language of metaphor, metaphor that needs to be deciphered. Many techniques are available to help decipher these messages, but one simple technique is to identify the feeling or emotion that is likely couched in the ecstatic experience. Identifying that feeling or emotion, and asking what part of me is experiencing that feeling, or where within me am I experiencing that feeling or emotion, can open the door to understanding the message.

But the messages from the spirits of the land may be of a different form. Frequently in my travels, the messages I receive from the ancient spirits of the land are images of the way the world and its people were in those ancient times. Are these images an accurate portrayal of the way the ancient world really was? That's a tough question to answer. I see these spirit images through a filter of my own experiences, concerns, questions, and expectations, often expectations from what I have read or seen. The ecstatic trance induction ritual also provides another filter, which we will examine in more detail in the next chapter, but briefly, the induction ritual is Earth-oriented. The ritual calls the spirits of each direction, season, and time of day, a ritual that I believe relates to how the hunter-gatherers related and relate to the Earth. These parameters likely give direction to and may limit what we experience in ecstatic trance.

Another major factor is how what happened in ancient times is of the universal mind or akashic field. Laszlo portrays the akashic field as a holographic matrix of information.[13] When I have examined a hologram, the image changes depending upon from which direction I am looking. But the question also arises, how is the information or holographic matrix stored in our brain? The information is modified and condensed, e.g. I hold in my brain the concept of a chair and not the images of every chair I have seen. Whether it is a plush office chair, a simple straight-backed kitchen chair, a comfortable upholstered living room chair, or a modern artistic chair, they are all chairs. Even a greatly oversized stage prop chair is a chair, though a tree stump upon which we can sit is not a chair. Yet, with intent, I can recall a specific chair that may interest me at the moment. We store the information in the universal mind in this condensed or summary manner.

I believe many factors influence what we extract from the universal mind and it is not a simple recording of an actual moment in ancient time, yet what we experience as the ancient spirits of the land is highly important and meaningful to us individually.

My ecstatic experiences often have a common theme, a theme that may describe my personal filter. That filter is my belief that the ancient culture of hunting and gathering people closely connected them to the Earth and all life on Earth. During that time, they venerated their Great Earth Mother, who is nurturing and compassionate. They lived in harmony and peace in their matriarchal world. When conflicts occasionally arose, they were more likely personal conflicts. But then came the time of transition to the world of the agriculturist and domesticator of animals, a patriarchal world where humans sought to control the Earth. Over these last 10,000 years, we have grown to believe that an off-planet god has given us the right of dominion over Earth such that we can take from her in our greed and selfishness whatever we want, calling what we do as progress. This attitude is leading us closer to our own extinction. Such writers as Eisler,[14] Gimbutas,[15] and Sahlins,[16] have portrayed this image of hunter-gatherers and the evolving place of humans on Earth. Felicitas Goodman has succinctly described this image:

"In a very real way, the hunters and gatherers open the first chapter of our human history. And fittingly, this dawning was as close to paradise as humans have ever been able to achieve. The men did the hunting and scavenging, working for about three hours a week, and the women took care of daily sustenance by gathering vegetal food and small animals. It was such a harmonious existence, such a successful adaptation, that it did not materially alter for many thousands of years. This view is not romanticizing matters. Those hunter-gatherer societies that have survived into the present still pursue the same lifestyle, and we are quite familiar with it from contemporary anthropological observation. Despite the unavoidable privations of human existence, despite occasional hunger, illness, and other trials, what makes their lifeways so enviable is the fact that knowing every nook and cranny of their home territory and all that grows and lives in it, the bands make their regular rounds and take only what they need. By modern calculations, that amounts to only about 10 percent of the yield, because *they do not aspire to control their habitat, they are a part of it.*"[17]

The ecstatic experiences of my last several books, *Baldr's Magic, Beowulf's Ecstatic Trance Magic,* and *Trance Journeys of the Hunter-Gatherers,* and now in this book reflect this theme. The ecstatic trance experiences that arise from the spirits of the land of those places I have visited reveal this nurturing and harmonious life of the hunter-gatherers, and the life of conflict and greed of the agriculturists. Hopefully, we will survive into the coming age, to return to the nurturing and harmonious life of a people who venerate and lived in oneness with the Earth, a new age of the *homo pacem* to use the words of Barbara Hand Clow.[18]

Thus, the experiences that come to me from the past in ecstatic trance reveal many influential factors that differ from those of someone else. The ways of the past differed from the present, and we will probably interpret them differently from how those of the time would interpret them. Yet my experiences bring me that which is important to me from the past. My experiences from the past are very parallel to each other in finding the magic in the hunting and gathering culture, experiences that are important to/for me.

CHAPTER 2
Ecstatic Trance

What is Ecstatic Trance?

Ecstatic Trance is an altered state of consciousness induced by rapid stimulation to the nervous system, like from the beat of a drum, the shaking of a rattle, or the clapping of hands. It is the form of trance that we often think of as used by the hunting and gathering cultures of the world in their ceremonial dancing to the beat of a drum. The research of the anthropologist Felicitas Goodman identified five basic requirements for producing ecstatic trance.[1] They are:

- Having an open mind and relaxed body, along with the expectation of a pleasurable but non-ordinary experience.
- Being in a sacred space, one separate from the activities of everyday life.
- Quieting one's mind with a meditative technique such as counting one's breath.
- Standing, sitting, or lying is a particular body posture that gives direction to the trance experience during the time of rhythmic neural stimulation.
- Rhythmic stimulation to the nervous system through rattling or drumming while standing, sitting, or lying in the particular body posture.

The story of Goodman's research that identified these five basic requirements is fascinating and inspirational. It is a story that I enjoy telling when teaching a person new to the experience of ecstatic trance, but it is a story that has been told frequently in such books as the book by Felicitas Goodman, *Where the Spirits Ride the Wind: Trance Journeys and Other Ecstatic Experiences*; and the two books by Belinda Gore, *Ecstatic Body Postures: An Alternate Reality Workbook*, and *The Ecstatic Experiences: Healing Postures for Spirit Journeys*. I have also told the story in my previous books, *The Power of Ecstatic Trance: Practices for Healing, Spiritual Growth, and Accessing the Universal Mind*; and *Baldr's Magic: The Power of Norse Shamanism and Ecstatic Trance*. I encourage the reader to go to any of these sources to read this story.

Initially, Goodman's research defined only four basic requirements to induce trance, and though these first four requirements were effective in inducing trance, it became apparent that something was missing because there was no clear direction to the trance experience. Goodman then read an article by a Canadian psychologist, V. F. Emerson on the physiological changes in a person as a result of different meditative body postures.[2] With this insight Goodman examined museum artifacts of the hunting and gathering people, both ancient and contemporary, searching for what she believed were postures used by the shaman of these cultures. She identified approximately fifty such postures and brought them back to her students at Denison University, where she had them sit, stand, or lie in these postures while she induced ecstatic trance. The results were very positive. She found some postures brought the student a feeling of healing and strengthening energy entering their body. Other postures brought to them a sense of metamorphosis or shape-shifting to some animals, birds, or fish. Some postures, the divination postures, led the students to find answers to questions. Other postures led them to experience spirit travel, some for going into the underworld, some for the middle world or this world, and some for journeying in the upper world or the heavens. Other postures produced an initiation or death-rebirth experience. Finally, she found several postures that produced a celebration experience or for calling the spirits.

Besides teaching at Denison University in Ohio, Felicitas Goodman founded the Cuyamungue Institute in New Mexico, located a few miles north of Santa Fe. I was trained at this institute to become a certified instructor of Ecstatic Trance, an institute that since Goodman's death has continued to promote her work and research. From these basic requirements for inducing ecstatic trance, she developed an effective method to induce trance that we refer to as the Cuyamungue Method.[3] It includes five basic steps:

- Preparation: The instructor leads a discussion regarding the appropriate attitude and what can be expected in the ecstatic trance experience. For newcomers, the story of Goodman's research is told. Then the particular posture to be used is described and demonstrated, with each participant practicing the posture. The instructor also answers questions the participants may ask.
- Sacred Space: We make the space in which the group meets sacred with two rituals. First, each participant, the ritual space, and the drum or rattle to be used are cleansed with the ritual of smudging with the smoke from burning herbs. Second, the spirits are called from each direction and offered a gift of cornmeal to welcome them to the sacred space.
- Quieting Inner Dialogue: The provided five minutes of silence is for the participants to focus on their breathing to assist them in quieting their mind. During these five minutes, the person may stand, sit, or lay in a comfortable position, though I suggest they place their hands on their lower abdomen in order to feel it rising and falling with each breath.

- Stimulation of the Nervous System: The instructor, or a designated rattler or drummer, then rattles or drums at the rate of approximately 210 beats per minute for fifteen minutes to stimulate the nervous system and bring the person into a state of ecstatic trance.
- The Ritual: The intent of the session is established or defined by the posture used during this fifteen minutes of drumming or rattling, a posture that gives direction to the trance experience.

The Postures

Of the 31 postures used in this book, nine are presented in this chapter. The remaining postures can be found in the book's appendix. The ones presented here are the ones I use most frequently, one from each category of intent, healing, divination, metamorphosis, spirit journeying, initiation, and celebration, with two underworld postures. These have become my favorites and with their repetition and frequency of use, they have become the most powerful to me personally. I expect that most shamans used only one or two postures, postures representing their strengths as a shaman. Some shaman likely healed through spirit journeying, some through death-rebirth experiences, some through divination, etc. They each developed and found their own special way of healing, their own special powers. I find particular power in a specific sequence of postures, a divination posture to identify a problem, then journeying into the underworld to find an answer, and finally an initiation/death-rebirth posture or a metamorphosis posture to incorporate within the individual the answer found.

As a psychologist, I have developed an awareness of what a client communicates nonverbally through facial expression, body posture, breathing rate, skin coloration, and other observable physical features. In examining these 'sacred' postures found from ancient and contemporary primitive art, feeling what each posture nonverbally expresses well leads a person to understand its intent and the direction it gives a person while in trance. Though this is not part of the Cuyamungue Method of inducing ecstatic trance, I find it very valuable to lead the participants to feel the non-verbal intent of the posture in the discussion that is part of the preparation for entering ecstatic trance.

Following are the nine postures I most frequently use:

Healing

The Bear Spirit

With the healing postures, healing and strengthening energy is felt entering the body, especially with the hands resting on one's abdomen where the participant feels it rise and fall with each breath when the person is breathing correctly from his or her diaphragm. The wood carving of this posture, the Bear Spirit Posture, found in the coastal area of the Pacific Northwest has been found in almost every hunting and gathering culture going back to as early as 6000 BC. In my collection of figurines I have two wood carvings from the Cuna Indians of the San Blas Islands of Panama standing in this posture, a posture referred to by the people of that culture as dreaming figures. Dr. Goodman gave it its name from the image she found of a man standing in this posture

Fig. 2.1

with a bear hugging him from behind. It has become the logo of the institute. I sometimes use this posture during the initial five minutes of quieting one's mind.

Standing in this posture, you stand with your feet parallel, about six inches apart, with toes forward and knees slightly bent. Your hands are resting relaxed on your abdomen with the tips of your thumbs lightly touching each other above the navel and with your fingers bent such that the first knuckle of your index fingers touch each other below the navel, forming a triangle around your navel. Your elbows rest easily at your side. Your eyes are closed with your head gently tipped back as though you are looking at a point where the wall meets the ceiling.

In the process of healing, journeying into the unconscious mind by using an underworld posture can lead a person to identify the cause or source of a personal problem. Often the experiences uncovered from the unconscious mind are painful experiences that may take extra strength to face, strength that can be accessed by using the bear spirit posture during the five minutes of breathing to quiet one's mind.

Divination

The Freyr Diviner

When I ask participants in my ecstatic trance groups what this posture reminds them of, their answer is invariably Rodin's *The Thinker*. It is similar to three other ecstatic trance postures that have the left hand raised to near the face. If I was deep in thought searching for an answer to some question, I would likely have my hand raised in front of my face like Rodin's The Thinker. The posture expresses a person deep in thought. I have found this posture very effective in providing me with answers to my questions.

This Nordic image of Freyr, a fertility god, sister to Freyja, and son of Njord, is from the eleventh-century found in Rällinge, Södermanland, Sweden.

In this posture, sit cross-legged with the right leg in front of the left. Your left-hand clasps the ankle of your right leg, while your right-hand clasps or strokes your chin or beard. Your right elbow rests on your right knee if your beard is long enough, otherwise, hold your elbow above your knee. Look straight ahead with eyes closed.

Fig. 2.2

Metamorphosis

Olmec Prince

The Olmec Prince was the very first posture I ever used. I was at a conference of the International Association for the Study of Dreams and sat at the back of the room against the wall in this posture during a drumming circle. I quickly became a high-stepping parade horse. It so happened that the drummer nearest me had been a drummer in his college marching band and was drumming with a parade cadence. Sitting cross-legged with the knuckles of my hands resting on the ground in front of me as if they are my forelegs makes the intent of this posture obvious.

The figurine of this posture is of the Olmec era in Mexico, found near Tabasco, Mexico, and dated somewhere between 1100 and 600 BC. The posture itself suggests an animal with four legs and has led me to shape-shift to a four-legged animal, but it also has led me to become a bird, snake, fish, and even a honey bee.

Fig. 2.3

In this posture, sit on the floor with your right leg crossed in front of your left. Stretch your arms, with elbows locked, straight in front of you, with your fingers curled inward, toward your body, such that only the middle segment of each finger rests on the floor. Your shoulders, elbows, wrists, and knuckles are held rigid. To maintain this position, you will need to lean slightly forward with your back straight, hinging from the hips. Lift your head with your closed eyes and look forward. Let your tongue protrude slightly from between your lips.

Journeying into the Underworld

The Hallstatt Warrior Realm of the Dead

This posture has been an especially powerful posture for me. It was the first posture to take me back in time to what I believe was an ancient ancestor, an ancestor from about the same time and location from where this posture was found, from the fifth century BC in Hirschlanden, Germany.

Standing in this posture, with your arms wrapped around you with your shoulders raised as if protecting yourself in apprehension from some impending situation, is likely the posture I would take while going into the realm of the dead.

In this posture, stand with your feet about five inches apart and toes pointed forward. Keep your knees locked. Place your right arm along your waist with the ball of your hand covering your navel. Your left arm rests along the side of your torso with the left hand resting on your right breast, fingers pointing toward the right shoulder. Face forward with eyes closed.

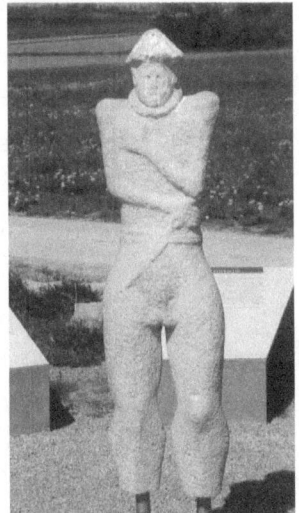

Fig. 2.4

The Tanum Underworld Posture

I found this posture while examining the large number of petroglyphs around Tanumshed, Sweden. This particular mural of petroglyphs on a large slab of rock across the parking lot of the museum at Tanum tells a story of a battle between two armies of ancient Nordic warriors.[7]

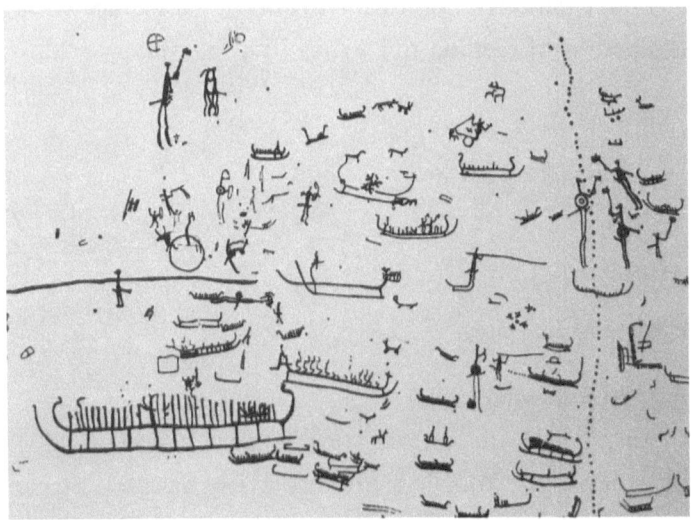

Fig. 2.5

Above the battle scene, Thor can be seen, riding in his cart pulled by two goats (see Fig. 3.1). At the top left behind the battleline can be seen a warrior hugging his girlfriend and behind him another warrior standing with a raised ax (see Fig. 3.2).[8] It is apparent that love distracts this warrior from the battle, and he is about to be hit. Below the figure of this hugging couple and below the outstretched arms of a sentry, this warrior can again be found, this time lying prone on the ground with his girlfriend kneeling above his head, and with a Nordic ship attached to his right foot, pulling him into the underworld (see Fig. 2.6).[9] Warriors who die as heroes in battle are taken to Valhalla by the Valkyries, but those who did not fight heroically go to the underworld, to Hel's domain. It is apparent that this warrior, distracted in the battle by his love for his girlfriend, did not die a hero, so is on his way to the underworld.

These petroglyphs, found on the west coast of Sweden, not far below the border with Norway, are from the Bronze Age, from between 1800 and 500 BC, well before the age of the Vikings. Each posture for journeying into the underworld is of the figure lying prone, the Sami warrior posture lying face down, and the Jivaro South American posture lying on her back, are lying close to the Earth as if seeking to journey into the underworld.

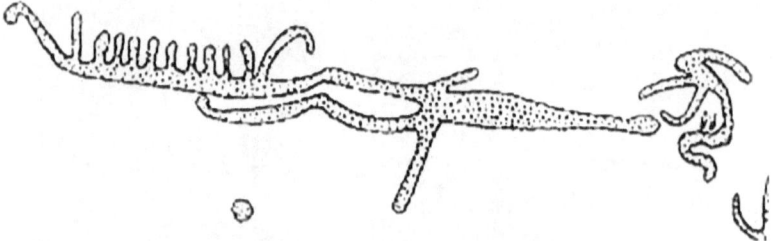

Fig. 2.6

In this posture, lie on your back with your arms at your sides close to your body. Your legs are essentially parallel. Stretch out your right leg as if being pulled. Relax your left leg with the knee slightly raised.

Journeying in the Middle World

Priestess of Malta

While journeying to the underworld you are lying on the ground, but for journeying into the middle world you are standing as the priestess of Malta, firmly planted to the Earth with your right hand pointing to the Earth, a posture that says I belong here.

The priestess was found on the Island of Malta, dating from around 3000 BC. She was found in the Hypogeum, an underground labyrinth of chambers carved into the limestone. Besides a burial mausoleum, some believe that the Hypogeum was a temple for worship and the training of priestesses in this matriarchal society. The priestess has taken me to many places upon Earth, both in the present time and also back in time to my ancestors in Scandinavia. In this book, I go to places where I have traveled, again both in present and ancient times.

Stand in this posture with your feet parallel and slightly apart, toes pointed straight ahead and knees slightly bent. Hold your right arm firmly to your side, locking the elbow, with fingers hanging down, pointing to the Earth. The palm of your left hand, with fingers and thumb

Fig. 2.7

together, rests against your waist with fingers over your navel. The elbow of your left arm is bent at 90° and held close to your body. Your face is forward, with eyes closed.

Journeying into the Upper World

Venus of Galgenberg

While journeying in the middle world you stand with your feet firmly planted to the Earth, but for rising above the Earth into the upper world, you are not planted but loosely connected to the Earth at a 37° angle to the Earth. For two of the postures, the Lascaux Cave and the Tanum upper world postures, you are lying at 37° on a sloping platform, but this is the angle of the Venus of Galgenberg's raised arm, extending to the heavens. Since it does not take the extra paraphernalia of a platform, I find it easier to use, and since I have used it frequently, I find it effective in carrying me into the upper world.

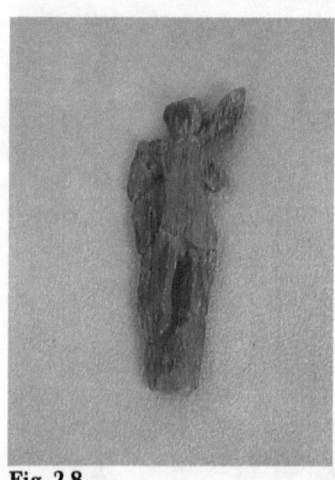

Fig. 2.8

The Venus is the oldest of the postures we use, from 30,000 BC, discovered along the bank of the Danube River near Krems, Austria. It is only two-and-three-quarter inches tall, with her upraised left arm.

In this posture, stand with your left leg straight and your left foot pointing forward. Bend your right knee slightly, with your right foot slightly turned out, away from your body. The fingers of your right hand are together and point toward the ground, possibly holding a stick that rests along your right leg. Your left arm is raised at a 37° angle from the vertical extending above your head, and that hand is cupped, with the palm of the hand turned toward that vertical line above your head. Your head is raised and turned toward the left, as though your eyes gaze at your raised hand, though your eyes remain closed.

With your left arm raised, this posture is difficult to maintain for 15 minutes. I suggest to participants that is okay to bring your arm down occasionally for a rest or to find something such as a wall upon which to rest the back of your upraised hand.

Initiation or Death-Rebirth

Feathered Serpent

The Feathered Serpent, also known as the Toltec deity Quetzalcoatl, was found in Zacatecas, Mexico, and is from around AD 100 to 650. This deity represents the cycle of life, from birth to death, to a new rebirth. It is the source of the breath of life and fertility.

When I ask our group participants what this posture expresses with its hands on its waist, their first suggestion is that it expresses a feeling of frustration or anger as when their mother stands in this way when she asks them as children to do something. When I have them stand in this manner themselves and describe the feeling, they recognize it is as a feeling of determination. When a person reaches a time of change in their life, when a part of them has to

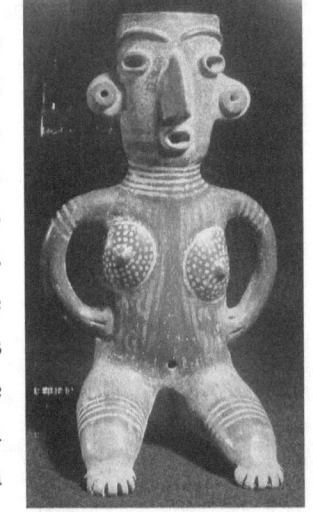

Fig. 2.9

die for a healthier part to be born, facing this change with a sense of determination is necessary, determination that is clearly expressed in this posture.

In this posture, stand or sit with your legs extended forward and feet parallel, about six inches apart, knees slightly bent with toes pointing straight forward. Cup your hands and place the backs of your fingers against your side at waist level, with fingers curling upward and your arms rounded outward with bent elbows pointing to either side. Your face looks straight ahead, your eyes are closed, and your mouth is slightly open.

Calling the Spirits

Calling the Spirits is a posture of celebration, as is easily recognized in examining the posture. It was found in La Venta, Mexico, of the Olmec era, and is from 800 to 400 BC. I often begin a series of experiences with this posture, a posture of bringing the spirits to the participants, a posture that sometimes brings a specific spirit guide to a participant.

Fig. 2.10

In this posture, stand with your feet parallel, about six inches apart, with your toes pointing forward. Keep your knees slightly bent. Position your widely spread fingers on your lower abdomen, with the middle finger of each hand in the crease where your leg joins your torso with your remaining fingers lying against your body, out to the sides. Eyes are closed and your head tipped slightly back. Keep your mouth open as though you are calling out, but make no sound.

Of these postures, all but the Freyr Diviner, the Hallstatt Warrior, and the Tanum Underworld Postures can be found in one of Belinda Gore's two books.[4,5] The Hallstatt Warrior is in the book *Where the Spirits Ride the Wind* by Goodman.[6] I discovered the Freyr Diviner and the Tanum Underworld Postures in Denmark and Sweden. They were first described in *Baldr's Magic*.

What Can a Newcomer Expect from Ecstatic Trance?

As you read the ecstatic trance experience in the following chapters, you need to realize that my experiences are just the skeleton of what I have written. From this skeleton, I needed to "flesh out" the story for better readability, and I fleshed them out while in a state of trance, often hypnotic. The newcomer to ecstatic trance cannot expect such a 'fully fleshed' story. Often the first experience is only of body sensations, e.g., of feeling hot, or feeling like you are swaying, about to fall. I suggest that while you are still in trance, ask, "What is making me hot?" or "What is causing me to sway?" This is a time to use your imagination. Maybe you are standing near a bonfire, or the sun is blazing hot. Maybe you are standing in a wind or someone is pushing you. Where are you when standing near the bonfire or when someone is pushing you? Your imagination is not from your five senses but from beyond, and it leads you into a deeper trance experience. What you imagine is very relevant to the trance experience. Whatever the content of your experience, take it further with other such questions, questions that bring you to build upon your experience. You cannot make up a story that is not relevant to you.

Experiences in recording and working with your dreams or experiences with hypnosis sensitize a person to the process of ecstatic trance and, they generally have fuller initial experiences. Artists who have an active imagination in visualizing what they create also have fuller experiences. I also encourage beginners to become part of an ecstatic trance group where they will receive encouragement in their trance experiences. With my extensive experience using hypnosis and dreamwork, I ventured into the world of ecstatic trance on my own before becoming part of a group, a group that I organized. Unless you have a strong background in dreamwork and/or hypnosis, for you to discover the power of ecstatic trance, being part of such a group is important. Developing the skill of ecstatic trance requires commitment and persistence. People who claim to not dream, when they make the commitment to remember their dreams, prepared with pen and paper next to their bed to record the dream upon awakening, soon discover that they do dream and with practice more and more of their dreams are remembered. Developing the skill of ecstatic trance requires commitment and practice.

Now, to begin my ecstatic trance journeys that take me to three continents, I begin first with Sweden and then Denmark.

CHAPTER 3

Living in Peace with the Goddess: The Ynglings of Sweden

My spiritual journey in Sweden began in Copenhagen, where we rented a car and left for Sweden. When we crossed the newly completed bridge between Copenhagen and Malmö, I began my first Swedish ecstatic trance journey near the eastern bank of the strait between the two countries. The three themes of my ecstatic experiences of my travels around Sweden are of experiences of current times, ancient times, and the stories of the Nordic Gods and Goddesses.

As I stand on the shore, my experience in the Priestess of Malta Posture (Fig. 2.7) follows:

I see ancient boats in the water with fishermen aboard. Stretched between two of the boats is a net that the men in each boat are dragging in. I can see fish thrashing around caught in the net. When the net is in and the two boats are pulled together, the men sift through the net, pulling out the fish, which they put in one boat as they pull the net into the other. The men then row into an inlet near what is now the harbor of Malmö.

I then see a large Viking ship with sails sailing from around the tip of Sweden and up towards Malmö. It is coming in open daylight, appearing not to be a threat. It is a merchant ship, something that greatly excites the people wherever it lands. The people of the settlement run to where the boat will dock, where they help the crew unload the ship.

The scene again changes. I see two ships coming down from the north. It is early morning, and the sun has not yet come over the horizon. The ships are of raiders seeking to attack the settlement and take whatever they find of value. One ship pulls in to the north of the settlement and one passes to come ashore from the south. There is a great commotion as the people of the settlement prepare for battle, some men running to the north and others to the south.

Then again the scene changes and two more Viking ships come from the north, but this time in the light of day with enormous banners flying from the masts of the ships, the ships of a visiting king, with his retainers to protect him.

That evening in Malmö I sit in the Olmec Prince Posture (Fig. 2.3), a posture of metamorphosis:

I quickly find myself digging in the ground with my snout and tusks, digging up roots to eat. I come to a rock and dig around it. The soil around the rock is loose, and the digging is easy, but then I move on to find other roots in the woods. There are many roots and the digging is slow because of the tangles. While digging I hear a noise. Men with spears are thrashing through the brush looking for a pig to kill. I move deeper into the brush, going in the opposite direction, but I soon come to men coming from that direction. I turn to the side but realize that I am surrounded. I find an opening in the brush, put my head down, and charge forward with my tusks towards the opening, but there are men there too. As I rush towards them I feel a spear piercing my side. I keep running, but I am hit by more spears and soon fall bleeding. I die and the men cut into me, taking out my guts before they tie me to a pole to carry me back to their settlement.

Our travels continue, as we drive south towards Trelleborg where we find ancient Viking ruins, the Trelle Fortress. A portion of the ruins is reconstructed with a high stockade of tree trunks with an entrance that leads into the field protected by the stockade. Inside the Trelle Fortress earthen ramparts rest against the stockade of logs, providing easy access to the top of the stockade for the chieftain's retainers to defend the settlement. Buildings are arranged in such a manner that if the enemy enters the compound, the chieftain's warriors will not be trapped inside. If the thatched roofs of the buildings are set afire or, if attacked, the warriors from the other buildings will have direct access to the building being attacked.

Inside the fortress, I stand in the Priestess of Malta middle world posture (Fig. 2.7):

Several of the chieftain's retainers stand at the top of the ramparts facing each direction, continually watching for the approach of an enemy. The feeling is of constant fear or paranoia of an attack. No trust exists between neighboring chieftains, and each chieftain is prepared for being attacked and prepares to attack the settlement of other chieftains to gain wealth, territory, and power. Families live in constant fear. At the center of the settlement is an open field where the retainers practice with their use of swords, spears, and other weapons. The lifespan of the people is considerably shorter than during the hunter-gatherer era several generations earlier. Many families live outside the stockade in small huts and farm the surrounding land to provide for themselves, the chieftain, and his retainers. A drummer sends an alarm at the time of an attack, and if time allows, the families rush into the stockade, otherwise, they run to hide in the forest above the settlement. The attacking warriors take anything of value from the village huts, and the huts are burned.

With these trance images, I feel the anxiety and fear of living in that time, the same anxiety and fear that many people experience in our present world of guns and terrorism.

The next day we leave Trelleborg and pass through Ystad, the seaside harbor city where ships took those immigrating from Sweden to America. I again used the Priestess of Malta middle world posture (Fig. 2.7):

I rise above the land and watch people walking, carrying their belongings in sacks over their shoulders, walking from their inland farms to this coastal city. They are leaving because the farms are too small to divide up between the farmer's children, leaving to find a new life that they have heard about with the available land in America. I am with one family, a young man with his wife and infant daughter as they walk along the road. With the help of the wife's parents, they have enough money to pay for passage on a ship to America and hope they have enough provisions for the trip. I see the crowd of people on the dock at the harbor who are boarding a ship and are being crowded into the unlit area below the deck that is lined with bunks. The air below deck is foul. During this journey many travelers become sick and some die, to be thrown overboard, but this family is healthy and strong enough to survive the journey. When they arrive in New York City, they are in great need of help and find ways to get by as part of the Swedish immigration in the late 1800s. Being with this family on their journey, I feel the anguish they must feel in leaving behind their parents and extended family, yet they leave with the feeling of hope for a new life.

* * *

That afternoon, as we leave Kristianstad we see several small farm gardens along the way. I use the Hallstatt Warrior Realm of the Dead posture (Fig. 2.4):

I am over the Atlantic and dive down into the depths of the water. I see an elderly woman and approach her. All she can say is, "I abandoned Freyja." She takes me to a small farm near Kristianstad. It was her farm. Her daughter marries a young man, and he moves to the farm where he grows what they need for their survival. He plants a large garden and raises several sheep on their small plot. His wife's aunts and uncles live on the neighboring plots. Her grandparents divided the land four ways for their children, and now the plots are tiny. The woman from the bottom of the ocean had only one child, her daughter, and she wanted her daughter and husband to have the land. She had been a popular person in the area because of her knowledge of the healing powers of the plants and herbs, something she learned from her mother. A new preacher in the local church called her a witch because of her knowledge of plants, and some church members started turning against her even though they went to her for help when they had some ailment. The preacher threatened her with hell and damnation and would not let her cross the threshold of the church, thus desecrating the church. If they crossed paths in town, he would yell at her with words of damnation. The mother felt the love and compassion of Freyja, and more decidedly she turned away from the church. In support, her husband also turned from the church, seeing that this preacher was not following Jesus's teachings of compassion and love. As this couple aged and their daughter grew into adulthood and married, they began to talk about moving to America where there was religious freedom, and they could start a new life.

They dreaded leaving their daughter but wanted their daughter to love their country and raise their grandchildren as Swedes. They eventually saw no other way for her daughter and family to survive except to leave for America. The mother had taught her daughter to love the plants of the Earth and of their healing powers. She believed her daughter would survive and could have a good life, thus she and her husband left for America.

On the way, the mother began feeling the pain of leaving her daughter and her home in Sweden, grieving more and more each day. She cannot eat, becomes sick with grief because she has abandoned Freyja, and soon gives up living. Her husband soon follows her in their death at sea. In communing with her at the bottom of the ocean, she, as my spirit guide, shows me around Kristianstad and the failings of the church in which she grew up. I realize that now few people in Sweden continue to go to church and some are turning to the old ways of Freyja and the other ancient Nordic deities by joining Forn Siðr.

As our travels in Sweden continue, we come to Kalmar and the bridge that takes us over to the Island of Öland. In Kalmer, while standing in the Venus of Galgenberg Posture (Fig. 2.8) on the bank of the strait between this town and the island, I have the following experience:

As I stand beside the water, I first see Freyr on his ship, Skiðblaðir. This ship, made by the dwarfs, the sons of Ivaldi, always has the wind in its sails and when not in use can be folded up such that it fits in Freyr's pocket. I then see Njord, the god of the seas and winds, winds that keep the sails of ships full while at sea. As Freyr's father, he looks after his son by keeping the wind in the sails of his son's ship. When Njord is away from the shore as when he is in the mountains that Skaði, his wife, loves so much, he finds it difficult to watch over his son, though when his son calls to him he hears and can blow from the mountain into his sail. I see these two gods of the Vanir, Njord and Freyr, watching over the sea as I am watching over the sea, feeling great reverence and appreciation for it. I see fishing boats going to and from the island, and as I watch, the wind comes up to fill the sails of those who have sails. Then the men pull in their oars to sit back to enjoy the sea. Njord and Freyr are much part of the lives of the Swedes both now and in ancient times with their lives on the sea.

In our continued travels, we cross the bridge and onto the island of Öland. We drive to the south on this narrow but long island where we see many sheep and other livestock in the fields surrounded by stone walls with an occasional bridge that crosses over the wall. We know that Carl Linnaeus spent considerable time on this island in his pursuit to classify the flora of the area. Parking the car near a pasture, we cross over the low stone wall to examine the flora where we are greeted by several cows who are in the field.

I stand among the flowers in the Tlazeoteotl healing posture (Fig. A.22):

I first see Idunn picking flowers for her hair and Bragi, who is sitting on a rock, watches her in love. She comes over and puts a flower in his hair over his ear too. Though Linnaeus was a botanist, I can't help believing that he must have had some love for Idunn, the goddess whose golden apples keep the gods and goddesses young and healthy. He knew the plants to heal various ailments. As I sit on a rock near Bragi, a woman comes across the low wall and walks towards me. She carries a basket and is picking plants. We greet and she tells me she is the local healer, a disciple of Idunn. She motions for me to follow her because she has something she must do. Just a few doors down the road she turns in to her place that is overgrown with bushes, trees, and other plants. She takes her basket into what may have been a garage but is now her storeroom of herbs and medicines. She reports that the plants she picks grow in the open pasture and not in her crowded yard, but the pasture is very convenient for her.

As she ties and hangs the plants from the ceiling of her storeroom, someone comes to the door, a mother with a young boy. The boy has a runny nose and a sore throat. The woman first wraps her arms around the boy, holds him to her, places her hands on his head, and closes her eyes. After a few moments, she moves her hands down to his belly and again holds him with her eyes closed. When she is satisfied with what she learns, she releases him. She puts a pot of water on the stove and waits for it to boil. As she waits she puts a couple of different herbs in the pot, and when it starts steaming she turns down the heat, brings the boy to the stove and places a towel over his head and the pot, and has him breathe in the steam. After a couple of minutes, she removes the towel and pours a cup of the tea that she has brewed in the pot and has the boy drink. She pours the rest of it in a jar and gives it to his mother with the instructions that he needs to drink the rest of it before he goes to bed, and that they should return the next day.

This disciple of Idunn has me sit and makes me a cup of tea while she tells me about the people of Öland, that many of them raise sheep and make things from the wool. She shows me a scarf made by the mother of the boy she just treated. She tells me how the women of the island respect and love her, and because of her, many of them have returned to venerating Idunn and Freyja. I soon stand to leave as a woman comes to the door holding her head and holding a towel over her mouth because she has been throwing up. I thank the disciple and leave to continue on my journey.

As we drive along the island we come to a store that sells woolen items. We stop and peruse the place. Soon we leave the island to venture farther north to Norrköping on our way to Mariefred. Norrköping is a harbor city at the mouth of the Motala ström river that opens into the Baltic Sea. It has been a shipbuilding town, though now the chief industry is textiles. Salmon also run the river.

Along the river I lay in the Tanum Underworld Posture (Fig. 2.6):

I dive into the river and swim downstream into the open waters of the Baltic Sea where I see a sunken Viking ship, fairly small in size. I think I see a treasure chest aboard it, but I know I cannot carry it up so leave it alone.

I then turn around to swim upstream and find I have become a salmon. I swim some distance upstream from the city where I am caught in a net and pulled up into a boat. I then become one of the fishermen and recall the story of Loki who makes the first fishnet, likely from the fiber of flax. Loki's plan is to escape from being captured in a fishnet by the gods. As the gods approach, he throws the net he is making into the fire and runs to dive into the river, shape-shifting to a salmon. One god sees the net's ashes in the fire and knows that it was for catching fish. So the gods make a net and go down to the river where they eventually catch Loki as a salmon. Having captured Loki, the gods take him to a cave and secure him to a boulder in the cave with a poisonous viper hanging above him, dripping its poison on him. His wife, Sigyn, is there with a bowl to catch the poison, but when she leaves to empty the bowl, the poison causes Loki to quake, making the earth quake.

Our travels then take us north with the next stop being Mariefred, the home of the Gripsholm Castle. Since Gustav Vasa, Gripsholm has belonged to the Swedish Royal Family, used as one of their residences until the 18th-century. It is now a museum.

After touring the castle I stand outside in the Calling the Spirits posture (Fig. 2.10):

I see unformed spirits rising from the castle, from village huts, from a cathedral in the village, and from an outlying farmer's hut. The spirits are of different colors. From the castle, they are a reddish-orange color, while the spirits from the farmer's hut are blue-green. The spirits from the cathedral are closer to being red or violet, and the spirits from the hovels of the villagers are a bluish purple. The king of the castle seeks wealth and power over the people of his domain and seeks to destroy others competing for his power. Underlying his seeking of power and wealth is anxiety and fear that he could lose everything, though outwardly he does not show this anxiety and fear. To defend his power and wealth, he has built his massive castle with thick walls, using as builders the people of his domain.

The farm families in their huts find peace and harmony in the way they live, though the peace and harmony were much greater several generations earlier before there were those seeking wealth and power. Now this family has to give an increasing portion of what they grow to the king, so they have to work considerably harder to survive. Sometimes a child of the farm family sees the wealth of the king and seeks wealth and power by moving to the village. This pursuit of power places him in poverty unless he is physically strong such that he can become a warrior for the king, but then his spirit turns towards being red.

The village people find a little comfort in learning some skill to provide some service for the king. They can become craftsmen such as blacksmiths, carpenters, or potters, and those who provide a service by becoming a seamstress, cook, maid, servant, or bartender. Their lives are marginal and they likely seek to rise above their poverty and misery by turning their allegiance to those in the cathedral in their fantasy of someday finding a better life in the afterlife. Again, like the castle, the massive and extremely ornate cathedral is built by the hands of men living in poverty.

In this age of seeking power and wealth, much of the nurturing and loving quality of life found on the farmstead has been lost. With this deterioration in life, I can see what drives our present age of terrorism. Rising out of the villagers are those who feel growing resentment towards the wealth and power of the king, and revolt ferments. These resentful villagers do not have the knowledge or wealth to become chieftains or kings, even if they should succeed in a revolution. Seeking wealth and power only destroys the sense of community between people.

In our journey towards Gamla Uppsala, we pass through the city of Stockholm, but I find having an ecstatic experience in such a setting next to impossible. I could likely find an enclosed place hidden away from the activity of the city as when I retreat to the kiva or a sacred cave, or even an enclosed hotel conference room, but I find the countryside much more conducive to ecstatic trance. Thus, we continue on to Gamla or Old Uppsala, where we find the remains of the place of worship of the ancient Ynglings. In Uppsala, we visited the museum home and gardens of Carl Linnaeus, who developed the taxonomy for classifying plants. This estate is near the University of Uppsala. In Gamla Uppsala, I sit by a burial mound in the Freyr Divination posture (Fig. 2.2). Partway into the experience, Freyr tells me to switch to the Feathered Serpent Posture (Fig. A.5), which among the ancient people of Scandinavia can be seen in a figurine of Odin:

While sitting next to the huge burial mound I see the masses of people building this mound by shoveling earth over the dead king, several of his wives, horses sacrificed for him for riding to the next world, servants, and other wealth. His followers treat him as if he is one of the gods. The remains of a thatched-roofed hall of the king are nearby, not the massive castle of later kings, but it is large enough to hold a great number of retainers as the king sits in his high seat, a seat likened to that sat upon by Odin. His retainers all wear a replica of Mjölnir, the hammer of Thor, on a thong around their necks.

Again, in the outlying countryside are the farm families who live in small thatched huts, who grow and provide food for the king and his retainers. Their lives are hard. The king or chieftain is the protector of these families in exchange for the food they provide him. Yet, the attacks of other kings and chieftains are a continued threat to the king, and not to the simple lives of the outlying farmers who can easily switch alliances to provide for a new king. These farm families call upon the deities Freyja and Freyr for fertility to help in their activities of daily life. If a king should fall to the strength of a rival king, the new king will depend upon these outlying farmers for their needed food supplies, so their struggle continues.

As I switch and stand beside the burial mound of the king in the Feathered Serpent posture (Fig. 2.9), I feel new energy, the energy of worshiping Odin and the warriors' worship of Thor. These gods are not dependent upon food provided by outlying farmers, but they have an endless supply from magical sources. When Thor's goats are butchered to eat, the bones regenerate into a healthy goat the following day. Similarly, a pig of Valhalla returns to life each day after being boiled in a huge kettle and cooked for supper the night before. Thus, the deities and their army have an endless supply of food. Both the goat and pig eat the leaves of the golden-leafed tree of Valhalla, while Idunn provides a supply of golden apples to keep the residents of Valhalla young and healthy. From Odin's high seat *Hliðskjálf*, he can see great distances, and likewise, the king from his high seat in his great hall can see over all his men. The king and his men seek to emulate the powerful Nordic gods, Odin and Thor, thus showing their reverence for them.

* * *

The next stop after leaving Gamla Uppsala is on the shore of Lake Vättern, the lake dug by the pig that pulled Freya in her cart, a story which is told in my book *Baldr's Magic*. On one occasion, when she pulled on the reins of the pig, he put his butt down in a skidding stop, thus digging the trench that formed the lake. She was searching for her wandering husband, Oðr, and thought she saw him.

I stand beside the lake in the Danish Realm of the Dead posture (Fig. A.4):

As I stand on the shore of the lake, I look out over the water and see rising lake spirits. I am back in ancient times, during the time of the worship of the Great Mother Goddess, soon after Freyja went searching for her husband. Many died in the flooding water, though their spirits continue to venerate the Goddess Freyja as they did before their death. These spirits rise when they have something to show or teach the person who stands and sees them. What does the spirit I see have to show or teach me?

As a simple farmer of the land beside the lake, fertile because of the lake, I go to the lakeside seeking advice for what I plant. Today, a day of midsummer, I have completed my planting and wonder what the spirits of the lake are going to tell me. The spirits have moved somewhat closer to the shore and I see one dancing on the water, throwing sprays of water into the air. She is telling me it is time to celebrate the planting by spraying it with water, something I already do when the garden appears dry. But, I need to do this watering with a sense of celebration for the fertile soil, for the seeds, and now the growing plants, and for the water that I use for the plants to grow. It is time for me to offer the spirit something in reciprocity for her message of wisdom. I call the spirit in the name of Freyja, the goddess of fertility, and throw to her a handful of seeds that land close to shore and will wash up onto the shore to grow into a bed of wildflowers, flowers that Freyja and the other goddesses love to put in their hair. I then turn to return to the garden to harvest a handful of early peas. Thank you Freyja, *Tack*, Freyja.

After this brief stop, we continue on down the east side of the lake to Jönkoping to spend time with a friend, Peter. The next morning I go for a drive in the country south of Jönkoping looking for tarns or *skogstjärn*, the sacred pools of water, the golden tears of Freyja when she does not find Oðr. In my previous book, *Beowulf's Ecstatic Trance Magic*, the priestess of Freyja, Vanadisdottir, returns to the sacred tarn of Freyja where she teaches the ways of Freyja. I explore the rolling hills at the end of Lake Vättern where the earth is scuffed up by the pig as he skidded to a stop.

I find several *skogstjärn* and park near one where I first stand in the Tlazeoteotl cleansing posture (Fig. A.22), but once I feel cleansed, I feel a need to change postures and I take the Freyja Initiation posture (Fig. A.6):

I stand next to the tarn and bend to take a scoop of water in my hand to wash over my face. I then go back in time and find a sauna or *bastu* next to the tarn, disrobe and enter the sauna. Once I take three cooling dips in the tarn and return to the *bastu* after each dip, I again dress and stand next to the tarn. Nothing happens for a minute or two, then I feel a need to move my hands to the Freyja Posture. For a moment I again see the castle, the cathedral, and the burial mound of the earlier experiences, and I again come to the edge of the lake and see the spirit of the lake. I realize that my place is farther back in time at the edge of the lake or the edge of a tarn, places that feel much more sacred to me. The simple places offered by our Great Earth Mother are much more alive, healing, and nurturing than a castle or cathedral that is cold and empty, though it may be protective. Mother Earth is most protective when I place myself in her hands. This new birth at the side of the sacred *skogstjärn* gives me a new strength to continue on my journey to new places that may include castles and cathedrals.

The next stop of my travel around Sweden is Trollhättan, a city on the Göta älv, a canal or river that runs from Lake Vänen to the sea at Göteborg. In the 19th century, locks were built, a lock system that provides the city with hydroelectric power and makes the river passable by boat. I stand in the Priestess of Malta middle world posture (Fig. 2.7) on the bank of the river. I so often find sacred places near water:

I stand on the bank of the river below the city. I rise above the river and float through the air downstream towards Göteborg. After a while, my experience changes, and I find myself upriver above the city and the locks that allow boats to travel between Lake Vänen and Göteborg. A replica of an ancient Viking ship resting in the lock is lowered as the water runs out. Men in Viking dress are at the oars as it travels down the river to a park on the river bank where people gather in their reenactment of Viking times. A shipyard on Lake Vänen built this ship as they built fleets of fishing vessels in ancient times to travel on the lake.

When the ship arrives at the park below the locks, a gathering of people greets it with cheers. There is much activity among this very diverse group of people. Many in Sweden are taking a great interest in the ways of the Viking era. The era fascinates many of the reenactors who are fighting with spears, swords, and shields. Some of these men are nationalistic and condemn the new diversity of immigrants to Sweden. Many are interested solely in the skills of their ancestors. There are those who are interested in the ways of blacksmithing, pottery making, and carpentry. Others are interested in the fabrics and clothing and the ways of making them. Others are interested in the foods and cooking of the time. Some are interested in the old herbs and medicines. Along with a few others, I am interested in the more magical ways of seiðr, the ways of seeing what others cannot see, seeing into the past, the future, and distant places. There is great wealth in this diversity of interests, and much to be learned of the old ways. I am especially interested in the ways of before the Æsir, of the ways of the Vanir, ways of compassion and nurturance, not the ways of strength and fighting as seen with some of the reenactors of the gathering. There is something for everybody in this gathering, a gathering like I experienced in several other places in Denmark and Sweden, such as the reconstructed site at Tanumshede, which we will visit next.

I am sitting in the reconstructed thatched hut in the Tanum Museum Center. As I come in the door, to the right is a wooden fence to keep the cow from wandering through the living area. To the left is a central fire pit and at either end of the thatched roof are openings for the smoke from the fire to exit. Along the wall are sleeping platforms, and at the end of the fire pit, to the left is a table with a couple of benches upon which to sit. I stand next to the table in the Priestess of Malta Posture (Fig. 2.7):

I find myself back in time sitting at the table in the thatched hut and across from me is my wife. She is pregnant and we are awaiting the birth of our first child. We have called upon the local volva to tell us about what she sees for our soon-to-arrive baby. We greet the volva at the door, and she comes to the table. To see into the future the volva sits on a raised platform, in our case on the table. She climbs onto the table and sits in the Freyr Diviner Posture (Fig. 2.2), sitting cross-legged, grasping her knee with her left hand and her right hand stroking her chin.

After sitting awhile she speaks, telling us that the child will be a healthy girl and will provide the family with much-needed help and be a joy to them. She will eventually marry a young man and become a farmer's wife, and she will provide them with three grandchildren. Farming life is compassionate and nurturing, but the work on the farm will increase because of the growing number of retainers of the local chieftain, but Freyja will watch over us and provide for us.

We then leave Tanumshede and drive south to Göteborg. Upon reaching this harbor city at the mouth of the Göta älv, I find a pleasant place to stand on the shore overlooking the broad expanse of the sea. I stand in the Venus of Galgenberg posture (Fig. 2.8) facing west:

The sunset over the water is beautiful this evening. I rise and find myself in Idunn's garden. In the center of the garden is her golden apple tree. I go to it and sit on a low branch in the tree and smell the lovely fragrance of the blossoms. The tree is very special because it has both fruit, its golden apples, and blossoms at the same time. It has apples that are ripe and ready to pick all year round. The story I know as told among the goddesses of the Vanir differs from the one told by the Æsir. The Æsir take credit for the golden apple tree growing in their domain, though in Asgard, they admit they cannot pick the apples. Only Idunn can pick them. The story I know is that the apple tree was in Vanaheim in Idunn's garden. She had to return to Vanaheim each day to pick the apples and while there, she would visit Moðir, telling her about the antics of the gods of Asgard. Sometimes they would have a good laugh as when the giant, Utgarða-Loki, tricked Thor. Other times they felt sorrow as when Thor was injured with a piece of stone embedded in his head or when the giant Thiazi held Idunn because of the antics of Loki. The gods of Asgard do not want to admit that they cannot pick the apples or that Idunn, who keeps them young, is faithful to and loves Moðir, so they continued to believe that the golden apple tree is theirs. But when Thiazi kidnapped Idunn, they go to find the tree and cannot find it. They then realized it must be in Vanaheim and know that they are not welcome there. If they should try to enter the domain of the Vanir, these fertility deities would stop them with their powerful magic.

While sitting in the apple tree, I can see Idunn with her basket picking the apples to take back to Asgard and the goddesses that live there. While there I recall the story of when the giant Thiazi kidnapped Idunn and the gods and goddesses of Æsir grew old because she is not there to give them the golden apples. Loki and Odin were visiting the middle world when Odin said that he was starving. Loki found a cow, killed it, and put it over a fire to roast. The hours went by, but each time he checked the cow it was still raw. He knew he was being tricked and then he saw an eagle in a nearby tree who told Loki that he would with the flapping of his wings make the fire hot enough to roast the cow if he could have his share. Once roasted, the eagle ate the entire cow, leaving nothing for Odin or Loki. Loki, in a rage, struck the eagle with a burning piece of wood and found himself stuck to the eagle as it flew away back to his home in Jötunheimr, for he was the giant Thiazi. While holding Loki prisoner, the giant told him he wanted Idunn's golden apples for his release. Loki at first considered this impossible, but with further discussion, Loki figured he could lure Idunn outside the walls of Asgard, and Thiazi as an eagle could come down and kidnap her. Thus, Thiazi, as an eagle, returned Loki to Asgard. When he was alone with Idunn, he told her about an apple tree he saw outside the walls of Asgard that he believed had apples shinier than the apples of her tree. She at first did not believe him, but then she became curious and went beyond the walls to see it. There the eagle took her to the hall of Thiazi in Jötunheimr where she was held prisoner.

As the gods and goddesses of Asgard grew old, they searched for Idunn and a way to bring her back. Eventually, Loki agreed to bring her back. So he shape-shifted to a falcon and flew to the hall of Thiazi, where he found Idunn imprisoned. He shape-shifted her to a walnut and flew off, carrying her back to Asgard. While in flight Thiazi saw him and knew what was going on. In the chase, the falcon Loki carrying the walnut flew over the wall of Asgard to safety where the gods quick lit a fire into which Thiazi flew to his demise. Thus, Idunn could return to Vanaheim to fetch more apples to bring the gods and goddesses back to their youthfulness.

With this ecstatic experience on the shore of the great sea of Western Sweden, we continue our journey, returning to Denmark for our flight home. Sometime after returning home from Sweden, I return to these experiences to reexperience and discover some of the important memories in my understanding of these ancient times. Returning takes me to the place that was especially sacred, to Tanumshede and the petroglyphs across the parking lot of the museum, which brought me to the experience of 10/21/15.

I use the Freyr Divination Posture (Fig. 2.2):

I am in the land of the Geats in the hall of the Geat King Hygelac, the land that will someday be known as Tanumshede. He is telling the story of his grandfather, King Gylfi of Sweden. He tells of his grandfather's benevolence, that whenever he saw someone in need he gave to them. Because of his benevolence, the people of Sweden loved him greatly. He would frequently wear ragged clothing to avoid recognition when mingling with the people as he wandered to help those in need. One day he saw a woman sitting beside the road below an apple tree, wearing rags and eating what she could of a rotting apple that had fallen from the tree. Gylfi sat with her and they talked. As they talked, the woman took another apple and cut into it, finding that part of the apple that was good and throwing away the rotten part. She then gave Gylfi the sweet apple. He appreciated her benevolence and told her he would give her as much land as she could plow in a day and a night. It so happened that she was the goddess Gefjon, also wearing ragged clothes to avoid recognition. The god Odin at the time was living on the island of Fyn, which was not big enough for him, so he asked Gefjon to find him a larger piece of land.

With Gylfi's offer, Gefjon went over the mountains to the land of the giants, Jotunheimr, to fetch her four oxen sons. With them attached to a plow, they dug deep and dragged a large piece of Sweden out into the sea to a place next to the Island of Fyn, thus forming the island of Zealand. This left a large hole in Sweden that began filling with water from the four rivers that flowed through the area. Pulling this piece of land through Sweden also formed a long valley from what is now Lake Vänern down to the coastal city of Göteborg. Through this valley flows the Göta älv River, so that the water from the lake runs to the sea. If you examine a map of Scandinavia, you can see that the size and shape of Lake Vänern is close to the size and shape of Zealand. The people of this new island soon see that they have a new island home.

As King Gylfi continued his wandering through his domain, he saw more and more people in grief. He asked them about their grief, and they told him about how they had lost part of their family when the Oxen plowed and pulled the land out to sea. The king felt the grief of his people and did not know what to say. When they learned what the king had done in giving the land to Gefjon, their love for him diminished. The king's benevolence was now the problem.

As the king wandered, he came to a point of land on the north side of the lake where his brother lived. Several chieftains or lesser kings ruled over this part of Sweden. His brother, Skjǫld, was the king over much of the west of Sweden, which included Lake Vänern. When Gylfi came to his brother's great hall, he could hear wailing coming from inside. Skjǫld's infant son, heir to the throne, disappeared when the Oxen plowed the land, and the family was in great pain. They did not know if Prince Scyld was alive or dead somewhere under the water of the lake. Since it was the Goddess Gefjon who took the land, Gylfi called the family together and asked that they pray to Gefjon to rescue the infant prince and care for him. Gefjon heard their prayer and felt their grief. In her compassion, she answered them, promising them that Odin himself would foster Prince Scyld, and Scyld would someday become a great king of the Skjǫldungs.

Gefjon also reminded them of the story of Nanna and Baldr. When Baldr visited the hall of Moðir, he felt deeply her compassion and love. As he sat in the garden of her hall, he dwelt upon the differences between the people of Vanir and the people of Æsir, of the compassion and creativity of the Vanir and the strength and violence of the Æsir. He respected his father, the god of gods of the Æsir, but he did not understand the Æsir's veneration of strength and their need for power to dominate the world. In thinking these thoughts, he felt sorrow for the Æsir.

As he sat in the garden, he felt the presence of someone sitting beside him, Nanna. She needed to say nothing because she could hear his thoughts, and he needed to say nothing because he could feel Nanna's compassion. With these feelings of love and compassion, he married Nanna before returning to Asgard, though Nanna needed to remain with Moðir, the mother of the Vanir. Though they could have grieved their separation, they knew they were together all the time, each with their ability to know what the other was thinking. This story was told by Gefjon to let the people know that even with their separation, the families of Sweden could still be together.

The grief of the Geats lessened when they discovered the value of the great Lake Vänern with its abundance of fish. Boatbuilding and fishing became major activities for the Geats. With the quiet water of the sheltered bays around the lake and with the large trees that grew along the edge of the lake, the boat builders found a home for the craft. They could row down the River Göta älv to the sea, and they became famous as seamen.

Over the years, King Gylfi had several children, and the oldest son, Hrethel, the father of King Hygelac, became a most benevolent king, though he gave away his wealth with more care to avoid causing grief among the people.

On 10/25/15 I return to Tanum while using the Calling the Spirits Posture (Fig. 2.10):

I am standing in front of the petroglyphic stone across from the museum in Tanum, Sweden. It is a battle scene (Fig. 2.5).[1] I find myself back in time, watching a man carving the stone. His sister is standing below the stone, watching him too. She asks him to show the scene of her embracing her warrior lover (Fig. 3.2),[2] and below that of her kneeling above his head as the ship attached to his right foot takes him to the underworld to the realm of Hel (Fig. 2.6).[3] The sentry, protecting the backs of the warriors in battle, misses one enemy warrior who sneaks by and kills her warrior, distracted from the battle by his love for her.

The battle is between the warriors of the King of Norway, King Sæmingr, and Gylfi, King of the Swedes. The Swedish volva sees the warriors of Norway coming south and reports what she sees to Gylfi, who has time to bring his warriors and ships up the fjord and along the river to fend off the warriors from the north. In this battle the warrior god Thor watches the battle from his goat cart pulled through the sky above the Swedish

Fig. 3.1

warriors (Fig. 3.1),[4] giving them the strength to win this battle against the Norwegian warriors. This battle takes place along the river Uddevallavägen, above the Gullmarn Fjord.

Then on 10/26/15 I again return to Tanum using the Hallstatt Warrior Posture (Fig. 2.4):

I am back at the settlement of King Gylfi. It is a day of festivity and feasting because a merchant ship has arrived. People are arriving from outlying steadings. Vigdis, a beautiful young woman, comes with her father, riding atop a card of wool to trade. One of the king's retainers is Thorsteen, maybe 17 years old, and a seasoned warrior. He sees 15-year-old Vigdis and immediately falls in love with her. There are other available young women in the settlement, but he sees something special in her innocence. The other women hang out in the king's great hall each evening, flirting with and seducing the warriors as they serve the mead. They are ready to lie with any of the seducing men, which is most of them. Some men do not find a woman because there are more men than women. Thorsteen is not a virgin, yet he thinks of these women as whores and is not especially interested in them. Vigdis is different. She has been a responsible daughter in working on her parents' steading and is still a virgin. Though her virginity is not an issue for Thorsteen, he loves her innocence.

He approaches Vigdis, and the greeting is warm. They are soon sitting on the ground under a tree talking. She tells Thorsteen about their sheep on the farm and what farm life is like. On the farm, they continually call upon Freyja and Freyr for help and to bless their life. He tells Vigdis about his life in the settlement of King Gylfi, about his father who is one of the king's strongest men, and about his training to become a warrior like his father. He likes the life of a warrior, of their daily practice with the sword and spear, and he helps the shipbuilders in building the king's fleet of ships. Sometimes their practice with swords is on the ships and between two ships. Ships are unstable compared to fighting on the land, so it takes more practice to keep balanced. He reports that there is always enough to eat and they have splendid feasts every night. He is thankful for the farmers of the outlying steadings for growing the food that they share with the king for his protection from outlaw raiders. This gives Vigdis a different view of the men of the king who come to their steading to collect their share of the harvest. She appreciates the thanks offered by Thorsteen for this food. Until now, her family has always felt resentment and anxiety about giving up half of their harvest to the king, not knowing if they would have enough to get through the winter.

Thorsteen is the first man she has ever felt this close to and wonders if her feeling is of falling in love. The other boys she knows are her cousins from other nearby steadings. The next day, after her father trades the wool for what they need on the steading, they prepare to return home and Vigdis is eager to tell her mother about Thorsteen. When they are ready to leave, Thorsteen tells her he hopes to see her again soon and kisses her with a hug. This adds to her feelings of excitement.

On 10/27/15, this story continues with the Tlazeoteotl Posture (Fig. A.22):

Vigdis arrives home in the evening and sits near her mother, who is stirring the kettle that hangs over the fire, to tell her about Thorsteen. Her mother listens with a smile and tells her that one reason she sent her with her father to the king's settlement was there she might meet a man. It was about time that she meets a man and starts her own home. Though this is a farming family, they believe that life in the settlement would be an easier life, if that is true. They work hard on their farm and think that where people did not have to farm, life would be easier. She is pleased that Thorsteen sounds so much like a gentleman and treated her daughter with respect. Vigdis's father also reports that when he met Thorsteen, he acted like a proper gentleman and not like the other warriors who were loud and drunk.

Several weeks later, two warriors arrive from the king's settlement to collect the king's provisions, and one of them is Thorsteen. He had made sure that he was the one to visit the nearby steadings. Vigdis had been dreaming over the intervening weeks of Thorsteen and wondered if she would ever see him again. In listening to her mother, she realized her feelings must really be of love. When the two retainers of the king arrived, Vigdis and Thorsteen run to each other and hug. The other retainer at first is all business and announces that they are there to collect food for the king and his warriors so that he can protect them from outlaw raiders. Thorsteen puts up his hand to silence his partner and tells him that this family is different, that they will collect the provisions, but first, he needs to spend time with Vigdis because she is the one he wants to marry.

With those words, Vigdis grabs onto Thorsteen even tighter. He can see over her shoulder that her mother and father are smiling in their approval. Soon one of the family suggests that Thorsteen's partner should leave and visit the other nearby farms with the announcement of the impending marriage while he collects the king's provisions. They assure him that with this announcement, her cousins would be friendly and that he would be in no danger.

As they sit and talk, Vigdis's parents learn about Thorsteen, and they welcome him as part of the family. Vigdis's younger brother is nearby in the farm field hoeing and soon comes to sit with them too. Thorsteen's Mjölnir, the hammer of Thor, was a sign to the family that he worshiped his namesake, Thor. With this the family feels the need to tell him about their love for Freyja and her compassion and love, and that when they get married, they will call upon Var, the Vanir goddess who listens to marriage vows and punishes those who do not keep them. Thorsteen tells of his disgust for the loud and drunken ways of the other warriors and their ways with women. He tells of how his warrior father and mother are different. Both had been farmers before they moved to the settlement, and they still value the loving and quiet family life that they had on the farm.

As they talk, they set the wedding for the fall equinox.

On 10/28/15, this story continues with the Venus of Galgenberg posture (Fig. 2.8):

I am flying through the air in a cart pulled by two cats. I see another cart being pulled by two goats near to me, the cart of Thor. I am in the cart of Freyja pulled by her cats. Then I am back with the family of Vigdis, and they are talking with Thorsteen about their differences in how they worship. Vigdis's father, Vivil, is talking about the cats and the sound they make when they walk. "They walk in silence, stalking, aware of everything around them. With this strength, they can sneak up on their prey without being heard. Heimdallr can hear the grass growing. The cats are even quieter than that. When the cats pulling Freyja's cart land, no one can hear it. But look at Thor in his cart, swing his hammer, making the crashes of lightning. He is just the opposite.

"You may wonder about why the army of Odin could not beat the Vanir. As much as they tried, the battles always ended in a stalemate. The Vanir didn't win the battle either. They were not trying to win but were only defending themselves. The Vanir used magic and one of the magical strengths was the sound a cat makes when it walks. For this silence, the Vanir go to a place within themselves, a place of harmony from where they can see what the warriors of Odin cannot see. They can anticipate and see from where the next swing of a sword is coming, they can see into the future, see the approaching army, and they can see the army retreating in frustration because they cannot win against the magic of the Vanir. This is just one of their magical strengths, but the most important. Their strength is in the sound a cat makes when it walks. Odin's army shouts and clashes their swords against their shields. They believe that the loudest army has the advantage, but the greatest strength is the harmony found in silence.

"When Thor flies in his cart pulled by his goats, he is watching the battle below, hearing the loud noise. He is there to give strength. When Freyja flies in her cart pulled by cats, she is looking for the people in need, of a woman in labor about to give birth, or of a farmer tending his fields, fields that are too dry and not growing well. She looks for those who are sick or injured so that she can bring them help. Her compassion and love is her strength, a much greater strength than the fighting between armies. We value the teaching of Freyja and do not understand her cousin Thor, who wants to fight all the time.

"The stories we hear about you from Vigdis tell us of your gentleness and softness. That is what she finds most attractive about you. You are not trying to impress her with the swinging of your sword and your shouts of victory. There are fewer men like you than there used to be. That is why we approve of your marriage to her. Maybe you can find a greater strength in fighting using the sound a cat makes when it walks, a way of the Vanir that she can teach you."

Thorsteen liked this story and loves the gentle and compassionate ways of this farming family, ways that remind him of his own parents and the stories they tell of the way life was on the farm.

We continue on 10/29/15 with this story of love using the Priestess of Malta Posture (Fig. 2.7):

I am again at the steading of Vigdis, and the visit with Thorsteen. Vigdis's mother, Vilborg, gets up to tend the fire while Vivil is telling the stories of the Vanir. As she adds a couple of pieces of wood, she thanks the Great Mother, Moðir, for providing the trees for their wood. She stirs what is in the cauldron that hangs over the fire and takes a piece of smoked lamb down from the ceiling, cuts it up, and puts it in the pot, again with words of thanks to Moðir who provides us with everything we need to live. She thanks the lamb for the wool it gives us and for it giving its life to sustain us. As she adds some turnips and other vegetables from the garden, she again gives thanks, mentioning how the vegetables depend upon us for pulling competing weeds and sometimes for water. The sheep depend on us for grain and protection from predators, just as we depend on everything around us. Everything of the Earth is interdependent and we humbly give thanks to our Great Mother, since we are no better or no less than the trees, animals, and vegetables.

As Vilborg quietly speaks these words while preparing the meal, Thorsteen listens to them, wondering if they were words spoken by his mother when she lived on the farm. At King Gylfi's settlement, the women in the kitchen talk about everything else with no mention of where the food comes from. The men in the hall are too busy eating and drinking while talking about their fetes of the day to think about where the food comes from. Thorsteen feels the quiet harmony of life on the farm.

Soon his partner returns from his collection of the food needed to sustain the settlement and is invited to join them for this meal. When the food is in front of him, he quickly holds the bowl of stew to his mouth and begins eating. With the family's sense of reverence for life, Thorsteen sits and waits for the others to sit down with Vigdis sitting next to him. She takes his hand and squeezes it with a smile and soon Vilborg sits too. She again speaks words of thanks to the Great Mother and the rest of the family begin to eat. Thorsteen's partner has put his bowl down, not knowing what to think.

While eating, Thorsteen looks out the door and can see the

cart and oxen loaded with food and to himself he gives thanks for where this food came from, thinking that the families who produce it feel no appreciation from the retainers who collect it. When finished with the meal, the two men prepare to leave to return to the settlement, Thorsteen thanks the family for what he has learned about life on the farm and tells Vigdis that he cannot wait until the next time he sees her as they hug. Hopefully, he will see her before the fall equinox.

Then on 10/30/15, the story of love continues with the Freyja Initiation Posture (Fig. A.6):

Thorsteen sleeps in the great hall at night, but on this evening after returning from his visit on the farm with Vigdis, he feels a need to spend time with his family. He has many questions about the farm and why they moved to the settlement of King Gylfi. His parents are happy about his love for a farm girl, and very much like Vigdis.

In talking, his mother explains that when they moved to the settlement, Thorsteen's older brother, Thorgil, out to seek excitement and adventure, had already moved to the settlement and was training to become a warrior. He felt impatient with the routine of a farm. The brother of Thorstain, Thorsteen's father, had also moved to the settlement and was becoming a warrior. His wife had died in childbirth and he could no longer manage the farm. "When my mother died, no one we loved lived nearby. It made sense to move to the settlement. You were just a baby, and I spent my time taking care of you. Your father, Thorstain, as big and strong as he is, had to take care of everything on the farm and that was too much for him too. We wished your brother Thorgil would return, but he was now committed to the king, so we moved to be near him and others of the family. Thorstain built a home for us so he would not have to stay in the great hall and I would not have to stay in the hall of the women. He would come home early from the hall to be with me. Our love and the vows we made before Var were important to us. I enjoyed spending much of my time with the women in spinning, weaving, and preparing the evening feast for the men."

"But what did the gods and goddesses mean to you?" asked Thorsteen. "Vilborg constantly praises and thanks the Great Mother, Moðir, for everything. Their life is so harmonious and peaceful."

"I still praise Moðir quietly to myself. Your father has a harder time with all the men chanting praise for Thor and beseeching his strength. That is why your father has become the captain of a ship. He depends on the winds and the condition of the sea. The sea has a will of its own and only Njord has control over it. He calls upon Njord, Freyja, and Freyr's father. Though Njord became one of the Æsir, he is still a Vanir at heart. Your father respects the strength of Thor and wears his hammer. He recognizes his authority over the outcome of the battles on land and will call to him in battle, but we live by the sea and raiders come from the sea. Njord protects us from the sea. In the drunken feasting in the great hall, he has a hard time remembering to praise and thank the twin children of Njord, but when he comes home at night, with my help, he remembers. When we first moved here, his job was to go to the farms to collect tribute, and he always thanked Freyja and Freyr with the farm family. In this way, they became friends and did not resent as much giving up half of what they grew and raised. I am afraid this is now forgotten."

Thorstein told them about what had happened and that Vigdis's family appreciated his words, though his partner did not understand. His family understands that King Gylfi still shows respect for the Vanir, though mostly out of guilt. His mother continues, "When the king sees a beggar along the road, he thinks of Freyja and gives the beggar something. He gives away a lot in caring for others, sometimes too much, but he is not taking a chance of losing the support of the Vanir. But in being a powerful king, he needs to venerate Odin and Thor. He is feeling the stalemate in the battle between the Vanir and Æsir, a stalemate that still is and will always be until the rebirth of Baldr. If we forget the magical compassion of the Vanir, with the death of gentle Baldr, there will be three endless winters and we will lose all. We still praise the ways of the Vanir."

Returning on 10/31/15 to the life of Thorsteen and Vigdis, I use the Freyr Diviner Posture (Fig. 2.2):

I become Thorsteen in his struggle with what life should be. I am respected by the king and other warriors for my size and strength and I am quite successful in fighting battles, but I feel very distracted by the harmonious and loving way of life of Vigdis. My parents live comfortably in both worlds, but I feel disgusted for the ways of fighting men. I know that for them they have to be one-minded, that their whole life has to be that of a warrior, but I am distracted and do not feel that one-mindedness.

My wedding to Vigdis is about a month away, and I have had only one opportunity to visit her again. I bring up the idea of becoming a farmer, but she feels that farm work is very difficult, and she has been looking forward to living in the settlement where she will have other women to relate to while spinning, weaving, and gathering food to prepare. I know that I have pledged my fealty to the king and know that I cannot break this pledge. He sees great things for me because of my size and strength. I could become one of his berserkers, which disgusts me the most.

"The other retainers thought it was strange when they saw me sitting on the hillside with the young shepherd, a place that is quiet and where I can think, but they would say nothing because of their respect for my size and strength. I was thinking about life after death, of fighting every day in Valhalla, which seems like a very bizarre wish, but life in Hel sounds very depressing. Why would anyone want to continue to fight every day, but if you are one-minded in being a warrior, in being the strongest warrior you can be and that is the only life you know, then the fighting in Valhalla maybe makes some sense. I would like to be more creative, creative in farming or shipbuilding, or blacksmithing, but the king and the other retainers see me and expect me to not be a ship captain like my father but to be a great warrior.

"Since I met Vigdis, one of my best friends has become her brother, Vitar. He loves the excitement of competition and fighting. He is smart, has learned the runes, and with his powerful arm he has become the king's carver of stone. He is both creative and a warrior, but his creativity is to tell the stories of strength and power in battle. These stories are told in the evening while the warriors eat and drink, but one cannot forget his telling of stories when carved in stone. He is a one-minded warrior. I tried to tell him about my thoughts, but he thinks I am crazy."

The experiences of the last several days bring me to believe that Thorsteen and Vigdis are my direct ancestors. This belief came to me today with the intensity of these experiences of Thorsteen's emotional struggle, and with it being All Hallows Day, the time that the spirits of ancestors visit. Some of my ancestral experiences, as recorded in *Baldr's Magic*, took place on the west coast of Sweden at Tanumshede just below the border with Norway, which adds support for this belief. These experiences take place again near present-day Tanumshede and began on October 25th, the morning after I returned from the Nordic Winter Nights Blot in Hagerstown, Maryland, where we celebrated the visitation of the ancestors.

Again I visited Vigdis on 11/1/15 while using the Tanum Underworld Posture (Fig. 2.6):

I become Thorsteen. I am laying against a large sloping rock with Vigdis laying on my shoulder. I found a reason to get away to visit her a couple of weeks before our wedding and we are talking. I am telling her of my thoughts about the absurdity of wanting to go to Valhalla, but the alternative of Hel doesn't sound any better. She tells me about Griðbustaðr, Freyja's dwelling place of harmony and peace. "Odin has forgotten or does not want to think about another place to go after death, and I think it is really the only place. Odin tells of the wonders of Valhalla because he wants men to be one-minded in becoming powerful warriors. I believe that where we go after death is Griðbustaðr, a place of harmony and peace."

"Where is that?

"It is here on Mother Earth. We become the air that all life breathes. We become the soil that provides the flora that all life needs. We become part of the fish that the bear needs to live, fish that join us in Griðbustaðr to become part of everything of the Earth. It is a beautiful place where we are part of everything of the Earth, part of the harmony of everything that depends upon everything to survive. I have been eager to tell you something special. This is the time. I am pregnant. We are going to have a baby, and we will become part of our child, part of a new life, both now and when we die. We will be everywhere like the ancestral spirits we talk to when we want to find answers to our questions."

Thorsteen rises on his elbow to look Vigdis in the eyes, kisses her, and his hand reaches to her belly to greet the baby. "Here is where life is created. This is the world into which we need to bring our child, a world that lives in peace and harmony with everything."

On 11/2/15 I journey back to the time of the wedding using the Calling the Spirits Posture (Fig. 2.10):

It is time for the wedding. Thorsteen has spent the last few days building their new hut/home for Vigdis. A small group of people from the settlement are preparing for the brief journey to Vigdis's farmstead, Thorsteen's parents, Vigdis's brother, and several close friends. With weddings at the king's settlement, everyone becomes involved. The people love celebration feasts, and the focus is on the feasting and not so much the wedding couple. With the wedding held at a farmstead, the focus is more intimately on the couple, while following the older traditions of the wedding being in the bride's home, and calling upon Var to listen to the wedding vows.

As all arrive at the farmstead, Vigdis's brother is carving a wedding stone, picturing the bride and groom embracing in their love. Others are preparing their places to sleep that night, building simple thatched huts. Some women are putting the final touches on the new clothing made for Vigdis. The parents of the bride and groom are visiting with their heads together, becoming acquainted. In sharing stories, both families appreciate their memories of the old ways of the Vanir.

The next morning, Vigdis joins the other women in taking a cleansing sauna where Vigdis receives womanly advice. Thorsteen goes down to the stream that flows near the farmstead to bathe and dons his new clothing brought by his mother. When the sun reaches its zenith, all gather around the new wedding stone, and the bride and groom each place their right foot on the stone while they speak the vows of fidelity, caring, and compassion.

At the conclusion of this ceremony, all retire to the feasting table set up in the field under several large trees. Thorsteen's father is at the side of Vivil, telling him the differences between the vows at the king's settlement and those spoken here. At the king's settlement, the man raises his sword in speaking the vow of protecting his wife and family, and the woman speaks of caring for the family with her spinning, weaving, and cooking. Fidelity and compassion are not mentioned. Both men value the old ways as carried on by the farm families and especially by the women. On the farm, the worship of Freyja and Freyr is most important.

Odin and Thor are not mentioned, though they appreciate Odin's beloved and gentle son, Baldr.

After one more night at the farmstead, Vigdis prepares for her move to the settlement, while the visitors also prepare for the trek. She has much to carry, yarn, loom, and some kitchenware, but there are enough people to lighten her load, and with all visiting with new feelings of closeness, her mind is busy with thoughts of grief and longing for the life with her family on the farm. Those thoughts will rise in the night when her husband is asleep beside her. She hears of the new home Thorsteen has built for her and looks forward to making it her home with the coming baby, who will be part of it. It is an exciting and joyous time.

On 11/6/15, the story of this newly married couple continues using the Freyr Diviner Posture (Fig. 2.2):

Several days later, after Vigdis has settled into her new home and is spending time with the women in their hall, Thorsteen goes to the practice field and half-heartedly practices. Soon his distraction tells him he should not be on the field and he goes to a spot where he can see the sea to the west. Just to the north he can see an island with the strait of water flowing beside it. The future name of this island will be Bohus-Malmön. Several fishing boats are fishing in the quieter waters of the strait.

Vigdis is sitting where she could see her husband on the practice field, but when he leaves she gets up to see where he goes and follows him to the spot where he is sitting, and they sit together. While they watch the sea and the fishermen, she tells him stories of the gods, of Njord's love for the sea and Freyr and his ship that he can fold up and put in his pocket, but when it's on the water it finds the wind it needs to sail. She grew up on a farm where she could not see the sea, but now she is seeing great beauty in it and feels a great reverence towards it. She wonders aloud whether Thorsteen would be happier following in the footsteps of his father, who is the captain of one of the king's ships.

Thorsteen remains silent and they embrace while looking out into the sea and the island across the strait.

And then on 11/7/15 I return to the settlement using the Tlazeoteotl Cleansing Posture (Fig. A.22):

We get up from where we are sitting and walk down the path that takes us to the shore. I take a scoop of the salty water and wash it over my face, smelling the salt in the water and the air. We stand and watch the fishermen and Thorsteen announces, "I want to be a fisherman, but I do not know how to tell the king that I do not want to be a warrior. Because of my size and strength, he wants me to be a warrior, and it is his decision."

Several days later in the night, the king's volva sees many ships coming from the North and reports to the king that there will be an attack by the Norwegians before sunrise the next morning. The alarm goes out and all the warriors gather to prepare for the attack. They plan to line the coast below King Gylfi's settlement, hiding back in the woods along the coast with Gylfi's ships prepared for water battle, with men hiding in the ships. Several of the king's ships cross the strait to hide in coves along the coast of the island. All feel prepared for battle. Thorsteen also prepares but feels apprehensive. Soon before sunrise, the Norsemen's ships

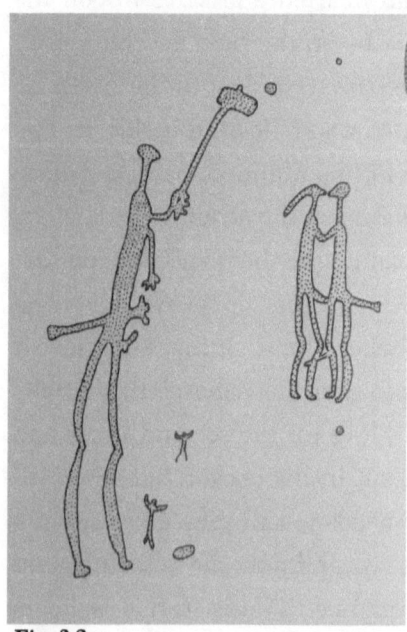

Fig. 3.2

come into the strait and quietly, the warriors come ashore. One ship unnoticed goes farther South to come ashore below the sentry that guards the southern flank of Gylfi's men. Thorsteen, ready for battle, gives Vigdis one last hug, but as he turns, one of the Norsemen, coming from the trees to the south, strikes him unexpectedly, unseen by him and the sentry. Thorsteen falls as the other Norse warriors from the south charge up the beach.[5]

Vigdis, in deep grief, kneels beside her fallen lover, and it is this scene that Vigdis's brother carves in the large stone, a ship carrying Thorsteen to the underworld, though Vigdis knows better (Fig. 2.6).[6] The king would want Thorsteen to go to Hel's domain because of his distraction from his allegiance to being a great warrior, but Thorsteen knows the way to Griðbustaðr, the dwelling of peace.

CHAPTER 4

Bridging the Two Worlds: The Skǫldung of Denmark

Gammel Lejre was the ancient center of worship for the Skjǫldung people. I first visited this site in 2004 and again a couple of years later. On both visits, I felt the deep spirituality of King Hrothgar and the three generations before him back to the first king, Sclyd, and his wife, the Vanir goddess Gefion. Caught in the middle of a struggle between the ways of Odin's warriors and the compassionate Vanir ways of King Hrothgar's wife, Queen Wealhtheow, the king struggled to find a middle road in order to keep his retainers in top fighting strength.

These two visits to Gammel Lejre were before I began practicing ecstatic trance, but because of the spiritual nature of my experiences, I returned to Gammel Lejre in trance from my home in Pennsylvania. With pictures from Google Earth before me, on 1/13/16, while using Tanum Underworld Posture (Fig. 2.6), I again visited this ancient sacred place. The story that follows is of the earliest king of Denmark, King Sclyd.

I find myself in ancient Lejre, Denmark, watching Gefjon with her oxen as she plows a field. She is showing the earliest Skjǫldung how to plant a garden, and how to train and use oxen. In watching her, I ask myself the question, "Who is Gefjon?" For one, she is the fertility goddess of plowing. This goddess of the Vanir wanders and, as she wanders, she sees life beyond the compassionate and nurturing lives of the other deities of the Vanir. She finds her way to the land of the giants and has four auroch sons to a giant, bulls that she trains as oxen. Training oxen takes the patience and nurturance of the Vanir. In her wandering, she meets Gylfi, the king of Sweden, who tells her she can have all the land that she can plow in a day and a night. Thus, with her four oxen sons, she plows a large piece of land from Sweden and pulls it out to sea, a piece of land that is now known as the island of Zealand, part of Denmark. On this land, she meets Odin, who she asks to foster Sclyd, the infant she found abandoned on the shore of Zealand after she pulled it out to sea. She also shows the compassion of the Vanir when she cares for and takes to her home in the upper world those women who die as virgins.

The Vanir deities are of the era of the hunter-gatherers. Ullr invented the bow and arrow to be used in hunting wild pigs and other animals of the time, and Idunn saw the Earth around her as a garden of nutritious and healing plants she gathered in caring for others. As Gefjon wanders, she learns how to control the Earth by plowing the fields and planting seeds. She becomes one of the first agriculturists, a bridge between the Vanir and the Æsir, the family of Odin. The people of the time had learned the skills of hunting from the stories of Ullr and of the nutritious plants from Idunn for how to live healthy lives, appreciating and thanking the Earth Mother for what she provides them. They live in peace and harmony in villages, working together in their hunting and gathering. As Sclyd grows to manhood and marries Gefjon, he sees life differently; he sees life through the eyes of Gefjon, who has learned to value the power and strength of Odin, so he strives to bring the people together in a powerful tribe, the Skjǫldung, with warriors to protect their land. Those who live in small villages and take care of themselves through hunting and gathering also need to support their king. They need to plant gardens and domesticate animals like the auroch and pig to provide for themselves as well as for their king and his warriors. The world is changing.

Before we go on, I have another question, "How did Gefion befriend Odin, and what was the nature of their relationship?" So on 1/14/16, I ask these questions while using the Freyr Diviner Posture (Fig. 2.2):

Gefjon continues to wander through the lands of the hunting and gathering people who turn to the deities of the Vanir from whom they learn the power of magic to sustain themselves. She is on the island that is now called Fyn, part of Denmark when Odin passes through on his journey of migration to the north from what is now Germany into what is now Scandinavia, a journey that will take him to what is now Uppsala, Sweden where he finds people who are ready to worship him, people who will praise his strength and who will become a great warrior tribe, the Yngling. Before these people turn to him, though, they are hunter-gatherers and worship the compassionate and nurturing deities of the Vanir.

When Gefjon meets him at what is now called Odense on the Island of Fyn, his strength and power impress her, but she feels intimidated too. She does not like feeling intimidated, so throws her shoulders back to show her strength. For Odin to move among people who do not know him and will probably feel intimidated by him, he needs someone that the people know and trust to go before him and prepare them for his coming. He asks Gefjon to be this person.

Being of the Vanir and appreciating compassion and nurturance, she has mixed feelings. She sees him as a warrior god and fears that he will lead the people to become warriors like him. She feels a need to give the people of the Vanir strength. This is one reason she takes the land from Sweden to form the new island of

Zealand, a land that she will protect for the people of the Vanir. When she finds the infant boy, Scyld, she wants him fostered by Odin in order for this new land to have a strong and powerful king, though she wants a king who also values compassion and nurturance. She sees into the future and sees what is coming with the people of Uppsala becoming the great Yngling tribe of warriors led by a very oppressive and greedy king, Atli. There are those who believe that King Atli was Atilla the Hun. Under Scyld, the people of Denmark will become a benevolent tribe, the Skjǫldung. As Scyld grows to become an adult, he returns to Zealand and Gefjon to become Gefjon's husband. He sees in Gefjon the power of the Vanir magic of compassion and nurturance. Thus he becomes the first Skjǫldung king and is a benevolent king, as are his son, Beow; grandson, Healfdene; and great-grandson, Hrothgar—the future king of Denmark. Because of what he learns from Odin, he also is a strong warrior king, but because of his benevolence, he rarely has to show this strength.

On January 15, 2016, I use the Tlazeoteotl Cleansing Posture (Fig. A.22):

Again, I am with Gefjon. Scyld has just returned to Lejre where he finds Gefjon waiting for him. She has visited him many times while he was being fostered with Odin and receives the report that this giant of a boy is exceptionally strong and excels in using the sword. Gefjon continues to have mixed feelings, living in two worlds as she is doing. Because she sees that the future is for those who are great warriors and wants the best for Scyld, she is pleased with these reports, yet she is of the Vanir and grieves the demise of the magic of compassion and nurturance as taught by Moðir, Odin's aunt. Moðir grieves too, seeing what Odin, her nephew, has become. Gefjon's hope is that with the return of Scyld, she can teach him the magic of the ways of the Vanir and that he will live in both worlds as she does. She tells him the stories of the Vanir and how Odin and his exceptional army of warriors cannot defeat the Vanir in battle.

The Vanir do not have a great army, but they have the magic of compassion that brings everything of the Earth to their side. As the army of Odin approaches Vanaheim, they see a large, immovable army that does not give way to their attack. What appears to Odin as a great army of warriors are the trees of the forest around Vanaheim. Trees do not move and cannot retreat. The trees with their great swinging branches throw rocks and spear-like branches at the oncoming army and repel them with each attack. The spears and swords of Odin's warriors do minimal damage to the trees that hang onto the swords that become embedded in them. The great bears of the forest also approached the warriors as great berserkers and Odin's army has to retreat. Odin sees that the strength of the Vanir and his own strength are equal, and this battle is a stalemate.

I am sure you have heard many stories of the great strength of Odin's son, Thor. Don't forget his foolishness in competing with Utgarða-Loki and when injured in a battle with the giant Hrungnir. These are only two of the stories of the blindness of Thor when he relies only upon his blind berserker strength and does not attend to his adversary. In his berserk-like rage, he does not see what his opponent is doing. Seeing and anticipating each move of an adversary is part of the magic of the Vanir.

Gefjon tells Scyld that people can live in harmony when they feel the compassion and nurturance of the Great Mother and that as a benevolent king of the Skjǫldung, by showing compassion and nurturance to the people of his kingdom, he will be a much stronger king than ones who value only the strength and power of a great army. She reports, it is a shame that men now rely on the strength of their army in trying to control all life that surrounds them, and that earlier, when people were hunter-gatherers, they lived a life of harmony and peace. But now in this new world, maybe Sclyd can be both compassionate and militarily strong, though she feels that this might be impossible. While valuing strength, others become envious and competitive, wanting to become the strongest, which leads to war and destruction.

We again return to the Gammel Lejre on 1/16/16 while standing in the Priestess of Malta Posture (Fig. 2.7):

Again, I am watching and listening to Gefjon and Sclyd. They are at the foot of what is now the Roskilde Fjord and are walking up towards the top of a ravine, to a prominent spot where they can see into the surrounding distance. This spot above the fjord is now the village of Gammel Lejre on Zealand in Denmark. When they reach the top, they sit down cross-legged and Gefjon tells Sclyd the importance of seeing. She explains to him that, like the Vanir, he can see into the past, the future, and distant places. "To see, you need to quiet your mind while listening to the rapid beat of the drum. Sit in this thoughtful way, stroke your chin as Freyr would sit and stroke his beard. Sitting in this way can bring you visions your eyes do not see and sound your ears do not hear. Let me show you." She beats her drum as he sits in this way before her.

As he sits, a vision of a nearby village, a village that sits below, near the edge of the fjord, comes to him. The men of the village are preparing to leave to go on a hunt. Gefjon has the same vision, seeing ahead of them a place where a hart is lying in the underbrush. She sees the hunters surround the brush and beat it with their spears to make noise, driving the hart out of the brush into the open. Sclyd sees the same vision, but he knows the men have not yet left the village. He stands and hurries down to the village to tell the hunters where they should go. They listen to Sclyd though they do not know this stranger. But because of his enthusiasm, they follow him, knowing they have nothing to lose. Sclyd takes them to the spot where he knows the hart is hiding.

He motions for them to surround the brush and beat their spears on it. Soon the hart jumps out of the brush and several of the men thrust their spears into its flank.

When they return to the village with the deer, they celebrate the success of the hunt, while treating Sclyd as a hero. Traditionally, the one who kills the deer receives the hide, but on this occasion, Sclyd receives it. Gefjon is with him, but the people of the village do not recognize her as the goddess. She takes Sclyd aside and explains to him he needs to practice seeing as he saw the deer and to see in this way he needs a drum made from the hide of the deer. That night Sclyd stays in the hall of the chieftain and Gefjon in the hall of the women. In the hall of the women, she reveals herself as the goddess when the women of the village tell of a young virgin who recently died. Gefjon tells them that this woman now resides in her weeping fields, Gratabjǫð, at the edge of Harmagil, the gorge of sorrow.

The next day, before Gefjon returns to her home in the upper world, she soaks the hide while hollowing out a piece of log over which she stretches and ties it. She then places it near the warm fire to help it dry. When finished, its sound pleases Sclyd and her. As she leaves, she reports she will be back to teach him more, and that he needs to practice using the drum while sitting in the Freyr divination posture to see what others do not see.

While standing in the Venus of Galgenberg Posture (Fig. 2.8), on 1/17/16, I have the following experience:

I am greeted by Gefjon, who has been wandering the island she formed in dragging the piece of land from Sweden out to sea. After finding Sclyd on the shore of the Island and after she places him in the hands of Odin to be fostered, she feels a responsibility to the people of the island who may have suffered some trauma in what had happened. In talking with the people, they tell of a massive earthquake but that they had survived. In greeting these people, she offers her compassion and nurturance by aiding them in what they need, whether in helping them in hunting, or in gathering foodstuffs and plants for healing. She teaches many of the women the power of different plants for healing and helps them in healing their children when sick or injured with the bruises and scrapes of childhood.

Though she spends considerable time in her domain in the upper world where she cares for the women who died virgins, she also wanders the Island. She soon becomes a welcomed guest in the homes of the people of Zealand. They recognize her as a goddess of the Vanir and make a central place for her on their home altars. They love and venerate her for what she has done for them, and forgive her for the traumas they may have suffered when their land shook as she pulled it out to sea. These people live in peace and harmony in their hunting and gathering ways and soon make friends with the people of the neighboring Island of Fyn and with the people across the strait in what is now Southern Sweden. They share with each other the successful hunts and what they are learning about the plants available for gathering. Their life is good and with little violence, such that they live to a healthy age as they learn and experience the magic of the Vanir.

Then on 1/19/16 while standing in the Feathered Serpent Posture (Fig. 2.9), Sclyd visits the people of the island:

I am watching Sclyd, who has been wandering Zealand, visiting the villages of the people living in peace and harmony. Their life's concern is in hunting and gathering and they are content in this life. In Sclyd's wandering, he helps the hunters find deer, wild pigs, and bears with his ability to see. Using his drum, he has been teaching the hunters how they too can see by quieting their minds, sitting in the Freyr posture, and following where their minds take them. He has become well known and popular in using and teaching this skill. He carries the sword given to him by Odin and impresses the hunters when he uses it to help in butchering the animals they kill, but they do not understand the concept of war or of using it to defend themselves. They live in peace. Each village has its elder chieftain, each is independent of the others, and none seeks power over other villagers of the island. When marrying, the men move to the village of their wives so the people of different villages are often related, thus adding to the peace between villages.

One day, while visiting a village beside the fjord, Sclyd sees a ship coming from the north, a ship of raiders. The village has never experienced raiders, but because of Sclyd's fame in being able to see, the villagers quickly follow his instructions, grab what they consider valuable, such as their iron kettles, and herd their few animals into the forest above the village where they watch the raiders come ashore and set fire to their huts. A side of deer is roasting over a fire. The raiders take it to eat but find no one in the village, so they soon leave and the villagers return to rebuild.

With this frightening experience of seeing about 20 men swinging their swords as they came ashore, swinging them ready to kill anyone they find, the villagers understand the sword Sclyd carries. He tells them about Odin and his army and that these gods of the Æsir are warrior gods who seek power over all the world before them. He tells them he sees this way of life as the way people will live in the future. In his visions, he sees another village not a great distance from this village that was attacked without warning the day before by these same raiders, and they killed most of the villagers, taking several young women as slaves. He sees the raiders take the side of deer that was roasting over a fire and celebrate an easy incursion that showed no resistance.

The people of the village have difficulty understanding all of what Sclyd sees in his visions and his stories of people swinging swords and seeking power over others, but they would not want to have to rebuild their village again or be in the village when raiders arrive. Soon a survivor of the nearby village that was attacked finds his way to this village and they hear the story from someone who experienced it. Many grieve deeply the loss of their relatives.

On 1/20/16, I see this transition to a new world of violence continue while using the Freyr Divination Posture (Fig. 2.2):

Everyone on Zealand has become acquainted with Sclyd through his wandering, and his visions of seeing into the future have brought him respect. Life on the island is changing. After the two raids, the villagers along the water that surrounds the island move some distance inland, where it is safer and sentries watch the shoreline for raiders. Until now, the occasional arrival of a ship would be of a merchant, something to celebrate and look forward to. The villagers have many questions of Sclyd on how to defend themselves, and though he has learned the way of Odin, he prefers the life of peace and harmony. He hesitates to form and train an army of warriors to protect the island, yet he knows things are changing, and training warriors to fight will be necessary.

The use of iron is very limited. The traveling merchants often carry iron ore from the mines in Norway, but it is heavy and thus very limited. Zealand has one blacksmith who makes kettles and knives for the women and spear points for the men, but he has not made swords. Sclyd struggles to figure out what he can do to protect the people. On one hunting trip, as he leads the men to a herd of deer, he finds several wolves stalking the same herd and watches as two wolves separate one deer from the herd. One wolf approaches the deer from the front, and the deer lowers its head to fend it off with its horns, but the wolf knows to avoid the horns. The other wolf attacks from the side, moving in to set its jaws into the deer's throat. This strategy impresses Sclyd, and he sees it as a way of defense against raiders. The men of the village need to fight in pairs, one facing the sword swing of the raider but jumping back to avoid being injured and the other to move in to wrap his arms around the raider but out of range of the sword. In close, he then can use his short blade knife to kill the raider. But this maneuver depends upon separating each raider from the others.

He also thinks of other possibilities. If men are standing on each side of the doorway of a hut, as the raider enters, unable to see in its darkness, the men can take hold of the raider and use their short knives. But the raiders are likely to just set fire to the huts. He then thinks of having sufficient trees and brush in the village behind which the men could hide in ambush, the trees, and bushes of the Vanir. From behind these trees, the men can use their short knives effectively. When Sclyd shares these thoughts with the men of the village, he receives their approval, a plan that they can now practice. In his continued wandering, he shares these ideas with the men of the other villages and suggests that they appoint a chieftain to lead them in practicing these ways of defending themselves, a defense that was unnecessary in earlier times.

The experience of 2/9/16 while using the Calling the Spirits Posture (Fig. 2.10) shows Sclyd's work in organizing the people of the island:

In one village, as in most, the chief selected is the strongest and biggest of the men. The warrior men selected him to lead the practice of defending themselves. The strongest of the warriors is the best fighter to defend himself. Until now, the men went hunting every few days, but in between they would work in the village garden along with the women, weeding and tending the plants for harvest.

Though the chief still enjoys hunting, now with his responsibility of leading the men in the practice of defending themselves, he has little time to help in the garden. The gardens are now left to the women, yet some men, usually the ones who do not excel in fighting, still like working in the garden. With this change in the way people live, the village garden has become small. But with the village's continued need for food, the chief suggests that the families with men who help in the garden move out beyond the edge of the village where they can find safety from raiders and plant larger gardens. When attacked, the raiders often set fire to the garden. If the garden was out of sight from the village, it would be safer from raiders. With this encouragement, some families move to build homesteads at some distance from the village.

Life on the homestead differs from life in the village. The men of the village grow close to each other in bonding as fighting men. Many of them now live together in the great hall of the village, the men's hall, and the women move to live together in a women's hall. The women have the responsibility of caring for the children, cooking for the men who now eat in the men's hall, where they spend their time bragging about the ability to fight. The women eat in the women's hall, where they also spin, weave, and sew. The families in the steadings are much closer as families, and the children know their fathers. The families live much more in harmony and peace, working together as they used to, following the ways of the Vanir. They work harder and their gardens are larger because a portion of what they grow now goes to support the village. The chieftain tells the homesteading families that his warriors are there to protect them, so what they give to the village is in payment for this protection. Some women of the village see the difference and would rather homestead. When they try to convince their husbands of this, a few, the ones who do not excel in fighting, move out of the village with the chieftain's support because he knows that the village needs what the homesteaders produce. But for the warriors in the village, there is honor and prestige in strength, something many men seek. They refuse their wives, who they no longer seem to value as much as the prestige of fighting. The wives feel more and more resentment but have the other women to commiserate with in the demise of the family. The way of life is changing, much to the unhappiness of the women who venerate the deities of the Vanir.

Still, Sclyd wanders the island and visits the villages and the steadings. He sees these differences in the way the people live and it pains him to see this unhappiness. He takes this concern to Gefjon. She tells him she sees this too and does not have an answer. The worshipers of Odin praise strength and power while the people who follow the ways of the Vanir value peace and harmony. They know the story of the war between the Æsir and the Vanir, of their fight to a stalemate, with no one winning. Gefjon predicts that this battle will go on for over two thousand years, but maybe there will be a time with the return of Baldr when the people will see the light and again live in peace and harmony. Some will never forget the ways of the Vanir and will continue to remind others that their wars are useless and destructive to peace and harmony.

On 2/5/16 as we continue on this journey, a journey of destruction that those of us of the 21st century well know, I stand in the Tlazeoteotl Cleansing Posture (Fig. A.22):

When Sclyd visits the farm steadings, he especially likes to sit with a son of the family while he is watching and tending the sheep. Sitting with the sheep is an especially quiet time to meditate and feel close to our Earth Mother. Sclyd tells the son stories of Freyja and Idunn, of their love for the Earth and of their ability to listen to the Earth to remember about how the Earth provides, of how the sheep provide us with meat to eat, with wool to spin and weave and with the many uses of the hides. One use of the hides is for making drums. "The beat of the drum is the heartbeat of the Earth and leads us to see beyond what our eyes see, and to hear beyond what our ears hear." He shows the shepherd how to see and hear in this way. He shows the farmer the magic he knows in helping plants grow by using the sheep manure to fertilize the soil and how to keep the soil rich for a successful growing season. He tells the family the stories of the Vanir and reminds them to be thankful for what the Earth provides as they sit around the dinner table. He feels the peace and harmony of the farm life and reminds the family to love and appreciate this peace and harmony. When he leaves, he tells the family how much he appreciates their way of life.

When Sclyd comes to a village of warriors and their chieftain, he thanks them for protecting the people of the island so that they can live in peace and harmony. He reminds them that their job is to defend the land, and warns them against seeking power and wealth from the land of their neighbors, like the raiders who occasionally raid the villages. When he hears the retainers of the chieftain brag and become competitive, he becomes scared that they are losing the ways of peace and harmony by valuing strength and power over others, yet he knows that to be most effective in defending the land, their feeling of strength and competitiveness is necessary. Yet in defending themselves against raiders, they have the advantage of being at home, knowing well the land they defend. The raiders are at a disadvantage in being in a strange land.

Sclyd hopes that with this message, the men will appreciate the land and what it offers. The land provides them with places and ways to protect themselves, and places to ambush the enemy when attacked. He teaches them tactics of defense rather than offense. Listening to the Earth provides ways of defense, but offense leaves them vulnerable without the Earth's protection. The trees of the Vanir were defenders of Vanaheim, and since they could not move, they were not offensive. The Vanir could not win, but their defense was such that they could not lose either. Sclyd hoped that the Skjǫldung warriors will follow the ways of the Vanir in defending themselves, and he reminds them of this whenever he had the opportunity.

We continue on this journey of transition on 2/9/16 while sitting in the Olmec Prince Metamorphosis Posture (Fig. 2.3):

I first became a bear, standing on my hind legs and roaring with its arms outstretched. I then become a berserker, a warrior that fights like a bear, who roars and swings his arms in uncontrollable rage. One warrior of the Skjǫldung had been a Yngling raider taken prisoner by the Skjǫldung. He told of many stories about his king, who was greedy and treacherous. He was happy to get away from this king and soon became one of the Skjǫldung's strongest warriors. One of his stories was of the berserkers. A king would often have twelve berserkers, men who would fight in a rage and would remember nothing about the fight afterward. Their strength and rage were such that they believed they were invulnerable and often would fight naked, unencumbered, fighting without a shield, but only a sword. Some of our men decided they wanted to fight like a mad bear in such a rage that they would feel invulnerable. Our new warrior who came from the Yngling taught them to at first sit and go into a trance and feel the frenzy built inside of them, and when they felt like they were going to explode in this frenzy, they were to stand and attack the enemy. We could not let them attack one of their warriors because of the potential for being injured or killed by the berserker, but there was one large oak tree at the edge of our practice field that the berserker would attack. The tree did not last long but for a short while was an effective target for the berserker.

In watching the berserker fight, I, as Sclyd, realized that in this blind frenzy or rage, it was best to have him fight on land that he knew well. If in a strange place, he could easily become confused in his blind rage and injure himself by running into a tree, tripping on a root, or falling into a hole. And, in that he would not remember what he did in the blind rage, he would forget the dangers of his rage. In between these blind rages, the berserker would likely be a very gentle and loving person. He could live with the others in the village in a peaceful and harmonious way. He could be nurturing to others in his willingness to help others, and he would not remember or recognize the berserker side of himself. He could appreciate the magic of the Vanir and could see beyond what his eyes could see. He could call the animals to him because he was not a threat to them or to anyone else. He was a threat only when he would sit and go into a frenzied trance.

Sclyd discovered he liked the gentle ways of the berserkers, and they added to the village's ability to defend itself. With this addition to his retainers, he and the villagers felt much more secure. The children of the village especially learned to love the berserker because of his gentleness when he would reach out to and play with them. They became an important part of the community.

Some men tried to become berserkers but failed because their frenzied rage carried over into the rest of their lives. They did not or could not disassociate from their normal gentle self when they went into a frenzied trance, so could not return to their gentle self. They carried their rage in their normal lives when they came out of the trance. Constantly irritated by everything around them, others did not like them, thus they could not continue as a berserker.

On 2/10/16, while using the Tanum Underworld Posture (Fig. 2.6), this journey of transition continued:

I became a follower of Sclyd. When I married and moved to my wife's village, I spent a lot of time with the shaman of the village and learned to respect him. Several years later, the shaman died and the people of the village started coming to me as their new shaman. Soon after his death, his daughter came to me with a concern about her son: "He is spending all of his time with his best friend whose father worships Odin. From this friend, he has heard the story of the people who die of illness and old age go to the realm of Hel. Disturbed by hearing this story, he cries a lot because he thinks his grandfather is suffering in Hel's realm because he died of illness and old age. He does not listen to me when I tell him about the Vanir and Griðbustaðr, the resting place of peace. I have told him that, since his grandfather knew and used the magical ways of the Vanir and lived in harmony and peace, he would go to Griðbustaðr. I don't know what else to tell him."

I suggest she bring her son, Alfdene, to me and that we could talk. In filling out the skeletal nature of ecstatic experiences, to help in the story's flow, I have given some of the new characters of the story names such as Alfdene. 'He seems to respect me when I have taken him for walks and he sees me calling the animals to me.' I again have an important opportunity to teach someone about the peace and harmony of the Vanir.

When she brings her son to me, I nod to her that she can leave and suggests to Alfdene that we go for a walk. When we sit, a rabbit comes close to us, and I tell him again about the way the Vanir live in peace and harmony, and I tell him about Griðbustaðr, the dwelling place of peace after death. I explain that the men who fight to protect us believe in strength to win victories in fighting and battle. They believe that to live this life of a warrior they need to believe that if they do not fight bravely in battle and should die of illness or old age, that if they have not been strong and brave enough to go to Valhalla and will go to Hel's realm. They have forgotten the place of peace that Odin's aunt Moðir tells about. Those of us who seek a life of peace, and your grandfather sought a life of peace, believe that they will go to the dwelling place of peace when they die.

With this story, Alfdene left with a smile and he was going to tell this story to his friend. When I saw him the next day, he looked downhearted because his friend did not believe this story. I have taken Alfdene's friend on walks too, and his friend seems to respect me, but that was not enough for him to believe this story. It is more important for him to look up to and believe his father, who is a retainer of our chieftain and Sclyd, our king.

We again talk and I explain to the friend that warriors who die of illness and old age will go to the realm of Hel, but others who do not live the life of a warrior and who remember the ways of the Vanir go to Griðbustaðr. Warriors who find the balance between being a warrior and being nurturing and compassionate in their personal lives will remember the magical ways of the Vanir and can still find their way to Griðbustaðr after death. Those warriors who know they have to stand up to raiders and others who want to take their land but still dream of a time of peace and compassion can go to Griðbustaðr. These warriors who remember the ways of the Vanir fight differently. They do not seek to kill the enemy but to restrain them and show them compassion, hoping they can see that compassion is more powerful than war. Sclyd tries to show our warriors this power of compassion, and some of our warriors who know it best are the berserkers who are very compassionate when not forced into fighting.

We continue on this journey on 2/10/16 while watching for opportunities to teach compassion and harmony, this time using the Priestess of Malta Posture (Fig. 2.7):

Alfdene comes to me again with other concerns, again about fighting. "How can you fight without injuring the other person or without making enemies?"

You ask about what the warriors learned long ago before they had long swords, to get in close and wrap their arms around the person with a sword, then he cannot swing it to hit you. While in close, you can use your short knife, but you don't need to. When you are close, you can talk to him and tell him you dislike fighting and that it would be better if we could live in peace and work together. Fighting wastes lives and everything else. We can live in peace. We have treated well our captive raiders, and some have come to our side when they see how we live. Their chieftain or King Atli was greedy and violent, and living for him was difficult. If you have to use your short knife, you don't have to injure him seriously. That is why I prefer to use a short knife, but there are ways of accomplishing the same thing with a sword.

I have taught a few of the young men how to see from where the next swing of the sword will come. Just as you can see animals at a distance that your eyes cannot see, you can see the next move of your opponent. For the men, while fighting, some have learned that they can see while breathing from their abdomen. They can feel harmony and peace within themselves, can see how the other person is about to swing his sword and easily fends it off. Fighting in this way feels very different; it feels like you are moving and fighting in slow motion. I like to see the men in practice fighting in this way, maybe at first with wooden swords, so that they cannot seriously injure the other person. When a man discovers that he can see in this way, see the sword coming and blocking it automatically without thinking, he gains much confidence from how this experience feels. Fighting in this way, you don't have to look for an opening to injure the other person and you can talk to him about not wanting to fight and about wanting peace. Fighting is such a waste of time.

On 2/11/16 while using the Venus of Galgenberg Posture (Fig. 2.8), we continue on our journey:

I am an enormous bird flying over the island of Zealand. I see several villages, about ten. The largest of these villages is at the foot of the large fjord cutting in from the north of the island, the village of Gammel Lejre. It was at the foot of this fjord that Gefjon found the abandoned infant Sclyd. This village, as with the other villages, had been near the shore, but during these dangerous times, each of the villages has moved some distance inland for better protection from raiders that come from the sea. Lejre is about two miles inland. Each village stations sentries near the shoreline who light a fire when they see the coming of raiders and other visitors, so the village can prepare for the raid or visiting merchants. I see other smaller villages, one to the east across the strait from Sweden. There is considerable swampy land between Lejre and this village to the East. Also along the coast of this strait, near the northern tip of the island, is another village. There are two villages along the strait between Zealand and the other large island of Denmark, Fyn. Then along the northern coastline west of Lejre are a couple of villages, and along the southern coast are three more villages. I can see the smoke rising from their cooking fires.

Also clustered around each village further inland are the homesteads of farmers who have cleared some of the land to plant their gardens, and each has a few grazing animals. Again I see columns of smoke rising above each of these homesteads, rising from their cooking fires.

I then watch or I become Sclyd, wandering around this island visiting each of the villages and the homesteads. As he meets the people of his domain, he praises them for what they have accomplished and the people now consider Sclyd their king. The people of Zealand love him because of his benevolent ways. He always thanks the homestead farmers for what they produce for the people of the nearby villages and reassures them they need to save enough for themselves to live comfortable and healthy lives.

When Sclyd visits a village, he watches the men practicing in battle and reminds them that their purpose is to protect the people of the island and show benevolence to the raiders, hoping the raiders will find a more peaceful and harmonious way of living. He visits with any of the captured raiders who now live in the village. He knows the life they have lived under the tyranny of their king, a life of violence and greed. He tells them of the ways of the Vanir. Sclyd also respects and supports the ways of the fighting men to protect the people of the island. He carries the words of Gefjon, the goddess of the Vanir that these people worship, a goddess who knows the ways of the two worlds, the world of peace and nurturance of the Vanir, and the new world of violence, of men who live the life of seeking power and strength, the world of the worship of the Æsir.

Our journey concludes on 2/11/16 with the Feathered Serpent Posture (Fig. 2.9):

As Sclyd, I feel an overwhelming responsibility to the people of Zealand, both the villagers and the homesteaders. I brought to them the ways of fighting out of fear, and the need to work together to defend themselves. Before, in a time of peace and compassion, they worked together in their villages to provide for themselves and live comfortably. With the coming of raiders and other warriors set upon conquering new lands, and making slaves for their king, I was the person who taught them to become warriors and to form armies to protect themselves, a much different life than before. I feel a great responsibility to lead them to be compassionate and benevolent warriors.

With this responsibility, I have constantly journeyed to visit the villages and homesteads of the realm. When I return to Gammel Lejre, which feels like home, there is one woman, Astrid, of the village, who calls me to her dinner table. I have not had the time or the thought of marrying or having a family. Gefjon visits me frequently, so I have two women who reach out to me and take care of me. I have greatly appreciated this support and their love for me, though I can't say that I have shown them the love they deserve. They both have given themselves to me and both have begotten children by me. My first child to Gefjon is Beow, a strong and healthy boy. Gefjon brought him to me and has encouraged me to find a woman to care for him on the island. She feels it is time that I find an earthly wife and thinks I should marry Astrid. It makes much sense to me since Gefjon has great responsibilities as a goddess of the Vanir and cannot settle down with me, but marriage has not been where my thoughts and concerns have been. Gefjon wants me to be part of Beow's life and wants the boy to live among the Skjǫldung. It is time that I make a commitment to Astrid. Thus, I propose marriage to her, and we are married. She is overjoyed to now have two children to care for, and I work to enlarge her hut to accommodate our growing family.

As Beow grows, I know he is to be king after me and needs to learn much to take this responsibility. So as the years pass and he reaches the age of 10, I take him on my journeys around the island to visit the other villages and homesteads. He enjoys these trips and has gotten to know the people of the island. Everyone loves him as they love me and they open their doors to both of us.

One day when we are visiting one village across the strait from Fyn, he asks about the land across the strait, and who lives on that island. The chieftain of the village is with us and tells us that raiders and warriors are a threat to them. Beow asks about their warriors and if they can defend their people. The chief reports their armies are not as strong as ours. Like us, they have sentries who watch for invaders, and they will light a fire like we do to let the people of the village prepare. When we see a fire burning across the strait, our warriors will cross in our fishing boats and help them in battle, as they have helped us. We do not have large ships as the raiders do, but we use the dugout boats our men use for fishing.

As Sclyd and Beow continue on their journey, they talk of these invaders. The king and his son know that there will be a day when both peoples will need to join together and become one to protect the people of both islands, but now Sclyd does not feel he has the strength or time to do this. This is something to be left to Beow for when he becomes the king. When at home, Beow practices his skill in fighting and learns to see beyond what his eyes see, like his father. Listening to the words of his father, he will become a benevolent and gentle king, remembering the ways of the Vanir.

CHAPTER 5

Learning the Ways of the Chumash Shaman of California

While visiting Goleta, California, I identified a sacred place on a cliff overlooking the Pacific Ocean and Santa Cruz Island, one of the Channel Islands off the coast. Anthropologists have identified the remains of a major Chumash village on or near this cliff. It is about four in the afternoon on September 20, 2013, and somewhat foggy. I watched two dolphins leaping from the water just a few minutes before I had the following ecstatic trance experience. While sitting in the Olmec Prince posture for metamorphosis, (Fig. 2.3), I experience grief for the dolphins:

As the drumming starts, I quickly become a dolphin swimming so freely and playfully as I move through the water with another dolphin. We break the water twice in our play. As we dive to the ocean floor, we turn and shoot up to break the surface of the water. It feels so good and so right. We are doing just what we were created to do, with no worry about food. As we swim through a school of small fish, I open my mouth to take in several fish with little or no thought.

But then I, as a human, have the thought from the news of several days earlier that dolphins are dying on Atlantic Ocean beaches, and I remember that a short distance up the beach from where I sit in this posture is a polluted river flowing into the ocean, polluted with sewage. I have walked along the river and have smelled the stench. I feel such sadness for the dolphins, swimming in sewage without an awareness of the danger it possesses.

Then on 9/21/13, the fall equinox, while again using the Olmec Prince Posture (Fig. 2.3), I feel the sacredness of this special place:

I am walking along the Goleta Beach at the base of the cliffs. It is sunny and hot, and I can see Santa Cruz Island. I start with the Jama Coaque Divination Posture (A.8), but the diviner tells me to use the metamorphosis posture again, so I switch to the Olmec Prince (Fig. 2.3):

I see a large land turtle and then a green sea turtle. I become the sea turtle, crawling along the sandy beach. I dig a hole, lay eggs in it, and cover them up. I return to the sea and find seaweed to eat. This is a very pleasant experience, again doing what I am naturally supposed to do. Then, as the land turtle, I eat plants along the beach and then dig a hole to lay eggs, again doing as I am supposed to do, but a coyote comes down onto the sand and digs up the eggs to eat.

The sea turtle's eggs hatch and the hatchlings crawl to the water's edge and dive in. It is cool and we are very comfortable swimming in the ocean as turtles do as creatures of our Mother Earth. We experience no depth of thought but are just being. There is the threat of the hatchlings being eaten, but that is life.

A couple of years later, on 12/5/15 I return to this sacred spot on the cliffs of Goleta near the remains of Chumash village where I stand in the Calling the Spirits Posture (Fig. 2.10):

I see the spirits of the gulls rising in a mist above the ocean and the dolphin spirits jumping from the water. The spirits of a school of fish rise from under the water. Turtles crawl up on the sand of Santa Cruz Island and dig holes to lay eggs. The eggs hatch and the hatchlings crawl back down to the surf. Some eggs and hatchlings become food for the foxes of the Island and for other fish. Some find safety by hiding in the seaweed and survive. The water around the Island is clear and healthy. The turtles that crawl up on the beach of the mainland have found the water polluted. Then I go back in time to the 1700s, when the water was clean. The turtles are laying their eggs and the Chumash Indians hunt for and eat some eggs and the turtles, though they respect and venerate the turtles, so only take a few eggs and an occasional turtle to let the turtles survive.

The Indians are sitting around the fire and eating turtle stew with vegetables, including seaweed. The kids are running and playing, a pleasant village scene. Nearby are the round thatched huts in which they live. Life is simple and there is plenty to eat. War and violence are rare. The people now are dancing to the beat of a drum to venerate Mother Earth. I go down the Arroyo to where the men are working, building and repairing their plank canoes while the children are playing in the surf. This is a perfect place to build these canoes, their *tomols,* since the cliff is of hard asphalt or tar, which they heat and use to seal the seams of the canoe.

On 12/6/15, I return to the Chumash village while using the Hallstatt Warrior Realm of the Dead Posture (Fig. 2.4):

Ancestral spirits rise above a burial site on the bluff to the east of where I stand. They drift down the arroyo to the sandy beach where at the bottom, canoes, *tomols,* are being caulked with tar from the cliff. A canoe arrives from Santa Cruz needing new caulking. A fire burns with a large stone bowl resting in it and the tar from the cliff is softening in the pot. A willow branch is then used to spread the tar along the seams of the boat where the planks were laced together. Another boat is sitting on the sand as the tar cools and hardens. Recently, the men found a piece of redwood driftwood on the beach. It has floated down from the north. The men are splitting it into slabs with wedges, driving the wedges along the grain, cutting planks for a new boat. Kids are running in the sand and surf. Several men with spears have waded out into the surf and are spearing fish. When they get one, they gut it, feed the guts to the other fish, and a kid runs up the arroyo with the fish to give to a woman who is tending a fire, to cook and smoke the fish they spear. These Chumash are hunter-gatherers and do not plant gardens, though they tend the wild flora by burning, pruning, and weeding. There is plenty, and though the white-men thought they were lazy, their life is harmonious and comfortable.

I continue my ecstatic visit with the Chumash on 12/6/15 using again the Olmec Prince Posture (2.3):

I become a stalking fox on Santa Cruz Island. Hidden in the grasses along the sand are nests of seabirds. I sniff out a nest and eat the eggs. Then I move on, returning to my burrow, bringing an egg to feed my young kits who are scampering near the entrance to the burrow. I see a shadow pass overhead, the shadow of an eagle. I quickly herd three of the four kits into the burrow, but the fourth is at a distance and I do not get it in time to save. The eagle dives and grabs it, thus the kit has sacrificed itself to the eagle.

On 12/7/15, the story of thankfulness continues while using the Priestess of Malta Middle World Posture (Fig. 2.7):

I watch the waves coming in, Mother Earth bringing the life of the ocean to us on the shore. The ocean is vast and powerful. The Chumash have to be awed by it. From the beach, they can see the island out in the Ocean that they have explored and settled, but they do not explore the ocean beyond the island. It is an open sea to the horizon. The Chumash thank the Great Mother for what she provides. They have all they need and do not need to go to other places.

While using the Feathered Serpent Initiation Posture (Fig. 2.9), on 12/7/15 I examine how the Chumash deal with waste:

I see at the back edge of the Chumash village a pile of waste, a dump. They live cleanly. They do not pollute the springs and creeks that run to the sea. They leave the innards of the fish in the ocean for other fish to eat. There is not enough waste to do damage to the Earth. Then I see a large pipe coming out of the hillside below a factory with much crap flowing out of it and into the river that flows down to the ocean. It is just a short distance to the west of where I stand. There is a substantial amount of sewage and we too easily let it flow into the waters of the Earth. We show no care and have conquered the seas with our large ocean-polluting ships.

The name of the cliff upon which I stand is Woqwoqo, meaning much tar.[1] The Chumash village on the cliff is 'Alkash.'[2] The Spanish first found the Chumash in 1542.

I again visited the sacred space on the cliff in Goleta, overlooking the Pacific Ocean. It is 2/3/16, and while using the Freyr Diviner Posture (Fig. 2.2), I asked what will I experience of the Chumash who lived here a century ago?

I find myself as a young boy in a small Chumash village west of, but near, Goleta on a small stream of water that runs down to the ocean. I am eleven years old and with my close friend who is close to my age. My friend's father has a plank canoe, a tomol, and we are out with him fishing in the channel. We bring home a few fish that we clean and put above a fire to dry and smoke before we hang them from the roof of his hut. His father is a woodworker and makes beautiful wooden bowls to give to the chief to be used in feasts when we go down to the big village, Alkash, to celebrate the Earth. This celebration brings people together from many of the villages. His father is a *paxa*, a leader of the special dances for when we call the spirits that we so much depend upon.

My father works hard fishing, hunting, and helping the other men of the village in building and repairing their huts and making tomols that take a lot of work. We enjoy the life of the village. My mother gathers plants, acorns, seeds, and nuts when in season for us to eat and to save to eat during other seasons. She gives what she collects to the chief to distribute to the people of the village as needed. He is to make sure that there is enough, preserving it in a safe and secure manner. We save acorns by burying them in large baskets. When she collects the acorns, she cracks them open and takes out the seed that she crushes and washes repeatedly with water to wash away its bitter taste.

I have spent a lot of time with my friend with our bows and arrows, practicing to become expert hunters. My friend has just turned twelve, and he is excited about becoming part of the *antap* society. His family has the money to pay the chief so that he can start learning the ways of the antap to someday become a *paxa* like his father. As a *paxa*, his father leads the ceremonies during the seasonal feasts. My friend now goes with the men and some older boys of the antap society to learn their secret ways. I am excited for him, but my father is not part of the antap society. We do not have enough money and are not as rich as my friend's family. When I turn twelve, I will go hunting with the other men to hunt for deer and other animals, and for seals and sea lions. Since my friend has turned twelve, he spends all his time with the other *antap* and especially with one *antap* who is a little older than him. I am hurt and disappointed to lose this friend. Now when we go to the feast celebrations, he gets to drum with the other men for the dances. I wish I could help in the mid-winter celebration, calling for the coming of spring by drumming, but I am not an antap. I do not feel this is right. The elitism of a special group of people brings resentment to the village.

Then later in the day, on 2/3/16, I continue with this journey using the Hallstatt Warrior Realm of the Dead Posture (Fig. 2.4):

Again I find myself as the Chumash 12-year-old boy. I am alone in my loneliness, and I think that there is something for me to learn. I feel some resentment, but I tell myself that resentment is a waste of time, that it accomplishes nothing. I go for a walk into the forest to the north of the village and sit by myself under a tall pine tree just to think. I decide that there are things to learn about being by myself, and when I return to the village I find one friend, another boy who is not of the antap society, and tell him I am going on a vision quest for several days. I ask him to tell my family when I do not come home at night, to tell them so they will not worry. I somehow expect that they would try to stop me if I told them of my thinking. They would want me to be at home, doing something productive.

Thus, I leave the village only with my bow and arrows. I find a place in the forest atop a large outcropping of rock and sit. The rock is warm from the sun, but I know it will get cold at night, so I collect some wood to start a small fire, and I wait for some understanding, wait for a spirit guide. Late at night, I see a stalking mountain lion. He is moving quietly and is alone. He is moving with great strength and confidence. When he finds his prey, he springs on it and takes it down. He does this with strength and not anger. I realize that the anger that comes from resentment is a weakness and not a strength. I stay there for a couple more days to feel that strength in being by myself and stalking the world around me, knowing I can take care of myself. With my bow and arrows, I stalk a deer and bring it down, something I have not done before with a hunting party of others from the village. While watching the deer, I sense one is ready to sacrifice itself to me. It stands still and at a distance from the others, and it takes my arrow. I bring it back to my campsite and find an appropriate rock to chip into a cutting blade and butcher the deer, suspending a piece of meat over the fire to cook, while I skin it. That night I look into the future and see myself someday moving from this village to start my own village, feeling the strength in becoming its chief, a vision I tell to no one. I am not born to the antap class, so I am not expected to be a leader, yet a chieftain, but I do not believe in this limitation. The following day, I take two poles over which I lay the rest of the deer and drag it back to the village where my family is happy to see me. I feel a new strength and confidence and my family now recognize me as a man and is proud of me.

The next day, on 2/3/16, I use the Olmec Prince Posture (Fig. 2.3) on my journey into adulthood:

I quickly became the boy and then a stalking mountain lion. The village is having one of its frequent dances with my friend's father leading the dance. I am dancing in the circle with the simple heel-toe dance of the common people showing respect for the Earth, while the antap dancers are bear dancing, acting out the movements of a bear in calling the spirits of the bear. I can feel the bear spirit while I stalk as the mountain lion spirit. I consider dancing the bear spirit dance, but that dance is for the antap and not for me. I can also feel the presence of the deer spirits when they dance the deer dance. These dances are to prepare the men for going on a hunt tomorrow morning. In calling these animal spirits, they are calling the animals to come to them on tomorrow's hunt and the men who are dancing in this special way are to be the leaders of the hunt.

In the morning, we get up early to leave for the hunt and I follow the men. As we walk, I feel the presence of the mountain lion spirit as I stalk. Soon my vision is of deer in a meadow not too far from us. Most of the men are following the leader in a different direction. I motion to my new friend who I have told about going on a vision question, motioning to him to follow me and we leave the others. I take him to the meadow where I see the deer of my vision, and we find a small herd of deer. One is standing to one side and I motion to my friend to circle around. We both take aim with our arrows, and we both hit the deer. We give thanks for the deer sacrificing itself to us, as we drag the deer back to where the other hunters are standing. They have yet to see any deer or bears and have just noticed that we are not with them when we return with the deer. They do not know what to think but are happy that the hunt was a success. With our success, my new friend becomes inseparable from me and we often go on walks together. He soon learns that I can see beyond what my eyes can see, and will take him to where we find animals. Though I want to keep this a secret, the word soon spreads about my ability to see and my antap friend wants to know how I do it. I do not tell him about my stalking mountain lion spirit guide, but he joins us on a walk and sees that I can see animals in my visions. This skill is one secret taught to the antap novices, but he has yet to have such a vision, a skill that I am not supposed to know.

The day after I return home to Pennsylvania, I continue this journey using the Calling the Spirits Posture (Fig. 2.10). At home, the energy is available for me to continue these journeys from special spiritual places where I often identify with a young person learning the ways of the shaman or medicine man.

Though I am continually surprised by what I experience in ecstatic trance, this and the past three experiences were especially surprising. Again this morning I find myself as the Chumash young man who has discovered his ability to see after his vision quest. He is having a good time showing off his ability to his young friends, and the word has spread about his newfound ability. Today I again become serious and question why I have this power, so take the question to the village shaman. As we sit and talk, the shaman reveals he is aware of what has happened and expected I would soon come to him. The shaman reports that not everyone has this ability, and it is something that is taught within the antap society but learning it is rare. After hearing my story of the vision quest, the shaman gives me the new name of "Stalking Lion," and assures me that my stalking ability is exceptional and valuable. The shaman asks me to take him on one of my walks. After we get well beyond the edge of the village, I sit down, grab his knees, and close his eyes. Soon I tell the shaman where I see a wandering bear. We then get up and the two of us walk to the place where we find the bear. There I leave a pinch of tobacco to the bear spirit for showing himself as I have done on previous walks with my friends. The shaman assures me I am doing the right thing in sitting with a quiet mind while calling the animal spirits and in offering thanks to the spirits when they reveal themselves. Though I am not antap as most shamans, the shaman tells me that it does not prevent me from becoming a shaman and that he will be happy to teach me more.

As they talk, Stalking Lion tells the shaman about his feelings of loneliness and resentment when his friend ignored him after he started his training to become a paxa and that he realizes that the feeling of resentment was a waste of time. The shaman tells him that recognizing and understanding these feelings is the first step in finding the power of seeing and that what he discovered is a powerful, new, and understandable thought to the shaman.

The conversation then turns to the periodic conflicts that arise between villages that cause occasional battles and deaths, and that these conflicts arise out of feelings of resentment when some people see themselves better than others because of their wealth and prestige. They talk of the fact that the most respected chiefs are those who remain humble and benevolent in caring for the people of their villages. Because of the diversity of the resources of the villages, trade is necessary to provide the villages with what they need to live comfortably. Trade brings the Chumash people from different villages together. But, some chiefs become greedy in trying to accumulate wealth, an attitude that is causing conflict and battles.

The shaman then tells Stalking Lion that the next thing he needs to learn is to see the coming of conflict. By listening to the people who come together for the seasonal festivities and trade, by watching for those who are greedy, his seeing eyes will see the coming of conflict, and he will warn the village to prepare. He suggests that when the villages come together, that he sits as he does with his eyes closed to see animals and listen to the surrounding voices to hear the sound of greed and of growing resentment. In this way, he will hear and see the sound of the coming conflict. As they walk back to the village with his arm around the shoulders of Stalking Lion, the shaman tells him that at the next village dance he will perform a naming ceremony to announce to the village his new name.

Then on 2/6/16, I use the Tlazeoteotl Posture for cleansing (Fig. A.22):

Again I am Stalking Lion. As I stand in this cleansing posture, I recognize my need to be repeatedly cleansed of resentment. I listen to the ancient stories of the shaman, of when all men were hunters, and they all worked together in all the tasks of survival. No man was better than any other man. There were the elders who all respected for their wealth of knowledge, but everyone knew that as they age, they too would someday become an elder of the village and they all lived in harmony. There was no feeling of resentment because everyone worked hard for the community. Now people have other feelings. When they become wealthy, they see how others live, and they fear losing their wealth. The poor resent not having what the wealthy have. This fear and resentment destroy the harmony that the people used to feel. Hearing this story I, as Stalking Lion, feel the grief that people no longer experience the harmony they used to feel, but feeling grief is also a waste of time. With this understanding, I realize my need to become a shaman. As a shaman, maybe I can help the people find harmony.

Stalking Lion now knows he does not want to be a chief nor even a paxa. He does not want to be wealthy. He is happy to learn to become an expert hunter and fisherman. He is happy to learn about the plants, the herbs that heal. There is so much to learn about the healing plants, but learning is exciting and the shaman is ready to teach him. His ability to see can also help him find what plants heal in what ways. But now what is most important is to listen to others without feeling resentment. Listen to them with understanding, to understand their feelings and what life means to them. I can learn from everybody. I also enjoy sharing with my friends what I am learning. Though they are not always interested, they sometimes are and I think then that maybe I can help in bringing harmony back to the community. My one friend's father complains about never having enough put away, enough saved, but I say that having enough for today is sufficient and that by listening to everything around you, you will realize that the Great Earth Mother provides enough for the next day.

On 2/7/16, I used the Feathered Serpent Initiation Posture (Fig. 2.9):

A couple of days later, the day before the men again go on a hunt, the villagers have a dance to prepare for the hunt. It is during this dance that the shaman calls for the attention of the people as he tells the story of Stalking Lion's vision quest and what he learned from his vision of the mountain lion. Though most of the village by now has learned of Stalking Lion's newfound power, how he learned this skill had not been told, and his new name had not been shared. Now they hear the name he is to be called from here on, Stalking Lion. Though he is not of the class to become antap, he has gained a new respect and all honor his ability to see. The shaman also announces that Stalking Lion is his apprentice and will learn the ways of calling the spirits of the animals in their dances. Then as the dance continues, Stalking Lion takes part in dancing the animal spirits.

The next day, as the men leave to go on the hunt, after they go some distance beyond the village Stalking Lion in his stalking way, sits and closes his eyes and soon sees a bear some distance from them at the edge of the stream that runs down to the ocean. He takes the hunters there and finds a mother bear and two cubs, but he calls to the hunters to save this bear and for the bears to run so that the cubs will have the chance to grow so that there will be bears in future years. Then Stalking Lion again sits and closes his eyes in his stalking way. He soon has a vision of an old male bear some distance upstream. This time, when the hunters reach the spot, the bear sacrifices himself to the hunters. With their success, the hunters offer the bearskin to Stalking Lion.

As we continue on the journey of Stalking Lion, on 2/8/16 I use the Priestess of Malta Middle World Posture (Fig. 2.7):

As Stalking Lion, I travel down to the large village on the island in the slough in Goleta. It is midwinter and the people are celebrating and calling upon the arrival of spring with dancing, singing, and feasting. They are also actively trading what they brought. The people from the islands have brought shell beads and fish, the coastal villages have fish and some animal products such as deer meat, bear meat, and hides. The inland villagers bring acorns, seeds, and some meat and hides too. The mainland coastal villages have been busy using the sturdy canoes, their tomols to carry the people and what they have to trade from the islands, and they will carry them back, making a considerable profit from such trips. Those families who can afford to make the expensive tomols have become the wealthiest of the Chumash and often the greediest. As Stalking Lion, I sit and listen to the conversations of the many people who have come together, and I quickly recognize this greed. Only with the tomols can they successfully hunt the large sea mammals, and they kill many more than they need in order to trade for the shell-bead currency that they horde in great quantities. The islanders especially depend on them and hold considerable resentment for them because of the way the tomol owners take advantage of them. The tusks and bones of the sea mammals are especially valuable, and again, the greedy tomol owners are resented because of the high prices they put on these tusks and bones.

Stalking Lion listens to the greediness and resentment in the voices of the surrounding people, which he finds depressing. When the dancing starts, though he is not an antap dancer, he still dances the animal-spirit dances, calling upon and honoring the spirits of the animals. He belts out the songs to these animals, thanking them for their sacrifice, proclaiming that he will take only what he needs to sustain himself and his village. Though these songs have been sung for generations, many people have forgotten the sacred belief of taking only what they need to sustain themselves. They have become greedy for preserving and saving more than needed. When Stalking Lion goes on walks with his friends and takes them to visit the deer, bear, and other animals, the animals come to him in trust, because he greets them in a quiet nonthreatening state. And now when he hunts and leads the hunters to their prey, he has made a promise to himself that he will do his best to make sure they take only what they need at the moment, trusting the Great Earth Mother to provide. With this promise made to the animals, he sees the animals will sacrifice one of their own to the hunters in reciprocity for this promise, showing their thanks. The animals are quick to know when the hunters are greedy and will hide to protect themselves with the loss of trust.

Then on 2/9/16, I use the Venus of Galgenberg posture (Fig. 2.8) in this continued pursuit:

I see a condor circling above and I become the condor. As I look down on the Earth, I see the coastal land and on a sandy beach, I see a young man, Stalking Lion, lying and looking to the sky. I become Stalking Lion, that young man. As I lie there, I am watching the condor circling with a quiet mind. In this quietness, I feel my abdomen rising and falling slowly as I breathe and I hear the rhythm of the sea waves washing onto the beach. I feel tremendous peace and harmony with the condor, the waves, the warm sand, and my breathing. I silently call to the condor to come to me.

At first, I think it is my imagination, but I see his circles coming closer and closer. As the condor, I hear the voice of the young man and I am curious about what he wants of me. I feel his harmony and do not feel threatened by him. He is asking me what I have to teach him. As I glide lower and lower what I have to show him is that I feel safe with the harmony he is feeling and I can go to him, that we are safe together and can share this sense of harmony, of two creatures of the Earth living in peace together. I land not too far from him and he turns his head towards me and we just watch each other.

As Stalking Lion, I am awed by his size and majesty and just watch him, thanking him silently for coming to me. He pecks at his wing in grooming and pulls a feather from it that drops to the ground. He then spreads his wings and again takes flight. I take the feather as a gift back to the village and show the shaman. He tells me to protect this sacred feather and that it will become part of my headdress that I will someday wear.

The next day I return to the beach again to call the condor, but this time I have brought him a fish in thanks. As I lay there, I soon see the condor circling and coming closer to me. He soon lands near me as our eyes connect and we watch each other. He comes and takes the fish in his beak and again takes flight. There is an understanding between us of harmony and appreciation.

Then, while using the Calling the Spirits Posture (Fig. 2.10) on 2/10/16, I show others how to call the birds:

Stalking Lion often walks with his two friends, one antap and one not. Today I again become Stalking Lion and walk with the one friend who is not antap. After the experience with the condor, I have sat and called other birds, carrying a pouch of seeds to give them when they come to me. I think this is something I can teach my friend. I have him sit with me and place his hands on his abdomen to feel his abdomen rising and falling as he breathes. I suggest that this will help him quiet his mind. I tell him that somehow the birds know you are not a threat to them when your mind is quiet and you are following your breathing. The birds have learned they can trust me, that I am not a threat, and they can trust the friend who comes with me. The birds soon come and peck at the seeds I have spread out near to us. My friend is a quick learner and can feel the harmony of his quiet mind while the birds peck the seeds near him.

A few days later my other antap friend joins me on a walk, and I show him the same thing about how to call the birds but the birds do not come. My friend mentions he could not quiet his mind. I think he was trying too hard and could not let go of his thinking. When we return to the village, I go to the shaman and tell him this story of what happened. He knows how to help my friend quiet his mind. He brings out his drum and starts beating it rapidly, telling me that this can help in quieting the mind. It distracts you from thinking. Then, over the next couple of days, he helps me make a drum. The next time I walk with my antap friend, I take my drum and beat it quietly as we sit to call the birds, and the birds come.

Stalking Lion thinks about the difference between his two friends and knows that his antap friend is always thinking about what he can do to accomplish things like his father. His thinking does not slow down to allow him to feel harmony with the world around him, but listening to the drumming and feeling his stomach rise and fall was enough to distract him from his other thoughts. Yet, his distracting thoughts would continue to limit his ability to see and to call the animals to him.

Then, on 2/11/16 while using the Freyr Diviner Posture (Fig. 2.2), I ask, "How can others learn to stop their thinking?"

I am again Stalking Lion, stalking the thoughts of my antap friend. We are sitting by an oak tree in the forest, sitting in trance and calling upon the spirits of the squirrels to come to collect some acorns that we lie around us. Though I have been drumming and have gotten lost in the drum's beat, my friend speaks up, saying that he cannot quiet his mind. Calling the squirrel to collect acorns is a call that he should collect acorns to put away for when he and his family may need them. In listening to his thoughts and the few words he speaks, I can feel his feelings of insecurity, the insecurity of not having enough to survive. To me, he and his family have plenty, more than enough. Hoarding acorns somehow should make him feel more secure, but just the thought of needing to horde suggests he believes he does not have enough. He does not have faith in Mother Earth and her ability to provide. He does not listen to and thank her for what she provides.

As I call the spirit of the animals to me or seek to see when they might be ready to sacrifice themselves to me, I find my growing faith in our Earth Mother's ability to provide. I feel one with nature, with everything around me. We are all in this together for our survival. We each depend upon each other. We are interdependent, and in this interdependency is our security. I pick up an acorn and throw it at him with a smile on my face. The acorn hits him on the head and he smiles back. His insecure feelings are a big hindrance to him in seeing and calling the animals to him. At least he realizes that I have something that allows me to feel free, to feel secure. He does not understand the value of having little. Having enough to survive for the day, knowing with confidence that Mother Earth will provide for the next day offers the security and feeling of freedom he needs for the animals to trust him.

As I feel Stalking Lion's trust and security, I can feel the sense of security within myself and feel confident that I have enough to survive comfortably in my faith that Mother Earth provides when I let myself be one with the surrounding Earth.

On 2/12/16, I use the Olmec Prince (Fig. 2.3) as I continue to learn much from Stalking Lion:

I became a young buck in a small herd of deer. A hunting party is stalking through the forests and sees us. I know that because I am young, they will not harm me and that the old buck of the herd is prepared to give his life to the hunters. I see the old buck fall, but then I am hit by an arrow and am confused as I try to run. I see the hunter who shot me fall as I run, but soon I fall, too. I hear shouting and see that there are two hunting parties, and arrows are flying between them.

The man who was hit by the arrow and fell, and the men with him are from another village and hunting outside of their own territory. After some shouting, the arrows stopped flying and the two groups of men come together to talk. The men with the man that was wounded had left their hunting territory when they could not find any deer and crossed into our territory. I am again Stalking Lion and see that these men are greedy because they killed two deer, more than they need for the next few days. I asked them in anger why they would kill a young deer and not leave it mature so that the herd remains healthy. They had no answer. I continued, "The deer in your territory have left because you have not shown care for them. The deer felt your greed and know other places are safer. Taking more than one deer, more than you need for a day or two is foolish. Now you seek to weaken the herds in our territory. You are not welcome here. We value our herds and the deer trust us to not take more that is needed for several days until we are again in need and ready again to hunt. Then we will find a different herd and take only one deer. Take your wounded hunter with you and leave. His wound does not appear too serious."

It surprised them to hear such strong words from such a young hunter, but they see all the men from our village nodding in agreement with my words, and they leave.

The men with Stalking Lion perform a ceremony of thanks to the herd with a handful of acorn meal and take the two dead deer back to their village. I take the story of what happened to the village shaman who compliments me on what I had done. It was my arrow that wounded the other hunter in the arm. The other hunters were about to take more deer if they could. They needed to be stopped.

I use Tanum Underworld Posture (Fig. 2.6) on 2/13/16 while I enter the sweat lodge:

After yesterday's experience, the shaman knows it is important for me to join the men in the sweat lodge. As we sit in the heat, we talk about what needs to be done. Another dance is important to ask forgiveness and to reassure the deer that we value and protect them. Our village remembers and lives the traditional ways of the Chumash, but the hunters of the neighboring village have forgotten these ways and think only in accumulating that which they believe they need for the future. They are not showing their love and trust for the Earth to provide. What can we do to bring them back to living in harmony with the deer and everything of the Earth?

The shaman does not have the answer, but he knows the shaman of the neighboring village and knows he needs to invite him to a sweat lodge and talk with him. The next morning the shaman along with Stalking Lion leave to visit the other village and invite their shaman to come for a sweat.

Stalking Lion and his shaman returned to their village, and when the neighboring shaman arrives, they climbed down into the sweat lodge to cleanse away the angry thoughts that both villages are feeling. The neighbor shaman reports their chief does not live by the old ways and tells the people that it is important to be strong and gather as much as possible to show his people that he cares about their security. The neighboring shaman had already listened to the story of what happened on the hunt from the chief, who was with the hunting party. He had been out of sight, and because of his embarrassment, he remained out of sight. He knew that the words of Stalking Lion were right. He was ready to seek ways to keep the peace between the two villages. Hearing this, Stalking Lion suggested their chief should come to a sweat.

The chief knows what to do. He will visit the other chief and let him know he wants peace. He will suggest that the two villages hold a feast and dance together to strengthen these ties. He will say nothing of what happened, knowing that it would only add to the chief's embarrassment. Stalking Lion's chief was also part of the hunting party and noticed the other chief was missing. Thus, the two shamans and Stalking Lion go to the other village to invite the chief and the villagers to a feast and dance on the following full moon. The chief knows that they now have plenty of venison to feed both villages.

Using the Tlazeoteotl cleansing posture (Fig. A.22) on 2/14/16, we prepare for this dance and feast:

At the time of the full moon, the people of the neighboring village arrive with many gifts of food. The women come together in preparing the meal, and soon the drumming begins, calling the people to come together to hear the words of the chief. He first welcomes the neighbors and gives thanks for what the Earth provides. He then follows by telling the story of Stalking Lion's vision and of his ability to see and lead their hunters on successful hunts. He then looks to the paxa to lead the deer dance before the feast starts. After the feast, the dancing resumes and continues late into the evening, but for this dance, the paxa asks Stalking Lion to lead it. Stalking Lion, wearing an antler headdress, begins and soon the other men joined in. One man has his arm wrapped where Stalking Lion hit it with his arrow. Stalking Lion goes to him and they dance side by side. So do the two chiefs and the two shamans dance side by side in an early circuit of the dance court, lifting the spirits of the deer. This dance removes any tensions remaining between the two villages and makes the continued eating a bonding experience.

The young children play and run together, and the adults renew friendships. Those who have parents, brothers and sisters, and other relatives from the other village are sitting together renewing their family ties and soon they will return to the dance to dance together. They repeated the deer dance several times throughout the evening, along with singing asking the deer for forgiveness. The message spreads of the importance of taking from the Earth only that which is necessary for the immediate future. The chief does not mention the need to respect the boundary between the villages' hunting territories because everyone knows that is to be respected. Thus, peace between the two villages grows, and all look forward to a renewed closeness of harmony and respect.

* * *

Stalking Lion continues to teach others as I use the Priestess of Malta Posture (Fig. 2.7) on 2/15/16:

During the feast, a young man from the other village comes to me and wants to learn how to see as I see. I am more than happy to teach him. He is staying the night, so we plan to go for a walk the next morning.

The next morning, another friend of mine joins us on a walk. As we walk, we talk, and I tell him that what is most important is to show the animals that we are no threat to them to gain their trust. To gain their trust, I visit the animals almost every morning. I have gotten to know the deer, bear, and other animals in our hunting territory. I know every nook and cranny of our territory and the habits of its animals. We come to a clearing and the three of us sit down with our legs crossed, and we grab our knees. I explain how it is important to clear our minds of all thoughts and to follow our breathing. We need to make sure that we are breathing from our diaphragm. In this way, we feel in harmony with everything around us and are nonthreatening. I beat my drum rapidly but softly. This young man is a talented student and quickly sees a deer in a nearby clearing near a gnarled Manzanita bush. We all three see the same place. As we walk to that place, I pick a handful of grass for the deer. When we get to the clearing, there are four deer there waiting for us. I lay the grass in front of us as we again sit in harmony, and soon the deer approach to nibble on the grass I brought for them.

As we walk back to the village, I explain it takes some time for the deer and other animals to trust, but that now they know me and trust me, trust me to bring them new friends that they can also trust. "When you return to your village, be patient in practicing what I have shown you, and eventually the spirits of the deer will show themselves to you and will trust you.

"Reciprocity is important. You need to have a gift for them to bring them to trust you and with this trust, they will come to you. When the day comes to hunt deer for food, one will probably be ready to sacrifice himself to you in reciprocity, probably an older buck, but you need to spend most of your time gaining the trust of the deer and the same thing with other animals. This works best if you have the cooperation of the hunters in your area to take only one deer while hunting."

Sometime later, this young man came to tell me of his success. The other hunters appreciate his ability to see, and he has won them over to the idea of taking only one deer to allow the herd to remain healthy.

On 2/16/16, we meet the family of Stalking Lion while using the Feathered Serpent Posture (Fig. 2.9):

It is several years later and Stalking Lion has started his own family. He is living in the nearby village of his wife and has become the shaman for the village. Living matrilocally is traditional for the Chumash. Stalking Lion continues to provide an example to the people by living simply. He continues to go for daily walks to be close to the animals, and he takes his young son and others for walks to teach them how to see. Hoarding wealth interferes with the life he believes in, but many in the village believe that wealth gives them prestige and security, including the chief. At least the paxa recognizes the power of the dances in being close to the Earth, but wealth separates people from their Mother, the Earth, and those who accumulate or horde that which the Earth provides are not appreciating her but take advantage of her.

Being the shaman, most villagers see Stalking Lion as different or strange in the way he looks at the Earth, but they respect him even though he does not think like them. By teaching others how to see, a small number also avoid accumulating wealth, but again, most villagers think of those few as also being strange. Most villagers do not live as true hunter-gatherers but live in the new world that has become competitive and violent in seeking to control and having power over others. Control and power have become the strength of this new generation, much to the chagrin of Stalking Lion.

He is proud of his son, who now can call animals and their spirits to him, loves that of the Earth, and is showing that he has faith that the Earth will provide. Stalking Lion's wife knows well the healing powers of many herbs and is the person of the community to whom the villagers turn for healing.

On 2/17/16, we return to the lesson of taking only one while using the Freyr Diviner Posture (Fig. 2.2):

Though the chief and many of the villagers put away much "for a rainy day," especially fish and acorns, they have learned from their shaman and from Stalking Lion the importance of taking only one deer, the deer that sacrifices himself to them on the hunt and only one bear, not a mother or her cubs. Some men remember when they had almost depleted the deer herds in their territory when it became very difficult to find even one deer. The deer dance and the bear dance are very important to them in calling the spirits of these animals. The dance shows them respect. They recognize that the deer and the bear feel this respect by coming to them, especially to some of the young boys who go on walks with Stalking Lion.

While fishing, the fishermen cannot be selective while using their nets as when hunting deer and bears with bow and arrow, but this does not seem to deplete the fish population. There always seems to be enough fish in the large schools in the channel. Whenever Stalking Lion has the opportunity, he reminds the fishermen to give thanks to the fish and to Mother Earth for providing. When collecting acorns, there always seems to be plenty. They know all the oaks trees in their territory and collect all the acorns they can find below these trees. The trees will always produce more. When they see a small oak, they protect it to allow it to grow large. Enough acorns escape being collected to produce these young trees. Again, when Stalking Lion or his wife has the opportunity, they remind those collecting acorns to leave something in thanks, a pinch of cornmeal or a pinch of tobacco, or some other gift available. The village always has enough to trade with the villagers from other parts of the Chumash territory, whether the islanders who are skilled in making shell beads and have the necessary shells or those who live inland who provide acorn flour and animal skins in exchange for fish and beads. Where they live is very productive as long as the people show respect for what they use. The village shaman and the paxa are important members of the village in reminding the people to show this respect. The dances and songs remind the people that all that is alive in the area are their ancestors.

As this journey ends on 2/18/16, we use the Calling the Spirits posture (Fig. 2.10):

This sequence of ecstatic experiences again takes me to a place, whether from a place within me or from the universal mind, of the ancestors of the land, a place where there are people who venerate our Earth Mother, a place of health, harmony, and sustainability. It may result from calling upon the spirits of each direction, but I believe it has taken me to what is most important in saving the Earth from the destruction we have put on it because of materialistic greed. We have forgotten what the Chumash and other indigenous people knew, that everything of the Earth is our ancestor and needs to be valued and respected.

Stalking Lion, his wife, and son, the shamans and paxa of the community, know this and work to sustain this knowledge through the ritual and hunting practices. We now see that the indigenous people of the world have maintained this awareness and are teaching us that this is what we need to return to in order for humanity to survive on the Earth. The Earth will survive and eventually recover from the destruction we have imposed, but we may not. Our only hope is to learn from Stalking Lion and others who believe like him. This has become a repeated theme in my ecstatic experiences and in my writing, a theme that has brought about a real change in my life. The spirits of the land and the spirits of my ancestors have become very real to me and I greatly value what they are teaching me.

CHAPTER 6

Learning the Way of the Huchiun Hunter of California

In June 2014, I attended the annual conference of the International Association for the Study of Dreams, where each morning I offered an ecstatic trance workshop. The conference in California was at a hotel on the Berkeley Marina at the edge of the Cesar Chavez Park. I found a place in the park on a knoll that overlooked both the San Francisco Bay to the west and a channel that separated the park from Berkeley to the east. This knoll, with its view, felt spiritual, a place where I took one of the ecstatic postures each morning and evening while I went into an ecstatic trance. On the first evening, the evening of June 5th, I sat in the Olmec Prince Metamorphosis Posture (Fig. 2.3):

As I sit, I see to my left the many yachts docked in the marina and beyond, to the San Francisco Bay and the Golden Gate Bridge. Off to my right is the expanse of the Cesar Chavez Park. During the silence, I have my eyes open and feel sadness because of the trash I see at the water's edge. When the drumming begins, I close my eyes and become a fish, coughing and seeing other fish with x-ed out eyes as if they are dead or sick. Then I become a catfish cleaning up the bottom, even so, I do not feel well or healthy because of the toxic waste. I become a worm used to clean up toxic waste and filth, a worm that I know will need to be destroyed when it becomes too toxic itself. Then I find myself by a stream of water at home that is burning because of the gas from fracking and wonder if the bay might catch on fire, though I know that is not likely. As a worm and a catfish, I am doing what I was created to do, doing it without thought, not knowing that I too would become toxic and sick. As a human, I should do better at my job of protecting the fish and worms from such toxins. I know better, but there are those who do not care. It is windy with the wind rippling the water.

The next morning, June 5th, I sit on the grassy knoll of the Cesar Chavez Park, and use again the Olmec Prince Posture (Fig. 2.3):

Today I try to make up for yesterday's very sad experience. The Park is a large part of this peninsula, protruding north into the bay. There is a narrow channel to the east that separates it from the mainland of Berkeley. The experience is slow in starting. I go back to before the white men came, about 300 years ago. I become a rabbit hopping through the grass, a tall grass much taller than the mowed grass that is there now, and I feel safe. I dive for my hole when I see the shadow of an eagle above me. The grass is tall and there are a lot of gopher holes around me. I briefly become a gopher, but I feel safe as a rabbit in this paradise. I sneezed once and opened my eyes to see three blackbirds within about 15 feet of me, just pecking in the grass without fearing me. This is a place where Indians hunt and two come by me hunting rabbits and looking for bird eggs. I feel that life here is paradise. I have heard stories of the California Indians as being lazy. In this paradise, life is peaceful, but not lazy. I can smell the grass in the wide-open space around me. When I return to my room in the hotel, I look up what Indian tribe inhabited this area and find it was the Huchiun tribe of the Ohlone.

* * *

That evening again on the knoll of Cesar Chavez Park, I use the Lady of Cholula Posture asking about the Huchiun people of the area:

Where I am sitting two Huchiun come walking by, hunting rabbits with their bow and arrows. We greet and when they start back to their encampment, they invite me to follow. They go up to what is now Strawberry Creek above the UC Berkeley campus, and around a curve in the canyon of the creek to a place sheltered from the wind, wind that is so common throughout the area. There I see several, maybe six, domed huts, covered with the tule rushes from down by the water's edge and there is a fire pit between them. The Huchiun are wearing next to nothing except for deerskin loincloths. They hunt deer, which are plentiful in the area. One woman of the encampment is next to a cooking pit in the ground in which a fire is burning. She is cooking a stew with herbs and vegetables to which they add the two rabbits that the men had killed and cleaned. Life is easy and unhurried, and food is plentiful. They do not need to kill or gather more than they need for a day or two. The weather, though it can be cold and windy, is not extreme. In their reed-covered shelters, they have beds of grass covered with deer hides. Animals are not afraid of these Indians because the Indians rarely need to hunt them and hunt only what they need at the moment. Other times they watch the deer, bears, rabbits, and other animals with a sense of respect and gratitude, watching them with a sense of meditative harmony. The animals feel safe around them when the hunters are in this state of mind. Living this peaceful and simple existence as hunter and gatherers, they are free to move from place to place. Having what we would call possessions is a hindrance, so they have only what they need at the moment.

* * *

The next morning, on June 6th, I sit in the Freyr Divination Posture (Fig. 2.2):

As I walk to my now sacred space on the knoll in the Cesar Chavez Park, three crows fly around me. When I arrive, a gull comes to sit nearby. I have a fairly empty mind. I start with the Freyr Diviner posture, asking what should I do this AM. I feel the spirits of children coming from the south. I am facing north. Soon, an antlered deer walks up to me. I switch to the Olmec Prince Posture (Fig. 2.3) and become the deer. I walk alone as the deer to the northern tip of the park. There I see gulls and become a gull to fly across the land to the Indian encampment up Strawberry Creek. Near me sits an elder with several children around him. He is telling them about the gulls and their nests in the grass. The children see me, a gull, and want to do something for me, so they pick some good-smelling grass and bring it to me for my nest. I don't collect grass for the nest but it is just there, an indentation in the grass where I would lay eggs, but I am pleased with their offering and take the grass. I then become a swallow and the elder tells them about my mud nest and about me eating insects. The children run off looking for some insects to bring to me. Again, I am pleased. Then I become a crow, and the elder tells the children about me pecking for seeds in the fields. The children run off looking for seeds, collect them and bring them to me. I am pleased. The drumming then ends. The time seemed so short.

That evening, I sit on the knoll in the Mayan Oracle Posture (Fig. A.14), asking for what I should seek next:

A seagull again comes to me and lands just about 20 feet below me on the hill, so I switch again to the Olmec Prince (Fig. 2.3) and become the seagull. I fly in expanding circles around the hill on which I am sitting. Soon I see the elder who had been telling stories to the children walk up the hill, and he sits where I am sitting. I come and land near him. He knows that I have shifted shape and starts calling to me, so I change back to my human form. He tells me about how special and sacred the water is that surrounds this peninsula, and how it provides abundantly for his people. The water beyond the bay stretches on forever, but the bay is a quiet sanctuary for many fish and birds. Besides the seagulls, there are cormorants, many ducks, and terns. As he talks about the sacredness of the bay, I hear a gull calling me from nearby. The elder tells me that the gull is calling me to join him and that it can show me more of the bay. I shift shape and we fly just above the water. I can see many fish below me. We fly a long way around the peninsula when he then dives and comes up with a fish in his beak. I do the same. We take the fish to the shore where we stand and flip up the fish to eat when the drumming ends. Again, I as a gull am doing as I should in living in harmony with the Earth.

The next morning is June 7th. I lay in the Jivaro South American Posture (Fig. A.10):

I first dissolve through the surface of the earth and into a cave where I meet four men who are my regular spirit guides from the four directions. One is wearing bird feathers, one wears a badgerskin cap, one wears a bearskin over his head, and the fourth wears deer antlers. I am not sure if they are my usual four spirit guides or if they are Huchiun. They feel and express the pain of what has happened to our Great Mother, the Earth, expressing a need to do something for her. I then join the Indians in Canada, fighting the Keystone Pipeline and other indigenous actions that I need to support. I realize I need to look closer at the mentioned Global Dream Initiative of the conference and talk in my morning dream group more about the need to leave this conference with a deeper sense of the spiritual side of becoming one with the earth. Today in my workshop I will talk about Gebser, Lazslo, and Sheldrake, and tomorrow about what we need to do in our rituals to bring spiritually alive the earth within us.

On June 8th I lay in the Sami Underworld Posture (Fig. A.16):
I should use this posture more often since it is apparently a posture from my ancestry. I shoot along the earth, close to the ground, like some cartoon character, maybe the Roadrunner, flying rapidly around the Cesar Chavez Park. I then slow down and become a rattlesnake. I go into a hole in a pile of rocks where I lay next to a human skeleton. The skeleton talks to me, telling me he died young because of all the packaged crap he ate. In dying, he found wisdom. He recalls all the stories of how his people used to live a lot longer before the coming of white man. It reminds me of when I sat at the water's edge of the bay with so much trash, of plastic wrappers and packaging, the trash that I saw killing the fish, but he tells me it also kills birds when they take it to their nests, and it kills all life. He tells me of spending time near the four corners where there are piles of radioactive rock. It was there that he first became sick, so he came home when he realized that his life was going to be short. He tells me the stories of how his people know they will survive and he believes that the time has come for their revival, for others to listen to these indigenous people and understand the better and healthier life they used to live. Their diet was healthy, and they protected the earth, taking only what they needed to survive and not the oil from deep in the earth that is used to make the plastics, the wrappers of food and the chemicals used that make the food toxic that is destroying the earth. As I lay next to this elder skeleton, I listen to these stories. He is telling these stories in confidence, trusting that I understand.

* * *

A few months after returning home, on 4/6/16, I returned to the Cesar Chavez Park in ecstatic trance while sitting on our sauna deck overlooking our pond. Again, while using the Olmec Prince posture (Fig. 2.3) I find myself as a young boy of 10 or 11 years, learning the ways of life. So often on the ecstatic journeys, I become a young boy learning the ways of the shamans.

Sitting on the knoll in the park, I look across the channel to the east and see the Indian dome-shaped huts made of the tule reeds. One low domed hut does not have smoke rising from it like the others, but there is a fire next to it heating rocks that are carried into this hut. It is the village's sweat lodge. I, as the young boy, walk near the sweat lodge and hear the chanting and drumming coming from inside the lodge. An old man sits outside the lodge, my grandfather, scarred from a bear attack. He is the fire tender and cares for the sweat lodge that is used daily by most men of the village. I look forward to the day when I am old enough to be part of the sweat lodge ceremony. My grandfather smiles, knowing my thoughts, and tells me I have much to learn first. Today he wants me to cross over the channel and sit on the knoll where I am sitting, and from there I can watch the bears, my totem animal. From where I sit, I can see several bears feasting on something. I wonder what the bears are eating. Since there are wolves circling beyond the bears, I assume that the wolves have brought down some animal, a deer, or maybe an antelope, but the bears have pushed them aside and eat of it first. The wolves are waiting their turn.

As the young boy, I leave to follow my grandfather's instructions, walking south along the channel to where the marsh is not deep, providing a way to cross the channel, I find a group of women cutting tules to repair the village's huts and for making other things such as the skirts they wear. They also make cordage from the spine of the tule, a very strong cord. The crossing, though ankle-deep in mud and water, is well trampled down because of the others who have crossed to hunt on the island. When I reach the knoll, I sit down cross-legged and watch all that is going on around me.

I see many birds, waterfowl nesting, and strutting around the area. I see a herd of deer in the distance, and I see the dead deer that the bears are feasting on. They soon get their fill and wander off, leaving the remains for the wolves, who are now attacking it. I sit there for quite a while, knowing that when the wolves leave, it will be my turn to collect the bones used by my family to make different tools, kitchen implements, and other ceremonial items.

There is peace in sitting among these animals with none afraid of me, and I am not afraid of them. There is no need for fear since I am not a threat, and they find plenty to eat with everything in balance. I carry my bola made from the ribs of the iris with bones tied to each of the three ends. After a while, I see a disturbance in the grass near me so reach for it. A quail comes bobbling out of the grass. I swing the bola as the quail takes flight. I let go, and the bird comes down entangled in the bola. I tie it to my waist and resume sitting, watching the wolves. When they are eventually finished, I collect the bones together in my loincloth, throw it over my shoulder, and return home.

As I walk, I take a wide circle around a bear that is now feasting on the larva of a ground yellow jacket nest. The bear's fur is thick enough for it to not get stung. But the bear has disturbed them, so my wide circle is to keep from getting stung. We too like to eat yellow jacket larvae, but we set a fire above the nest and fanned the smoke into the nest, quieting the yellow jackets before the nest is dug up to roast the larvae over a fire.

When I return to the village, I stop by our family hut to give the quail and some bones to my mother, who is pleased. I then leave to go to the sweat lodge to tell grandfather about my day's experience, giving him the skull of the deer to prepare and use in ceremony. He may give it to a young person whose totem is the deer, though usually the young person is expected to find his own skull, tail, and hide. The men whose totem is the deer wear the skull in the deer dance.

The next day, 4/7/16, again on the sauna deck, I use the Freyr Diviner Posture (Fig. 2.2) as I return to the Ohlone village:

I quickly find myself back in the Indian village as the young boy. My routine each morning is to first go to the sweat lodge to check in with grandfather. He always looks forward to seeing me. Today he asked me to collect some firewood for the lodge fire. I go out to where trees are growing, some distance to the east towards the hills and our summer village along what is now called Strawberry Creek. I find below one of the live oak, a dead branch and leave it there for when I come back past it. I am going to some large pine trees. The bottom-most branches of the pine are dead, being shaded by the higher, newer branches. They hang down and are easy to break off. I like to grab on to the end and walk it around the tree until I hear the loud snap of it breaking. The pine always smells good when it burns. I collect several large branches and drag them back to the sweat lodge, picking up the oak branch I left below the tree. This is enough wood for grandfather to start a good fire, but the other men who come for their morning sweat know to bring more wood because the fire needs to last for much of the day for all the men of the village to enter the sweat.

With this, grandfather points down towards the channel edge where I see my father collecting tule reeds he ties together to make a boat. I go down to help him because it takes two people to hold the reeds tight to tie them together with the strong rib of the iris and tule leaves. When I get there, I know what I am supposed to do. I hold the bundle of reeds together as my father ties them with the iris rib. After tying a few bundles, we then tie them together at the end and weave the fiber cordage in and out through the bundles to tie them together for the middle of the boat where the people will sit. We wove the middle section fairly flat, with the sections at each end pulled together and tied into a point. Made of tule rushes, the boat is quite light and floats easily on the shallow waters of the channel. We then drag the boat down the well-trampled path through the marshland to the channel. It takes a good part of the morning before we drag the boat down to the channel where we get in to try it out. Father gives me the oar and I paddle out to the middle of the channel from where we explore along the shore and find among the tule rushes an otter that he shoots with an arrow. The splash made by the dying otter flushes out many birds that live in the rushes. I am ready with my bola and throw it among the rising birds. There are so many that I am quite assured that I will get one and I do, a coot, not the best tasting bird, but still appreciated. Mother will be happy to see us bring home meat for dinner.

Another eventful day has passed of learning how to be a man, of learning the healthy ways to live at one with all life on Earth.

This morning of 4/8/16, I will learn of the trust animals have of us while using the Hallstatt Warrior Realm of the Dead Posture (Fig. 2.4):

I wake and smell the acorn mush steaming over the fire just outside of our hut. I go out and eat a bowlful before I venture towards the sweat lodge where I know I will find grandfather. I wonder what he will have me do today. When I get to the lodge, I see him with his hand over his eyes, looking to the south. When I turn to see what he is looking at, I see in the distance a herd of deer, about ten, a beautiful sight. We then sit next to the lodge, and he beings telling me a story.

When we kill one of the deer, the others of the herd become afraid of us and run off if we get too close, but the deer are the curious type, and if we don't threaten them, they may come closer to see what we are doing. When we kill a deer in the sacred hunt and give thanks to the deer spirit for sacrificing itself to us, the spirit hears us and the deer learn that most of the time they can trust us. It is important to show the deer that at other times when we are not hunting, they can trust us and that we are not a threat to them. To become a good hunter, it is important to show them they can trust us. Grandfather tells me, "Today you need to go see how close you can get to the herd and not scare them. Watch them carefully and when you see them becoming anxious, sit quietly and just watch them, sending them your thoughts of how beautiful they are and that you love them."

I then leave and walk south to where we saw the herd of deer. They have moved out of sight, but I expect they have not moved far. When I get there, I continue on beyond where we saw them, following the tracks in the spongy earth alongside the bay. I soon come to a ravine and see them at the bottom. Startled at seeing me at the top of the ravine, they stop grazing and move about anxiously, so I sit on a rock at its edge and watch them, and they soon return to grazing and ignore me. So I quietly creep closer. They look up and begin to prance around, looking nervous, so I again just sit motionless until they again become quiet in their grazing. I again crawl a little closer before I again stop until they return to grazing. We repeat this dance several times as the deer watch me, and I watch them. They seem to be curious about what I am doing, crawling towards them on all fours. Why am I not walking like other humans? I resume crawling and they move in my direction, just watching me. After a while, I am close to the edge of the meadow in which the herd is grazing, and I just sit and watch them in appreciation. They do not seem at all afraid of me. I pick a handful of grass and hold it out towards them. They stop and watch me, but they do not come closer, though I think that if I did this enough that they might come and eat out of my hand.

As the sun goes down over the bay, I get up to walk back to our village. As I do, I throw down the grass that I held in my hand. As I walk away, I turn to look back and the deer have come to where I sat and are smelling the grass I left there. When I get back to the village, I go to grandfather to tell him what happened. He just smiles and then asks me how long do I think it will take before the deer will eat out of my hand. I know he wants me to do what I did today again until they are eating out of my hand.

Today, on 4/9/16, I will continue to show the deer they can trust me as I stand in the Priestess of Malta posture (Fig. 3.7):

It is my job to learn to be a man of the Huchiun. Again this morning I first check in with the sweat-lodge grandfather, then I go out into the meadow where I find the deer and sit to watch them. They let me come closer today before they appear nervous. Gradually, I crawl closer and sit with a clump of grass in my hand. They seem to remember me from yesterday and watch me with curiosity. They seem especially interested in the grass in my hand. I put it to my mouth and pretend that I am eating it and they take a few steps towards me. I move a little closer to them. They seem more curious than afraid, thus our relationship of trust grows. I am not expecting that they will eat out of my hand today, but I think the day is getting close.

I taste a few blades of the grass and think the flavor is pleasant, but the stringy texture and toughness are not pleasant. I don't think I could be a grass eater. One stalk of the grass had a seed head, and I found the crunchiness of the seeds more enjoyable. That is why we are seed eaters. From where I sit, I can see a couple of bears wandering up along the water's edge. I know they are looking for fish, something I can understand because I, too, like fish. Thinking about the other animals, I know that wolves and mountain lions eat deer, something I like the most, but they eat it raw. I once tried to eat a piece of deer meat raw and it was very tough, though juicy. I could not bite through it. I have watched two young wolves tugging together on a piece of meat and they could not tear it apart. Other smaller animals mostly seem to eat roots, plants, and insects. The bear likes insects too, the grubs of the yellow jacket and other grubs they find under the bark of a tree. I like roasted grubs too, but not raw. I am most like a bear in what I like to eat.

While I have been deep in thought about what other animals eat, I am surprised when I look up to see that the deer have come considerably closer and are grazing only a few feet from me. When I look up, they jump back but stay close by. The grass is still in my hand and I reach it out towards them, offering it to them. One is close enough to sniff at it but does not take it. I lay it down in front of me and move back from it. It is not long before the closest deer takes it as he continues to look at me with curiosity. I think about the other men back in the village and realize that I am not the first person to feed the deer. The deer hunters sometimes wear a deer costume with antlers as they move as close to a deer as they can. I am sure that they have done just what I am doing to gain the trust of the deer. This is not the first time that deer have ventured this close to eat what a human offers them. With this thought, I feel a closeness to the deer and other animals that live around us. They are our ancestors and one day, hopefully soon, I will learn which one is my special ancestor, to which animal clan I will belong. Since it is the deer that I am now befriending, maybe I will be of the deer clan. Again I return to grandfather and tell him what has happened and ask him about which clan I will belong to when I become a man. He tells me I need to watch for a sign, a special sign, maybe in a dream, but someday I will know.

Today, 4/10/16, while using the Venus of Galgenberg Upper World Posture (Fig. 2.8), I will have fun collecting grasshoppers:

I have been looking forward to this special day, a day that is a lot of fun, but still, I need to go first to my grandfather. Being the fire tender for the sweat lodge, he is busy making an ember bundle because as we leave the village, we will need an ember to start a fire. He too is looking forward to this day and will carry the ember bundle with a hole carved into a piece of hardwood with the hole partially covered to control the air that gets to it. If it gets too much air, the hardwood will catch on fire. If it does not get enough, it will go out. He adjusts the covering so that it burns slowly into the hardwood because it needs fuel to keep burning, but slow enough to last a couple of hours.

We then join the rest of the people of the village, men, women, women carrying babies, and children as we begin our walk along a well-worn path to a grassy meadow. Someone the day before went to this meadow and in the center dug a large shallow hole and filled it with the brown, dry grass. The women have been to this meadow many times with their baskets that they ran through the grass to collect the seeds that fall from the grass when brushed. But now it is late in the season, most all the seeds have been collected, and the grass is brown and dry.

Today, as we get to the meadow, we spread out in a circle around its edge, maybe 80 of us, for this fun party. As we look around the circle, we see many smiling faces as we take a step towards the center of the circle. The circle slowly becomes smaller and ahead of us are jumping many grasshoppers, more and more as we approach the center of the circle with the hole covered in dry grass. Soon as we crowd around the circle, the lodge grandfather throws the burning ember he carries into the dry grass and it quickly ignites with a flash into a low burning fire, singeing the wings of the roasting grasshoppers. The fire soon burns out and the women carrying baskets go into the hole to collect baskets full of grasshoppers for a tasty feast of celebration. Each person had brought a token of thanks, tobacco or acorn meal, to leave in the hole, thanking the Great Earth Mother for providing.

The tribe then returns to the village in a joyous mood, looking forward to repeating this fall ritual in a couple of days in another grassy meadow. I again identify with the bear who I know seeks grasshoppers to eat. Where we live, there is plenty of food and life is easy. Each season we eat what our Great Earth Mother provides us and take no more. Taking more would be a burden to carry with us as we move from place to place, and there is always enough. Besides the grasshoppers when the grasses turn brown, and grasses that have given us plenty of seeds, there are many oak trees with their acorns. These foods, along with all the animals, fish, birds, and other insects that abound, make where we live paradise.

Then the next day, 4/11/16, while using the Feathered Serpent Posture (Fig. 2.9), I return to the deer herd:

I return to being the young boy among the Huchiun. I wake this morning feeling very troubled. If the deer learn to trust me and I show them they can trust me, how can I ever kill one without losing their trust? I take this concern to my grandfather and he just tells me to go back out to be with the deer. They have now learned to eat out of my hand, and I feel I am part of the herd. I know each deer personally, the alpha buck, the other younger bucks, the does, the ones that are pregnant, and the new yearlings. They all turn to the alpha buck for his wisdom and strength, though he is getting old and may not have the strength to continue matching the challenges of the younger bucks.

They also know me and know that today there is something wrong. Maybe they can read my mind and know about my thoughts of killing one of them. In their nervousness, knowing that I am troubled, they come to me and, in this way, I feel their reassurance. I am sure that other men have struggled with the same troubling thoughts. They have killed deer and apparently, they have not lost the deer's trust. The deer can feel the respect I give them and know from our deer dance how the entire tribe respects them as an ancestor. The deer have a right to fear the wolf and the mountain lion. They know that when the hunger of these predators is satisfied, they can again live together in peace, but sometimes they need to sacrifice one of their own to satisfy the wolf or mountain lion's hunger. In this way, they can return to living in peace with these predators. The wolf and the mountain lion do not nurture the deer's trust like I have been doing, and the deer keep a respectful distance from them.

I know that among the deer, the younger males are jealous of the alpha buck and likely wish he was out of the way so that they could exert their manliness in pursuing a doe. They probably would not resent me if I should help by killing him. The younger does too may appreciate me by saving them from the advances of this dirty old buck. If I am honest with them in telling them we prefer their meat and that we will take only one of them when we need one, maybe they would accept me taking the old buck and we could still maintain the trusting relationship.

The men who hunt deer watch them to learn how they move and practice moving in this way. They will wear deer horns when hunting and try their best to move like them. I cannot imagine that the deer thinks this imposter is a deer. They are very sensitive to everything that is around them. I wonder what the deer are thinking. They know we try to protect them from the wolves and mountain lions. Maybe they see this like they see our sacred deer dance and feel the respect we are showing them. In this paradise, the deer want to maintain this respectful relationship, know that each day may be the day to die, and will sacrifice one of their own for this relationship. These thoughts are troublesome, but with experience, I may know better how to answer this question. I know that gaining their trust now can only help when I join in the hunt.

When I return my grandfather that evening and tell him of my thoughts, he answers that this has been a struggle for all the men and the reason for their elaborate preparation for hunting deer, elk, and antelope.

The next morning, on 4/12/16, my experience was one of those that I would call extra profound. I enter ecstatic trance using the Calling the Spirits Posture (Fig. 2.10):

Again I walk to the sweat lodge where I find grandfather. He indicates for me to sit down because he is going to tell me a story. He begins: "The deer and all other animals are our ancestors, are our brothers and sisters. How can we kill a brother or a sister?" He is silent for a few moments before he begins again. "How can you kill another member of our tribe, your family? I know you would likely give your life to protect your family. There are many stories of our people giving their lives to protect others in their families. When a bear attacked me on a bear hunt, another of the men ran at the bear, distracting it from me. The bear attacked him, and he died several days later. That is how I was injured, but I am sure you have already heard that story. If you have chased a wolf away from the deer to protect them, your brothers and sisters, how could you kill a deer?

"Other animals, rabbits, birds, mice, are all a bigger part of what we eat than the deer, but the deer is delicious and very special, eaten on special occasions. The animals we eat do not have the spiritual power of the deer, elk, antelope, wolf, bear, or mountain lion. When preparing for the sacred deer hunt, the men deprive themselves of many things. They do not eat meat, fish, birds, or anything greasy. They do not talk to or look their wives in the face when preparing for a deer hunt. They spend several days in the sweat lodge preparing themselves for the sacred hunt. They dance the special deer dance and make a special deer costume to wear on the hunt, a costume with deer horns. They look to their dreams to see signs for what else they should do to prepare and signs for the success or failure of the hunt. From a young age, they study the habits of the deer and how they move, just as you are doing. They have developed a very special and sacred relationship with the deer and can truly call them brother and sister.

"The deer have also learned that man is their brother and they know they must protect them. When deer see a man wearing deer horns and moving like them, they know he has something he wants to say to them, that he is asking for help, and they are ready to listen and provide that help. They are ready to sacrifice one of their own to help their brothers and sisters, the same way a man might sacrifice himself to a wolf to protect a deer. We sometimes say, 'today is a good day to die.' We are ready to die for our brother or sister.

"With all the things that a hunter denies himself before going on the sacred hunt, he is asking for forgiveness from the deer, and the deer feels this deep connection. When the sacrificed deer dies and the hunters carry it back to the village, the hunter will probably eat none of it but give it to the rest of the family for their health and sustenance, again a sign of the pain he feels in having to kill his brother or sister. He truly feels the pain of his brothers and sisters giving one of their own to him, as I did when my brother died in protecting me. All are very thankful for the deer and show this thanks through their dance and prayers,

prayers of thanks to the Great Earth Mother for providing and to the deer. She expects us to love and cherish all our brothers and sisters, all of her children."

With this story, one of my experiences from the 20th century came back to me. On one occasion, as I was practicing tai chi in our yard, two deer came up within 15 feet of me and just stood watching me, knowing that I presented them with no threat of harm. They reached out to me, showing me they wanted me to be their brother. On another occasion, I was sitting in the woods talking with my son when a young deer came to just a few feet of us and just stood listening or watching. The deer and all other life on Earth greatly miss this communion with humans that they used to have when we were hunters and gatherers. So often while I sit on our sauna deck in ecstatic trance, rabbits and birds come close and watch me as if curious, but they are also seeking the trust they used to have with humankind. Putting ourselves above them in our relationship is a great pain to them and is leading to their extinction.

With these stories, the young boy better understands what lies before him in becoming a man and a hunter.

I used the Freyr Divination Posture (Fig. 2.2) on 4/13/16, and my relationship with the deer continues to grow:

I, as the young boy of the Huchiun, again upon waking go to my elder grandfather, who tends the fire of the sweat lodge. This experience has become an integral part of my ecstatic trance induction over the last few mornings. After yesterday's experience, I know that I have to return to the deer herd to call them my brothers and sisters. I feel this new understanding deep within me. Grandfather understands my deeply felt need and waves me off to go to the herd.

When I get there, I sit as I usually do, now quite close to the herd. They show no fear of me and even come closer as I hold out a handful of grass, which they take from my hand. As I look into their deep brown eyes, I call each one brother or sister, and we feel a special closeness. This is what my relationship with my brothers and sisters should be. It feels so right.

As I sit there, I see a wolf and then several wolves at a distance on the other side of the herd, stalking the herd. I stand and the herd is not fearful as I stand. I walk around them to the other side. I untie my sling from my waste, a sling I use for throwing stones with which I have been practicing. My aim with the sling is improving. I find the right size stone on the ground, place it in the leather cup and swing it over my head several times before I let go of one of the iris rib cords and let the stone fly. It hits the wolf closest to me, and he yips off with the other wolves following. They know that this herd of deer is being protected and leave to find a meal elsewhere.

I again sit down and the deer come close. I sense they appreciate and thank me for protecting them. I sit with them most of the day and feel good about my brothers and sisters. I can't imagine trying to kill one of them when they trust me as they do. As the sun goes down, I stand to leave and they all look towards me with their deep brown eyes. When I get back to our village, I find grandfather still sitting near the sweat lodge. I tell him about my day, and he simply smiles in understanding and support for what I have been doing.

When I return to our hut, mother has our evening meal ready and when we sit down she looks towards me, a sign that she is ready to hear about my day, and what I have learned about life. My father has returned from fishing in the bay and has brought fresh fish for us to eat. He hangs several from the ceiling, drying in the fire's smoke. I tell them the story of my brothers and sisters, the deer, and how I protected them from stalking wolves. They both smile in appreciation and we begin to eat. I am doing what all expect of me in my journey towards adulthood.

* * *

Then, on 4/14/16 while using the Priestess of Malta Posture (Fig. 2.7), I realize I am again protecting my brothers and sisters:

This morning when I arrive at the sweat lodge I hear singing coming from the lodge. The men are preparing for a hunt with my uncle in the lead. Grandfather has laid out the body paints for my uncle to be painted with the designs for the deer hunt. The antlers and costumes for the deer hunt are lying nearby. Again I want to go spend time with the deer, and grandfather is supportive. He is busy with the men in preparing for today's hunt.

I leave to find my new brothers and sisters some distance from the village. When I arrive, the deer come to me. They were waiting for me to arrive. I just sit and feel this newfound trusting closeness with them. After a while, I look up and see my uncle and several other men walking towards me, but then they turn and walk away. They know what I am doing, know of its importance, and leave to let me commune with my brothers and sisters. Each of the men did just what I am doing when they were young, and they appreciate what I am learning in life about life on Earth. There are several other herds in our territory. Sitting by this herd is a sign to them that the deer they hoped to take today is not from this herd.

When I return to the village that evening, the hunters have already returned from their successful hunt. My uncle is sitting by the fire in deep meditation, thanking the herd that sacrificed one of their own to him. All are in a somber mood as the deer is butchered and offered to the others of the village. Everyone comes to my uncle to thank him and to thank the herd. Some of the meat is cooked and shared, but my uncle sitting in deep silence takes none of it. I can feel his deep sense of guilt for having taken one of his brothers, but, with this deep spiritual feeling of thanks and affirmation, the sacred bond between the men and the deer deepens with the sacrifice, a sacrifice that my uncle will never forget, the affirmation that when the time comes, he will be ready to sacrifice himself in protecting the deer, his brothers, and sisters.

As I go to bed that night, I feel a strong urge that tomorrow I need to find the herd that sacrificed one of their own to show the herd that I can be trusted. As I sleep, I have a dream, a dream that the deer are mourning the loss of one of their own, but in doing so feel safer from other predators. With this payment to the world of the humans, they can trust the humans to be on their side and be ready to protect them from wolves and mountain lions. With this sacrifice, they paid a price to ensure that they and the humans will continue to live as brother and sister, a relationship that supports the interdependency of all life of Earth.

While using the Hallstatt Warrior Realm of the Dead Posture (Fig. 2.4) on 4/15/16, I journey to the herd that sacrificed one of their own:

Last night, while talking with the returning hunters, I learned that the herd from which they killed the deer was to the east, up along Strawberry Creek. This morning when I visit grandfather next to the sweat lodge, he tells me that this herd stays close to the creek and is maybe a mile upstream from the village. I leave to visit it and find it where he directed me.

As they see me coming they know, they can feel, that I am a brother, that I feel a deep caring for them. They can feel what I have learned from the time I have spent with the other herd, a feeling of harmony and compassion. They let me come quite close and then I sit, reaching out to them from my center of harmony. I see the young bucks prancing around, making a nuisance of themselves in front of the does. The older buck is not there to protect them. It is the does who first come to me seeking some protection from the energetic bucks, protection for them during a time of mourning. They sense I know what is going on. The bucks do not seem especially afraid of me but keep their distance, sensing that I disapprove of their sexual energy. I feel the herd needs me in this time of mourning the loss of their alpha buck.

As I sit with the does, I see a wolf approaching the herd from the south and when these rambunctious bucks see it, horns come down and they charge, letting the wolf know he is not welcome. The wolf, along with the rest of the pack, disappears into a grove of trees and does not return. In this way, the bucks show their manly and protective strength to the does, hoping they will win their approval. They give the mourning does a respite from their newly released energy.

Yet, the does stay near me and when I reach out to them with a handful of grass, they readily take it. I am surprised how quickly they began to trust me, and I have to assume that what I have learned from my brothers and sisters in the other herd is apparent to these sisters.

When I return that evening to tell grandfather the story, he assures me I have changed in a real way, that the deer have taught me something very important, a feeling that is coming from me. Deer, and all animals, are very sensitive to the energy coming from different feelings within a person, and they can feel my new inner quietness and compassion. This trait has become part of me and will be very important as I continue through life in everything I do. It is this trait that brings me to be one with the Earth, Our Great Mother Earth, and all of her children.

Finally, on 4/16/16, while using the Feathered Serpent Initiation Posture (Fig. 2.9), this journey comes to its conclusion:

To bring this series of ecstatic experiences to a close, I use the Feathered Serpent Posture for initiation or death and rebirth.

This morning when I greet my grandfather he reports that my uncle, who has been grieving the death of the buck of the herd, thanks me for going to his brothers and sisters of the herd and wants to meet me with the herd to offer his condolences too. Thus, I go up the creek to where I again find the herd, and again the does come to me without hesitation. As I sit there with them, offering them handfuls of grass, soon my uncle appears. The bucks begin to prance nervously when he arrives, feeling his manly strength as a hunter, but when he sits with me and the does. they soon quiet down. One buck, the strongest among the herd, has become the new alpha, at least for the time being, until possibly a buck from some other herd shows up who is stronger. The bucks have spent much of the time clashing horns to see who was the strongest.

The does can feel the quiet compassion coming from my uncle as they feel it coming from within me. They can appreciate and accept his grief as they experience their grief in the loss of their aged leader. We sit together with these feelings and accept each other as brother and sister. Though my uncle has not killed many deer and has felt compassion in this brother-sister relationship, this is the first time he has come to the herd from which he has killed a deer, and being with them begins to heal the pain of death. This is something that he realizes he should always do after a successful hunt. We both watch the new leader and soon our eyes connect. The buck quickly senses that we are not a threat and wanders over to us to accept a handful of grass, a sign of acceptance.

We are all one of Mother Earth. We need to accept and trust each other for us to live in union with all life of the Earth. We sit together for most of the day before we rise to return to our village, feeling healed from the hunting experience of two days ago. Upon returning, uncle calls for a deer dance, and the songs we sing to the deer reaffirm to all the men that their relationship with their brother and sister deer is healthy and not lost. With the songs and dance of thanks, the spirits of the deer rise above the fire. Uncle now accepts a bite of the meat of the deer, incorporating within him a piece of the aged buck that sacrificed himself to strengthen the relationship between man and deer.

CHAPTER 7

Venerating the De Danaan's Circle of Light, Ireland

In May 2014, my wife and I toured the northern half of Ireland with Mick Moloney, the Irish singer and musician. Along with the music of Ireland, we toured many archeological sites. I selected places along the way that felt especially spiritual. Again, I attempted to connect deeply with the spirits of the land twice a day using ecstatic trance.

On 5/15/14, our first evening in Ireland, we are in the Boyne Valley and just returned to the hotel from a tour of the Newgrange. I am standing in a grove of trees near the hotel and can hear owls hooting. I begin this journey using the Hallstatt Warrior Realm of the Dead Posture (Fig. 2.4):

I stand at the entrance to the Newgrange, beating my drum. I am looking down into the valley where, in the distance, I can see a much smaller burial mound. Someone has died and I am drumming to call the people together, maybe fifteen of them. I see them walking up through the valley, coming from different directions. Several are together, carrying the body of the person who died. The drumming sounds very sad and dirge-like. As they arrive, they place the body on a pyre, and the pyre is lit. As it burns, they add more wood. It takes the best part of a day for the body to burn and we sit or stand around waiting. Periodically, someone wails out and others join in. I continue beating the drum. Finally, they place the ashes and unburned bones in an urn and take it into the Newgrange, laying the urn in the chamber to the right. The people continue to wail along with the sound of the continued drumming.

The next morning on 5/16/14, I return to the grove of trees and lay in the Jivaro South American Underworld Posture (Fig. A.10):

After several years, I have been rereading *Gods and Fighting Men*.[1] I have been wondering or questioning the nature of the De Danaan, the people of the otherworld. The De Danaan reigned over Ireland until the coming of the Sons of the Gael. After their coming, the De Danaan go into the otherworld, though they frequently revealed themselves to the Gael, especially Manannan, who reveals himself in different forms and by different names to entice the stronger and more beautiful Gael to come with him into the otherworld. In this otherworld, the people live forever, do not need to eat but enjoy eating an unlimited supply of food. They could take a bite of an apple and the apple would remain whole, or eat pork yet the pig would live and remain whole. But this otherworld has other curious characteristics. Why would the De Danaan entice the Gael to come to it? In one story, Tadg was captured and taken from his land. He then escaped and went looking for his homeland. The winds of the sea carried him to the otherworld, to Manannan's island. There he sees the beautiful plain of the two veils of mist of three hills. There is a strong dun or fortress on each hill. White-bodied women lived in the first dun. The second dun is the color of gold where every king, chief man, and noble person who ever lived and died in Ireland now reside. The third dun of silver is for the kings who are yet to rule Ireland.

I use the underworld posture because my questions concern the De Danaan who are in the otherworld: I first met Manannan dressed in green with green upturned toes, like a huge leprechaun. He dances joyously towards me, joyful in my readiness to come to the otherworld. As he leads me into the otherworld, I can see on top of each hill a fortification. I ask, why does he want to show me the otherworld? What is this otherworld, the world of the Sidhe, the world of the De Danaan, but also why is it where the dead nobility reside and a place for future nobility, a paradise with duns of gold and silver? From the story of Tadg, I realize the reason they kidnap Tadg is that the De Danaan wanted to show him that their world is paradise, the earlier era of compassion and harmony. The DeDanaan want the Gael to know that there is a better way to live, a life of peace and harmony, rather than a world of greed and war. I see the place as on the Earth but in a different dimension where the people live within the means of what the Earth provides, the Garden of Eden, with its abundance.

This experience pushes me to explore more deeply the nature of the Sidhe. Manannan, the trickster, shows me what heaven is like, what life could be like. The wars between these people are wars of powerful magic, not of spears and swords. Differences and jealousy cause Gaelic druids to use their rods of magic to shape-shift others or protect themselves through shape-shifting, a magical form of battle. In my experience with this magic, while using ecstatic trance to shape-shift, I can change myself but not shape-shift others. Shape-shifting others, if possible, is black magic.

I continue to seek answers to these questions, so on 5/17/14 I sit in the Lady of Cholula Divination Posture (Fig. A.11) in the garden patio of the Boyne Valley Hotel facing the sunrise:

I call for the ancient spirits of Ireland to show me the way: During the period of quieting my mind by focusing on my breath I flow out to the East over the Irish sea to the UK and on to Europe, to the roots of the Celts. But during the drumming, not finding these roots there, I am pulled back to the Newgrange about 5000 years ago at the time of the winter solstice. I feel I am only an observer/questioner but feel the energy of the people huddled from the cold winter and lack of sunlight, huddling in the womb of mother earth, experiencing her consistent warmth/temperature while waiting for the sunrise, the sun to penetrate the womb with its light of regeneration for the new birth of spring, a gestation that will take 3 months. The sexual energy of the solstice celebration feels powerful, bringing the people together in the womb of Mother Earth. As I sit, I can hear crows cawing. On this shortest day, the sun rises at about 8:30 a.m. and sets around 4:24 p.m. Ireland feels more like the origin of the Celts than across the channels to the mainland of Europe.

On the afternoon of 5/17/14, I kneel in the Tandragee Idol Posture (Fig. A.20), a figurine that I found in the museum in Belfast, a Chiltan Spirits Posture:

From my examination of the ancient art of Ireland and exploring the Irish museums, I was starting to believe that the ancients did not believe in graven human images until I found two ancient human sculptures in the Belfast Museum. I use the posture of this image found near Armagh, the Tandragee Idol, with my right arm wrapped around me, grasping my left shoulder, feeling its self-protection.

After our trip to Belfast, we travel to Lough Allen, where I kneel in the Tandragee Idol posture at the edge of the lake. I have been questioning the fact that archeologists have not found evidence of ancient battles, even though the ancient myths report them, for example, of the invasion of the Sons of the Gael fighting the De Danaan.

I find myself observing the so-called battle with the Gaelic druid and the son of Danu facing each other. The Gaelic druid raises his rod, but the son of Danu quickly shifts his shape into a woodpecker and flies away. He then comes up behind the Gael druid and pecks him on the head. The son of Danu then retreats to the cave of Danu and stands before her throne. She tells him we just need to avoid the Gael. By knowing the land so well, we know where and how to hide.

Also, while looking out over the Lough Allen, a concealing mist provides limited visibility, the mist from which the de Danaan would appear to others. The trickster god, Manannan, frequently shape-shifts to entice the Gaelic heroes to come through the mist to the lands of Danu. The battle is of magic and does not leave the signs of a major battle of spears and broken swords. The De Danaan blend into nature and disappear. The myth suggests that the Sons of the Gael won and that the De Danaan had to go underground, but the De Danaan know better. They chose to live inconspicuously, at one with the Earth, unless they seek to trick the Gaels with magic. I see some shape-shift to flies, another way to become most inconspicuous.

I again use the Tandragee Idol Posture (Fig. A.20) on the morning of 5/18/14 while at a hotel on the edge of Lough Allen. I walked down to the edge of the lake in the rain. While following my breathing, I watch a duck followed by 8 or 10 ducklings on the lake. In calling the spirits, I call Mother Earth by her ancient Irish name, Danu:

My experience is slow and quiet, with the thoughts of spring, of the Earth, and Danu waking up, coming alive with the rain and everything green. I feel very inconspicuous and small while kneeling at the edge of the southern tip of the lake. The drumming takes me to the gate of the underworld at Newgrange, where I watch people, 10 or 12 of them, walk up the hill in the rain wearing hooded robes as they enter the womb of the Earth. When I see the ducks, I hear the mother duck's name, Danu. This is a silent and enjoyable experience in its magical quietness.

* * *

One thing that our tour guide told us was that the Creevykeel Cairn was 7,000 years old, and life expectancy then was 50 years. The Carrowmore Cairns, near Sligo, were 6,000 years old, but life expectancy was only 35 years. This fits with my belief that the earlier age of the Great Mother was paradise when the hunter and gatherers lived within the means of what the earth provided.

On the evening of 5/18/14, to journey into the underworld, I use the Jivaro South American Posture (Fig. A.10):

I find myself at the cairn atop the hill at Carrowmore. On October 31, early in the morning, others come to the cairn and kneel in the Tandragee Posture while they call upon their ancestors. I am again an observer. While at this central hilltop cairn, they quake and moan in ecstasy. The sunlight brings alive the spirits of the ancestors. I feel myself going further back in time. I see a funeral pyre burning on the hilltop. Some men are feeding wood to the fire. The smoke rises, carrying the spirit of the person who died into the air. From the hilltop, the mourners watch where the smoke drifts and again lands on Mother Earth. They then take the ashes to where the smoke fell back to the earth and build a cairn or use a nearby cairn, where they place the ashes. These outlying cairns are not aligned with the sun but aligned to the cairn on the central hill where the cremation took place.

On the morning of 5/19/14, I stand at the edge of the Lough Allen in the Hallstatt Warrior Posture (Fig. 2.4). Using this realm-of-the-dead posture, I expect to have a more personal experience:

I again go to the cairn on the hill at Carrowmore, where I see Manannan. There in the cairn, I find an opening that leads into a lower cave, where I meet the four men I have frequently met before, who are my regular spirit guides. This time, one is wearing blue, one green, one brown, and one white. The one wearing blue leads me to the East to the water's edge of the Irish Sea. There we dive in and he takes me deep to the bottom of a trench where I see a lot of human bones. We then come back up and the one dressed in green takes me south, where everything is green with lush growth. Then the guide dressed in brown takes me west to the autumn world of the harvest. I am invited into a large thatched hall where I partake in a feast before the king. The guide in white takes me north, passing by the NE where I experience the presence of ancestors. With this, I feel my place now is to return to the East, where Manannan takes me back down into the depths of the lake and the pile of bones. There I see one small bone glowing red among the others. I dive towards it when the drumming ends.

I feel that I have been an observer to this point, but the glowing bone tells me I am connected to the bone. Of the Irish Celtic Gods, I seem to resonate most with Manannan. I see him as a shape-shifter, trickster, or enticer. I have often thought of the Nordic god Loki as the trickster, the psychologist of the Nordic gods. Now I find Manannan playing that role. One thought is that the glowing bone takes me back to a distant cousin on a distant branch of my genealogy, but I now feel I am connected. This evening I need to ask the diviner to tell me about this ancestor.

Thus, on the evening of 5/19/14, I use the Freyr Divination Posture (Fig. 2.2) as I pursue this ancestor:

I am again at the edge of Lough Allen and ask the diviner about the glowing bone that I feel is an ancestor. On today's tour, we went to the grave of Turlough O'Carolan and heard the story of how bones were often dug up and crushed for treatment of various disorders, including epilepsy, and that O'Carolan's bones are not likely in the grave.

I again dive to the pile of bones in Lough Allen and find the one that was glowing, pick it up, and feel it pulsing or throbbing. I swim to the surface with it, and it flies out of my hand as I shape-shift into a blackbird, a raven, and fly. I follow it. It flies south along the West coast then up the Shannon River and across Ireland to just below Dublin, where it turns south and flies down the East Coast, covering much of Southern Ireland before it comes back to my hand, and I shift back to me. I get the message that I am to search the island to find a place of resonance. I then ask the bone how old it is. It takes me back to 6000 BCE to my first Hallstatt, Germany experience of several years ago and then to the Viking raids along the Shannon River. I am not sure what the message is when the drumming ends.

I felt my first experience of connecting with an ancestor when I used the Hallstatt Warrior in January 2010. I went back to about 5000 BCE in Germany and met men in a hut preparing to hunt the next morning.

On 7/28/16, over two years later, I have another experience using the Hallstatt Warrior Posture (Fig. 2.4). Since it is again of the glowing bone, I am inserting it here:

During the five minutes of quieting my mind, I see the glowing red bone I saw in Ireland. I am again in the realm of the dead and the red glowing bone is in a pile of other bones. When the rattling starts, the other bones rise as skeletons and start dancing around the glowing bone. After a while, the skeletons lift their arms to the heavens and collapse back into the pile of bones. The glowing red bone then rises and forms a skeleton. The glowing bone is the breastbone, the sternum. The skeleton comes over to me and hugs me. The hug felt warm and soft, not boney like you would expect from a skeleton. Then it steps back and collapses back into the pile of bones. I rise out of the realm of the dead into a sunny meadow, where I lay down and feel the pleasant warmth of the sun shining on me.

This experience brings a sense of closure to my connection with the glowing bone, a connection to my heart, a death-rebirth experience.

Returning to our journeying in Ireland, on 5/20/14 we visit an art museum in Carrick on the Shannon where I sit in the Freyr Divination Posture (Fig. 2.2) on the edge of a planter in front of the museum, a place from which I can see the Shannon River. My experience was an experience of synchronicity. That morning I had read the introduction to a book on ancient Ireland where it mentioned the Hallstatt Iron Age of 600 to 500 BC in Hallstatt, Austria when the smelting of iron first began:[2]

I sit on the bank of the Shannon and see a Viking ship coming up the river hidden by the trees along the river, but I am also hidden from them. I first think, maybe I am hidden by trees, but when I heard the name Carrick means the rock, I think it could have been a rock. I run up and over a low ridge to warn the others of our small settlement that the Vikings are coming. I sit on the hillside in a state of meditation that gives me the vision of the Viking ship. The warning leads others to run further inland with all that they can carry. The Vikings come ashore and take what they can find, but they do not seem interested in searching for us. We have little, but they take a recently killed pig we are roasting. They throw a piece of burning wood on a nearby thatched hut, setting it afire. They are looking for the gold found in monasteries, not in a settlement of poor farmers.

The book I am reading reports that in Ireland, iron was first mined and smelted at Lough Allen, a process that was first developed at Hallstatt. Lough Allen happens to be where I used the Hallstatt Warrior posture. I think the answer to my question is that my Irish heritage goes back to Hallstatt, but it connects me with the Vikings at Carrick on Shannon. On this trip, I learn that the first Viking raid was in 795 and the first Viking settlement was in 888 in Dublin. The Norman invasion of Ireland was in the late 1100s after the battle of Hastings of 1166.

This time on 5/21/14 with so many questions for which I seek answers, I again use a divination posture, this time the Lady of Cholula (Fig. A.11):

We are on an island of the Aran Islands, climbing to the top of the hill of Dun Aengus. There I sit on a wall overlooking the Atlantic Ocean. I am back in time as an observer, observing people coming and going from the fort. Though it is a fortification, the people living there live a relaxed and peaceful life. There is no battling or wars. A few huts and grazing animals are outside the fort, and the men are leaving to go fishing. Fires are burning in the cooking pits in thatched huts. It is a peaceful scene as I am looking south and west over the ocean. I wonder about the need for such fortification, 1100 BC to 800 BC since the Viking raids did not start until about AD 795. The fortification was likely for protection from the elements of overlooking the ocean.

Then on 5/22/14, while lying in the Jivaro South American Posture (Fig. A.10), I wonder about the Irish image of the Mother Earth Goddess. I feel my experiences of 5/19 and 5/20 break through to my heritage, bringing me into this experience at the hotel garden in Galway of the magic of the otherworld, of the Sidhe:

I am walking along a road and through the mist when I see a beautiful woman walking towards me. When she gets close, I see she is Miss Piggy. She takes me on a tour of the otherworld where I meet several people: a woman jealous of her lover's paramour, a man seeking the power of kingship, a warrior seeking strength, a young boy much bigger and stronger than others his age. I meet each of these characters of mythology with curiosity, but I remain at an emotional distance. Being with Miss Piggy keeps me at that distance. I then retreat to my thinking self and think about the meaning of this experience. I realize I need to reread *Gods and Fighting Men* to identify these archetypes and give them names. Another character is the King who is trying to retain his power. I need to understand Danu to understand the myth, Danu, the mother of the De Danaan.

My experiences have two sides, one to understand the ancient myth, and second, to find in these stories my Irish connection that now seems to be an ancestral branch from Hallstatt, Austria of a distant cousin who ends up in Ireland when the Sons of the Gael had to face the raiding Vikings. It so happens that today we will visit the home of Lady Gregory, whose books have told me the ancient stories. Miss Piggy shows the two sides of each story, of an unattractive pig made into a thing of beauty. According to one person on the tour, Miss Piggy tramples on others, but she herself has no shame. She speaks no "should" or "musts," as created by Jim Henson. She expresses feelings of jealousy, strong in dependency and not content with self, feelings of being unloved, though some believe that jealousy shows love. Her power is of strength versus the fear of being a servant or slave, the fear of weakness. She shows us our shadow. There is gold in our shadows, as the sun casts the shadow.

From *Gods and Fighting Men*, the strengths of the ancient people include being skilled in healing, battle, writing, crafts, and smithing. Lugh was greatest as a carpenter, smith, champion, harper, poet, magician, physician, cup-bearer, a worker in brass, and at the chessboard, the greatest in all skills.

On 5/22/14, using the Tandragee Idol Posture (Fig. A.20), I journey into the Realm of the Dead, where I find more of the magic of the otherworld:

While kneeling in Ennis's Old Ground Hotel Garden, I ask what else Miss Piggy has to show me in the otherworld. I return through the all-present mist in Ireland and find Miss Piggy, who takes me down a path. I first see the giant, Lugh, who stands and pounds his chest and roars in an intimidating manner. Piggy just pushes him aside and we go on, and next, we come to a very skinny frail man, a poet who speaks, telling us fanciful stories of history that he claims are true and have much truth to them. Then we come to the magician, a short ugly troll who shape-shifts first into a crow and then a bear that stands on his hind legs and dances, but he then vanishes as he dances. Then we come to a healer with a bag of many kinds of plants and herbs. We follow him to a grove of trees where others come to or are carried to him, some with wounds. For the wounds, he makes a poultice that he places on the wounds. For other problems, he makes teas or other concoctions for them to drink. In one case, the tea made the person vomit, and then he stands up, smiling. I was again just an observer. The poet who is still with us tells us that the people live forever in this place and food is plentiful because when eaten, it quickly regenerates and became whole again, a paradise. He tells the story of Danu, the Mother Goddess, who people go to for her blessing. He tells us, too, of her husband, Dagda, who is creative and skilled in hunting. I hear these stories with my third ear, I just know them. In some of the ancient stories, Dagda is Danu's father and in others, her son. In any case, he is the "All-Father."

On the morning of 5/13/14, while standing in the Hallstatt Warrior Posture (Fig. 2.4) in the garden, I return to the world of my ancestry:

I begin with wondering what track I will be on this morning, of going into the underworld or of my communing with my ancestry that began on the hill outside of Carrick on the Shannon. I become a Druid, sitting on a burial mound. I have led the people of our small village into the mound to hide from the Vikings. As we come out, we see one hut burning near where the pig was roasting. They had thrown burning wood on the hut. I frequently go to the mound to talk with my ancestors, especially my father and grandfather who were also druids. Some people of the village are Catholic, though they still come to me, a druid, for healing and divination. Though there is a monastery at some distance from our village, since the Vikings raided it, the people questioned the power of the Catholic god, who did not protect this place of worship. I still call upon Danu for my strength, understanding, and compassion. The village respects me as their protector, as on this occasion where her womb provides protection. A few of the men of the village respect strength and see themselves as warriors. They stand close to the entrance of the mound, ready to fight off the Vikings in these close quarters if they find us. The villagers feel quite safe. My ancestors came to Ireland several centuries earlier, before the Catholic saints arrived.

That evening, 5/13/14, while sitting in the Jama Coaque Metamorphosis Posture (Fig A.9), I return to the world of the Great Mother Earth to commune with Nature:

I sit on the Cliffs of Moher on this very windy afternoon. The wind has blown me off course. I am a black-capped tern with eggs laying in a crevice of the cliffs. I need to eat, so dive down to a small pool of water in a large creviced cave to eat some sea creatures swimming in the pool. The waves breaking on the rocks below the cliff are dangerous, but I fly out a distance to dive for fish. The water creatures in the pools are eating the moss and algae that are plentiful on the rocks. There is plenty of grass in places on the cliff and the manure of cattle in the fields above the cliff is full of seeds and other food for other smaller birds, but it is too windy to fly up there. Other birds are flying back and forth along the cliff, some catching flying insects.

Often I have experiences of nature like this and I seek an experience of nature today by using the metamorphosis posture. At the Cliffs of Moher, there is much of nature to see.

On this last morning in Ireland, on 5/24/14, I lay in the Jivaro Underworld Posture (Fig. A.10) as I journey to an ancient Irish settlement:

Lying on my back, I slide down head first, but then roll over and spread my wings like a bird. I fly in an expanding circle around our settlement and soon I see three grazing deer. I am again the druid who shape-shifts into a bird. I return to the settlement and tell the waiting hunters who have prepared for the hunt the direction in which to go. I then return to being a bird and watch their progress as they hunt for the deer. I switch back and forth twice to give the hunters who I am following further directions and when to start the drumming to drive the deer toward a hedge of whitethorn. At the end of the hedge, a hole has been dug, covered with branches. The hunters drive the deer towards the hole. One falls in and is speared by the hunters, who gut it and carry it back to the settlement with thanks to the Great Mother. They use everything of the deer, hide, meat, and bones.

After returning home and sometime later, I return to my experiences in Ireland. I ask the diviner what about my trip was most important to me in learning of the magical ways of the ancient people of Ireland. I call upon the Freyr Divination Posture (Fig. 2.2) on the tenth of March 2015 to lead me to the answer:

I find myself at Carrowmore sitting on the hill upon which the Listoghil cairn eventually will be built. It is just before sunrise on around the end of July. I am guessing it is around 5000 BC. There is a group of people around me, though I don't think they see me, a spirit from the future. There is a large bonfire burning and someone is drumming. We are all staring towards the Ballygawley

Mountain ridge to the east, and towards the north end of the ridge is a shallow valley that in later years will be called the saddle. We are all waiting for the sun to rise above the saddle. As the people wait, they slide into a trance with the beat of the drum. Someone near me turns and smiles. He can see my spirit self and soon almost everyone in trance notices me waiting with them.

The sun shows itself above the saddle, and the people stand with their arms raised in praise of the sun, the beginning of a new day at the time of year when the days grow shorter and the Earth begins to sleep. Birds begin to fly south, and soon some of the animals will go into hibernation in their burrows. The leaves begin to fall from the trees and other plants are turning brown. Some bushes still have berries and nuts for which the people are grateful. They have stored in their huts dried meat and dried fish along with dried berries and nuts that they hope will get them through the winter. Other herbs and plants are hanging from the smoked-filled ceilings of the huts. After a while, the people leave to return to the small winter settlements of their bands, bands of maybe five or six families and maybe twenty to thirty people.

One person stays on the hill where the bonfire burns, the drummer, the wise elder of the area. In later years, he will be the village's druid. I can now see his small hut below the fire. He comes to greet me and we sit and talk. He points out to me the four mounds that rise to the south of the saddle on the Ballygawley ridge and tells me that the mounds are of Danu, their Great Mother Earth, her head, breasts, belly, and thighs, and with this sunrise just above her head, she is looking forward to falling asleep for the winter. She is our Earth goddess who provides for us through the year but now needs to rest.

With this experience, I am set for this series of experiences, a series that arises out of my experience at Carrowmore, one place we visited while touring Ireland. The next morning, 3/11/15, I use the Hallstatt Warrior Posture (Fig. 2.4) to continue on this journey of ancient Carrowmore:

Again, I am on the hill near the center of the Carrowmore valley. It is some days later. The wise elder of the area drums as a few men climb the hill to be near him. It is a hunting party of one band who is going out to hunt auroch or deer to provide fresh meat for their band. As we wait for the sun, it will rise above the head of the sleeping goddess to the south of the saddle. They bring with them food for the wise elder and a few armsful of firewood for his fire. As the sun rises, we all stand, chanting praise to Danu, thanking her for what she has provided, and asking her to lead them to success on the hunt. Her long flowing hair flows above her head towards the saddle.

Each day, groups of men arrive before sunrise, men from different bands in the area, hunters or fishermen. Sometimes women come to ask the advice of the wise elder of the mountain, and later that morning a young boy arrives to sit with him. Again, I find myself with a young boy who is learning the ways of the shaman. Though I am in my eighties, I am young in learning the ways of the Earth and find that I have much to learn from the young boy and his time spent with the wise elder of the mountain. I was wondering if I would have a young spirit in this sequence of ecstatic experiences as I have had in others.

As we sit and talk, the elder explains that when the sun rises above the head of Danu, our Great Earth Mother, she offers us the knowledge of the surrounding Earth, the Earth to which we need to listen to learn what she has to teach us. We need to attend to the ways of all life of the Earth, to the animals, and to the flora, especially this time of year when many of the animals have left or gone into hibernation and the flora has turned brown for the winter. This time of year, fish are still available, as are deer and rabbits. Though we may know where bears hibernate, it is unfair to hunt a bear now when they are defenseless. At other times of the year, when a bear offers itself in a hunt, it is his will that we should take him. The elder tells the boy that there is much to learn about everything in the area in which he lives. He needs to know every nook and cranny of the area, to know every rabbit burrow, every place where the bears hibernate and the habits of the deer, from where they sleep to where they go to forage for food and drink, to know which fish come up into the bays that are on each side of Carrowmore and at what time of year, and to know the habits and nests of the birds and when they leave to fly to warmer weather. The plants have so much to teach, too. He then sends the boy out to search around the hill to find the burrows of rabbits and to watch to learn when, during the day, the rabbit comes out of his burrow. There is so much to learn, and I am thankful that I can follow along with this young boy to learn as he is learning.

On the morning of 3/12/15, while using the Priestess of Malta Posture (2.7), a middle world posture, with the young boy, I visit the life of our finned ancestors:

While standing in this middle world posture, I again walk up the hill at the center of the Carrowmore valley to where the wise elder of the mountain is tending his morning fire. It is before sunrise and the families of one band of fishermen climb the hill to ask for success in their fishing venture and success for their wives in their walk to find the herbs to spice their meals. By now, the sunrise has moved further south along the Ballygawley ridge. The families face the beginning glow of the sun as it rises above the full breasts of the Mother Earth Goddess, breasts with up-turned nipples. They wait in anticipation for the sun to show itself, honoring the nurturance of Danu, the Great Mother. This is a most auspicious time for these men who are about to go fishing and the women to find herbs to nurture their families. As the flaming sun rises into view, they raise their arms with chants of praise and thanks. They then return down the hill to begin the day of fishing and gathering, but the young boy who is part of this band remains to learn from the wise elder of Carrowmore.

As they talk, the boy does not remember nursing from his mother's breasts, but he has often seen the younger children of the band being nurtured by the breasts of their mothers. This reminder brings alive within the boy the nurturance of their Great Earth Mother. Again, they talk of the animals of the area and the boy remembers watching bear cubs nursing off their mother's breasts. He asks if young fish nurse off the mother fish, and the wise elder tells the boy to go down to the water's edge, peer into the water, and see what he can learn from watching the fish.

I go with the boy and we watch the tiny fish in a pool of water at the edge of the bay. The young fry are swimming close to their mother through the sea plants around the pool. We do not see them nursing from their mother, though. We do not see breasts available to them, but we see them nibbling on the leaves of the plants around the pool with their mother close by, watching. Mother Earth has different ways to provide for her young offspring.

We return to the wise elder to tell him what we saw. His smile assures us that what we learned was correct, at least for most fish. While sitting there with him, we see a woman from the band climbing the hill. She brings a concern to the elder that her young daughter is sick. She is having trouble breathing and has a sore throat. He turned to me and says that this was a very common problem because of the smoke in the huts, though the mother could not see me. He told the mother to have her daughter spend most of her time outside of the hut in the fresh air and to make a steaming tea of hyssop and have her daughter breathe the steam. The mother knew about the use of hyssop but could not find any because everybody was using it, so the wise elder took some from his hut to give to her. The boy was watching a spider crawling over a rock and then looked up, reporting that he saw some hyssop on their walk down to the water's edge. He motioned for the mother to come along as he took her to the place where he saw it, not too far away. He is learning well what the elder is teaching and showing him.

As the days shorten, I use the Venus of Galgenberg Upper World Posture (Fig. 2.8) on 3/13/16:

The sun continues to rise farther and farther to the south. Each day, people climb to the summit of this low mound to visit the wise elder of Carrowmore. I find myself back on the summit several days later, this time for when the sun rises from the belly of Danu. She has brought life to the world and is the Mother Goddess to those women who are pregnant. Lying along the ridge above Carrowmore, she too appears to be pregnant with her enormous belly. Today is the day for pregnant women and those women who want to become pregnant to greet the glowing sunrise, just as those women who are pregnant glow. Again, as the sun rises above her belly, all arms raise with the chants of praise, thanksgiving, and petition.

These women come from some half dozen bands that roam the area, though this place is especially special with the Great Mother Earth reclining for her winter sleep along the Ballygawley ridge, so women from more distant places who seek to become pregnant have made the trek to this hilltop. Among them are several women who help in the delivery of newborns, and they are there to help these women in need. They suggest a uterine tonic, a tea made from red raspberry leaves, as the remedy. For many of the women, this is a time for celebration and some brought their husbands and children to help in the celebration. These families bring bouquets of flowers to leave for Danu, the Great Mother, and others bring songs or poems that they will sing. Some women who cannot get pregnant have a hidden fear of pregnancy and fear the pain of childbirth, but watching and listening to these women celebrate help them overcome their fear and open them to become pregnant. On this special day, the people are slow to leave the hilltop. Before, when hunters and fishermen came, they were eager to leave to get on with their plans.

My next visit to the Carrowmore knoll is the next day on 3/14/16 when I use the Olmec Prince Posture (Fig. 2.3) for shape-shifting:

The people from the hunting and gathering bands in the area continue coming to visit the wise elder of Carrowmore. But as the rising sun continues moving to the south along the Ballygawley ridge the visiting crowd grows until the sun rises over the fourth mound, Danu's thighs from between which all life is born, life that sustains these people but also of all beings that are interdependent upon them and each other. The people of the time live healthy lives with sufficient food and a life relatively stress-free because the people follow the instructions of the Great Mother Danu. These instructions include taking from her only what they need for their survival at the moment and protecting all other life of the Earth by protecting the young and the mothers of the young for the future, taking only those animals who sacrificed themselves to feed the people. They know to give back as much, if not more, than they take from the Earth to maintain a healthy relationship with the Earth. These are words well known to the people and words repeated by the wise elder of Carrowmore to the young boy who follows him and to me.

The day that the sun rises over the center point of the fourth mound is especially important because it is the day to praise and thank all life that came from Danu, from between her thighs. With care, the people select the food they can spare, knowing that there are still a few more weeks of winter, and bring it with them to the hilltop, food for the feast to Danu. The men have been busy hunting and fishing to prepare for this day and all express joy in the life that comes from the Great Earth Goddess.

As I watch the happenings of winter from the vantage point of this hilltop, I can feel the deep love and respect that these people have for the Earth and all life on Earth. Now they celebrate and dance around the bonfire that blazes on the hilltop, celebrating the life that Danu brings to the Earth. The celebration lasts late into the evening when the hunting and gathering people light torches from the fire to help them find their way back to their huts.

Then, on 3/15/16, I return to the Carrowmore valley using the Feathered Serpent Posture (Fig. 2.9) on the day that the sun stops moving south, the shortest day of the year:

On this day, using this posture of death and rebirth, I again returned to the hilltop of Carrowmore. In a few days, the rising sun will stop moving south and its birth each dawn will be from the same spot to the south below Danu's thighs. When that day arrives, the wise elder of Carrowmore tells the young boy and me it will be a couple of weeks before the sun again starts moving, this time northward, passing over the sleeping body of Danu as the days become longer, bringing her awake as she again wakens the Earth. It will soon be time for the boy to watch for the signs of spring.

As the sun moves north and again reaches her thighs, we will see the new birth of the young of all animals that inhabited the area, the swelling of the buds on the branches of trees, and the return of the birds from the south. We will again see young deer and bear cubs nursing from their mother's breast. As the sun continues on its journey north and rises above her belly, the time comes to move, to follow the deer, sheep, and aurochs to their spring grazing grounds. The people of Danu will leave the valley of Carrowmore as they do every year, knowing where to go as taught them by their ancestors and the Great Earth Mother. It will also be time for the wise elder to leave his hut on the hilltop and begin his wandering to visit the moving bands of people in the area. As the young grow and the buds flower, they will be too busy with their summer activities to petition in their need of the wise elder on his hilltop.

But until then, when the sun is still to the south of the sleeping Danu, her bands of hunter and gatherers continue coming to the hilltop to praise and thank the Great Earth Mother for all that she provides and to find answers from the wise elder and the spirits of their ancestors who reside around the hill of Carrowmore.

As the sun moves north to rise over her breasts, the Earth becomes productive for hunting and gathering. The aged animals will be ready to sacrifice themselves as the young replace them in the herds, and the herbs, fruits, and nuts will be ready for harvest. Soon, the elder will return to the hilltop as the bands return to the Carrowmore Valley below. Their huts will need repair, and the collected meat of the deer, sheep, aurochs, and bears, along with the collected herbs, all to be used during the winter, will again hang in the smoke above the hearth fires. As the rising sun passes over Danu's face, all know that the longest day of the year is soon to arrive when it again rises above the saddle above Danu's head. With the return of the celebrations of the autumn and winter as the sun again moves south, the people of Danu will live in peace and harmony, as they have lived for many millennia.

While using the Freyr Divination Posture (Fig. 2.2) on 3/16/16, the journey moves forward in time as we continue to go to the hilltop of Carrowmore:

Again, I find myself on the hilltop of Carrowmore, but I have moved forward in time to the agricultural era, somewhere around

3000 BC. The area is quite different, now inhabited by the Gael. A large burial mound sits atop the central hill, a passage tomb that is now sealed off with light of the rising sun sealed inside. It is the time of Beltane when the sun will soon rise again over the saddle of Ballygawley ridge. All around, down below the mound, are cairns of the dead. Off to the west, upon a hill, is another large mound, the burial mound of Mebd, the queen of Connacht. She was the enemy of the king of Ulster and stole the Ulster king's prize bull, as told in the famous cattle raid of Cooley.[3] The Gael's arrival in Ireland brought an end to the peaceful and harmonious way of life of the people of Danu. The people of Danu, knowing every nook and cranny of Ireland, sought peace by moving underground into the magical world of the Sidhe, where they could live forever in peace. Seeking the return of peace and harmony to the land, they, with their magical ways of shape-shifting, entice the Gael to follow them into their world where they can live without the fear of death and always with plenty to eat, a world of paradise, the Garden of Eden. Many stories of their enticements are still told.

    The Gaels' arrival brought to Ireland the cultivation of land and the domestication of animals. They settled down in larger villages, where they raised the animals and planted their fields. The aurochs were now domesticated and became known as cows. The cows were important for their milk and the bulls important for their meat and breeding. The boys of the village tended herds of sheep and goats on the hill pasture land. Even domesticated pigs wandered the villages. Because of the controlling nature of these people new to the island, animals lost their ways of independence and could no longer survive on their own but depended upon humans to feed and care for them, and to die eventually at their hands. The balance of nature was lost. Because of the people's fear of wolves, large cats, and bears that preyed upon these domesticated animals, very easy prey for them, these carnivores were hunted to a point of extinction or near extinction.

The flora that is now cultivated, barley, oats, wheat, and other vegetables, no longer offered the wide breadth of foods eaten when gathering was the way of life. This dietary restriction led to a loss in the health of the people who began dying at an earlier age of around 35 years instead of 50. They no longer depended upon the now-forgotten Great Earth Mother. The people depended upon their own hard work, which added to their shortened lifespan.

But the people still come to the hilltop for Samhain to commune with their ancestors, a time of expected frost and the end of their harvest. There, they celebrate the success of their harvest around a large bonfire. Over the next three months, they do not wait and watch as the rising sun moves north to rise above the four mounds of Danu. The forgotten Danu is only for the people of the underworld. The people now worship the world of kings and power as they struggled to control the Earth. Their world is no longer the Garden of Eden.

This ecstatic journey in Ireland now ends on 3/17/16 while using The Feathered Serpent Initiation Posture (Fig. 2.9):

The Gaels are aware of the seasons as they related to their agricultural ways. At the end of winter, when their ewes give birth and lactate, the sheep and cows go to the pasture lands, and the people know that spring is on its way. Around the first of February, they celebrate Imbolc and the Goddess Brigit, the goddess of fertility and birth. Then around May first is the biggest celebration of all, Beltane, the celebration of spring when the people dance around the largest of bonfires, bringing new spring light to the world. Around these fires, the people frolicked to show their own virility and fertility and the virility and fertility of their herds of animals by indulging in the rite of sexual freedom. Sacrifices ensure a fruitful year in raising their crops and animals.

The fourth celebration occurs on the first of August, the summer celebration of abundance and the harvest, Lughnasadh. Lugh was the master of all crafts, crafts that the people have grown to depend on in their agricultural and warrior ways. Lugh's warrior ways give the warriors of the kings' armies their chanting of spells for encouragement and to ensure victory.

Thus, from my vantage point atop the hill of Carrowmore, I watch these wild celebrations of the virility of the men and the fertility of the maidens of the Gael, and of strength and violence in their control of life and of the Earth, celebrations that the people of Danu would have found very intimidating and fear-inducing. Lost are the ways of nurturance, peace, harmony, and cooperation of the people of Danu, the hunter-gatherers of the earlier era who know the ways of the animals and seasons of the Earth, showing all that is of the Earth respect in their veneration of it, ways that led to a longer and healthier life in their Garden of Eden.

CHAPTER 8

Learning the Esopus Way of Oneness with the Earth, New York

The Dutchman, Henry Hudson, sailed up the Hudson River named after him in 1609, sailing as far as Fort Orange, now Albany, to lay claim to the area for the Dutch. Settlers coming from the Netherlands to the New Netherlands soon came to Fort Orange and to New Amsterdam, now New York City. In 1614, the settlers opened a trading post at Wiltwyck, now Kingston, on the land of the Esopus Lenape. Two of my 9xgreat grandparents were early settlers of Wiltwyck, arriving in the 1650s. The indigenous Esopus of the area were a subgroup of the Lenape. During those early years of Wiltwyck, two major conflicts with the Esopus came to be known as the first and second Esopus wars. Because of my ancestral connection to the area, I have returned to these ancestral roots using ecstatic trance.

My daughter and her family now live in the area close to where Lambert Huybertsen Brink settled in 1658, in what is now Hurley, NY. My son-in-law has built a pleasant and attractive treehouse in the woods near where they live, a place that feels quite spiritual. This ancestral journey begins on 12/23/15 while sitting in the Freyr Divination Posture (Fig. 2.2) in this treehouse:

I feel the breeze in the trees, otherwise, it is silent. I see a village of the Esopus, with 6 or 8 domed shelters or wigwams and a longhouse made from bent saplings and covered with woven mats. Smoke is rising from a hole at the top and people are beginning to stir in the early morning. The men come out and stretch their arms towards the sun. A smokey outdoor fire is slow to start because the Earth is damp. The people are standing around the fire and see a herd of five deer at the edge of their dance court. They watch the deer eating the grass with its tassels of grain and thank the deer, their ancestors, for teaching them about the grain, which they collect and grind into flour. They also see and thank a bear that stands at the edge of the woods, praising these animals for their beauty. The animals hear this message and are thankful for the peace and harmony that exists. The Esopus presently have enough, so they are not excited about hunting these animals for food. All feel at peace and harmony and a young boy stands next to his grandfather with the grandfather's hand on his shoulder, a relationship that I am invariably drawn to in these experiences.

While standing in the Calling the Spirits Posture (Fig. 2.10) on the evening of 12/24/15, I return to this Esopus village, on a creek now with the same name, the Esopus Creek:

It is warm with a beautiful pink sunset. Above the herd of deer and above the bear I see rising the spirits of these animals. I feel the harmony and peace that exists between them and the Esopus. They each have an awareness of this relationship and know that there will be a time when one of them will need to sacrifice itself to the Esopus to feed them, but the animals also know that the humans will take only what they need at the moment.

That evening, the Esopus give a dance to prepare for a bear hunt. This being the wolf clan, the dance is of a wolf stalking a bear. From the dance, the bears learn or know that it is their turn for one of them to be sacrificed. The following day, as the Esopus leave for the hunt, they are sensitive to and recognize the one bear that will sacrifice itself and know to show their thanks with offerings to the bear. With a successful hunt, they butcher the bear, using every part, and continually give thanks throughout the process. The harmony that exists between all the living creatures of the Earth ensures the success of the hunt.

Then, on 12/25/15 while using the Sekhmet Initiation Posture (Fig. A.17), I return to the experience of life in this Esopus village:

I am the Indian boy in the domed hut of the wolf clan of the Esopus. It is warm and comfortable near the fire. I crawl between the furs on my sleeping platform, where it feels so peaceful and comfortable. Grandmother is tending the fire, and I fall asleep. In the morning, a new day, it is bright and cold. The men are meeting around the fire, and I sit listening from my sleeping platform. People from across the ocean are taking their land, cutting trees to build their houses, and hunting their animals, indiscriminately taking more than they need. We at first welcomed these strangers and took them turkeys and other food we had hunted, but they are not friendly. Since then, they have shot and killed one of our own who ventured too close to their village. The men around the fire are trying to decide what to do. They talk and deliberate all day. They call the grandmothers and other women to their council to ask them what they think. The women only shake their heads and say they do not know, but they want peace. The women hope to keep the peace but understand what the men are thinking. They think that if they attack and burn the village, the white people might just leave and go home.

They cannot decide what to do, but the next day, on 9/20/1659, a group of young men who had been drinking too much brandy goes through Wiltwyck on a drunken rampage. They shoot flaming arrows into the thatched roofs of the homes of the white men, and the homes burn. From then on, my sleep is not peaceful. The white men do not leave. With the continued unrest, we do not know what to do. The First Esopus War I is history, but we know that 4 years later we try another attack, The Second Esopus War, which again we lose in the end, so we retreat. A few of us moved further west, near what is now Binghamton, New York, far away from the white man.

I return to this journey with the Esopus later that day, 12/25/15, while using the Tanum Underworld Posture (Fig. 2.6):

I am a snake crawling into an underground hole. I am the Esopus moving west. The snake is sacred wisdom, the wisdom that needs to survive for the survival of the Earth. The Esopus realize this and know that if they remain where they are, they will not survive to carry on the sacred wisdom of their people, so they move west, as did the people of all tribes, moving to survive, signing treaties, and moving to reservations, knowing that there will be a day when they can again share their sacred wisdom with all the people of Earth, sharing that is beginning to happen now in the 21st century. Some Esopus move and again set up their village near what is now Binghamton, living in oneness with the deer, bear, and mountain lions of the Earth as they had before, and as their dreams tell them how they should live. As we know, they have continued to move to survive for the last several hundred years, but they will survive and they will show others how to live. As I crawl underground, I will again arise into the daylight to share my wisdom.

My experience of the life of the Esopus continues the next morning, 12/26/15, while using the Olmec Prince Metamorphosis Posture (Fig. 2.3):

I become an oak tree, a burr oak. Several young girls are collecting the acorns from below my branches. I can feel their respect for me in the way they occasionally reach out and touch my trunk. Both when they begin and when they finish, they offer me a pinch of acorn meal in thanks. As I stand as an oak, I watch the people of the village moving through the forest. Close to me is a chestnut tree and nearby a hickory tree. Again, there are the young people of the village picking up the nuts. Others are picking up broken and dead branches to use as firewood for their fires over which they cook and warm their shelters. They all show us, as trees, respect and thank us for what we give them. Some are looking for a special ash tree. There are many ash trees in the forest and they seek a straight one that they can use for many things including strips of bark for covering their huts, strips of wood to make baskets, wood for their bows and arrows, for making bowls, and for snowshoes on which they walk in the winter. They are very thankful for the ash that they select and they make sure that there are many young ash in the area to replace the one that they take. They also look for long willow branches from along the creek to make and repair their wigwams. The willow is fast-growing and in thick abundance along the creek. They give thanks to the willow. To make a dugout canoe, they select a large and old pine tree, and this takes a lot of work to cut it down and burn to hollow out the trunk. They are very grateful and thank the pine tree too. They sometimes used bark from the birch tree to make canoes. The forest remains healthy and productive, used by the people but also by many animals for food and shelter, and where birds build their nests.

On 12/26/15, my experience with the Hallstatt Warrior Posture (Fig. 2.4) takes me to my 9xgreat grandfather Brink:

I am watching and listening to Lambert Huybertsen Brink, my 9xgreat grandfather who lives in Nieuw Dorp, the village that is now Hurley. This and the following experiences feel somewhat different from usual because the characters in the experience are my known ancestors from the area around Hurley. My ecstatic experiences are from a tree-house in the woods near to Hurley (c. 10 miles away). In 1663, during The Second Esopus War, a band of Esopus capture Lambert's wife, Hendrickje, and three of their children, Huybert, Jannetje, and Cornelis, and hold them in a Wappinger Lenape village for three months. Cornelis, the youngest, was only 4 years old.

Lambert cuts down trees indiscriminately and in great numbers for building his home. Earlier, others have cut down many trees to build the stockade around Wiltwyck. Their iron axes make the job easier than it is for the Esopus, who use stone axes and burn the base of the tree to fall it. The Dutch give no thought or thanks to the trees because of their belief that they have dominion over the Earth, and taking from it is their right. Their God gives them the right to use the Earth as they see fit. This is appalling to the Esopus, and they feel threatened by the Dutch, which is one reason for their attack. Though the women of the villages seek and hope for peace with the white man, the Indian attackers were young men who had been drinking brandy given to them by a local Englishman, Thomas Chambers, in exchange for work done on his farm.

While holding Lambert's wife and children captive, the Esopus treated them well, showing them respect. His wife, Hendrickje, sees how the Esopus showed respect for the land, animals, and trees, calling the animals and trees their ancestors. With their release, Lambert thought of the Esopus as savages and the enemy, and his wife could not tell him of the respect she had gained for them. To this story, we will return.

Then on the next day,12/27/15, while using the Priestess of Malta Middle World Posture (Fig. 2.7), I find myself again in the Esopus village:

I go to the Esopus Village. The men have their heads together, discussing what needs to be done. A scouting party goes out to visit other outlying villages with the thought that we need to move to the West. But other tribes inhabit the West. We are one of the largest villages, being on the edge of a large river. Moving would impinge on the hunting territory of the other villages, though in some villages we have relatives, the parents, sisters, and brothers of our husbands who would most likely welcome us. But such a move tears us away from the land we know so well, from the animals and trees who are our ancestors, animals, and trees who we have protected and who trust us, our Garden of Eden. We have continually thanked them for what they provide, but now some of us decide to abandon them and leave them to be destroyed by the coming of people from across the ocean. As we leave and walk slowly in sorrow, we know the Earth provides. Many of us stay, hoping to get along with the white man.

Then I find myself in the home of a Dutch family. We have a large supply of firewood to keep us warm and more than enough food stashed to last us for weeks. It is warm and we praise God for what he has provided us, though we ignore the Earth that has been the provider and of whom we have taken advantage. We are happy to see the Esopus leave the land to us, the Esopus who are savages and do not believe in God, a God that has sent them away and given us dominion over this land along the river. There are a plentiful number of deer and other animals in the area, but the animals are quick to learn to hide and no longer trust humans with guns. This is no longer the Garden of Eden.

On 12/27/15, I use the Venus of Galgenberg Posture (Fig. 2.8) for journeying into the upper world:

I fly over the Esopus village that has moved further west, still along the Esopus Creek. They are busy and have gotten into the routine of living as they had farther down the creek. Then I fly over the Brink home outside of Nieuw Dorp, now Hurley, where

Hendrickje is inside talking to her children, who are now older, telling them about their capture by the Esopus. "The Esopus had burned the village of Nieuw Dorp and were leaving when they passed our house a half-mile out of town. Your father was in town fighting the Esopus. I was home alone with you when an Indian came to the door and grabbed my arm, and pulled me out of the house. He then took us, blindfolded me, and led me away with the three of you following. You were crying and scared, but the Esopus were gentle with you and one was carrying Jannetje and another Cornelis. When we got to a rocky area of the path, they took off my blindfold. I did not know where we were. We kept going for maybe another hour or two before we were lifted into a canoe and taken some distance downstream before we reached their village. I think the Esopus in the battle were from several villages and this one was far away, a Wappinger Lenape village. They took us to one wigwam where there was a squaw and several children about your age. She brought us a bowl of stew that she had cooked and it tasted good. Everyone in the village showed us respect and was gentle with us. They knew we could not leave because we did not know where we were and how to return home, so they really did not hold us like prisoners. After a while, you were playing with the other children, and I was helping some with the cooking. I wanted to go home, but after a while, I was not afraid of the Esopus because they were treating us well."

Hendrickje continues with her story as I journey with the Calling the Spirits Posture (Fig. 2.10) on 12/28/15:

As I told this story, I had several thoughts. Why did they take us and not any of the men as prisoners? Why were they so gentle with us? What did they want from us? There was no ransom. And when some scouts returned, telling of men coming, they easily let us go, and we went out to greet them. One was your father. It was so good to see him. I think they only wanted to show us how they lived and how they took care of their families. They showed a lot of respect for the animals of the forest and for what they took from their garden by leaving a gift of tobacco or cornmeal for whatever they took. They were very gentle with everything, especially us. At first, when they took us, they tied my hands together, but soon took off the strip of hide and examined my wrists to make sure they were okay. When the squaw nursed her youngest, she pointed to me, showing that I should nurse Cornelis. I could not understand her words, but we smiled a lot. I think they wanted to show us they were gentle.

Using the Lady of Cholula Divination Posture (A.11) on 12/28/14, I return to being Hendrickje:

I find myself again as my 9xgreat grandmother next to the cooking fire. After the story I told the children yesterday, I realize that as I cook I most always take a moment to thank the Lord for what I am cooking, a silent prayer. Lambert leads us in a prayer of thanks before we eat, as is our tradition, but he does not thank each thing that went into the meal and where it came from. I did not learn many words of the Indian language, but one word was their word for spirit, *maytscheetschank,* and not just one spirit, but of the spirits of everything. In their dances, they wore different costumes for different animals they hunted, calling the spirits of those animals. These spirits seemed very real to them, and they seemed to talk to them all the time, thanking them. The Indian mother thanked the spirits of everything she cooked as if the spirits were real and could hear her. The way the deer and other animals came near and into the village made me think they could hear the words of thanks spoken by the mother. They showed no actual fear of the villagers. When Lambert hunts, the deer hide and are hard to find. The Esopus have a very special relationship with everything around them.

* * *

On 12/29/15, while using the Tlazolteotl Cleansing Posture (Fig. A.22), I join Lambert, my 9xgreat grandfather, on his farm:

I am on Lambert's farm in Hurley, only a few miles from where I stand in the Tlazolteotl Posture. He is working in the field harvesting barley. He has one black slave to help him and they work hard. They then carry the threshed barley to the mill to be ground. He is thankful for being blessed by God for his success, but it takes hard work on his part and he takes pride in his harvest. The Earth is quite fertile, which he attributes to the off-planet God. Though many farms need to be cleared of trees, his land was a large treeless meadow at the edge of the Esopus Creek, occasionally flooded by the creek, so he did not have to clear the land. Yet, when he expands his fields, he will need to do some clearing. He also has a field of wheat and one of oats. He thanks God in church on Sunday, in his prayer at the dinner table, and at bedtime. He believes God has provided him with the land over which he controls in planting, and it is his responsibility to work hard to make it productive. He does not thank the Earth for providing for him and his family.

I return to the farm using the Olmec Prince Posture (Fig. 2.3) on 12/29/15:

Again, I am taken back to the farmstead of my ancestors, Lambert and Hendrickje Brink. I am his first slave who works the farm with him. I look to his God who promises a heavenly afterlife if I remain humble and faithful. The Bible says that it is easier for a camel to go through the eye of a needle than for a rich man to get into heaven. But my master believes he is rich because of God's blessing, and since I am a slave, I am not blessed. My master takes care of me and is not abusive. He shows me the love of God, even so, he looks down upon me because I am not blessed. I am confused. I don't understand what it means to be blessed when a rich person cannot get into heaven. He believes he will go to heaven because he is earning his way by working hard, praying, and going to church. As a slave, I don't have a church, but we get together and pray. I heard the story of Hendrickje being captured by the Esopus, how they lived, and of the Esopus gentleness. I wonder if they will get into heaven. My master believes they need to be converted to be saved, but believing in the love of God, I can't imagine that God would turn anyone away.

With the Hallstatt Warrior Posture (Fig. 2.4), on 12/30/15 I explore the Esopus medicine ways:

I am with Hendrickje, her daughter Jannetje, and her daughter-in-law, also named Hendrickje. Her young grandson, Huybert, has an earache and sore throat. Hendrickje recalls her time with the Esopus family and values what she learned from the mother in treating illness. One herbal remedy she remembers is using the bark of the black locust to make a tea for sore throats. Since the time of their capture, she and her three children have learned to trust and value what the Esopus teach, and she has developed a friendship with an Esopus woman who lives in a nearby village. She leaves to visit her to ask about how to treat earaches and learns to take a piece of wood, the best is from the persimmon tree, and place it in the fire until it sweats. Collect a few drops of the wood sweat to drop into the ear with the earache. These Esopus medicines were effective in treating Huybert. The three women have become known as respected healers by the Dutch families for their ability to heal various illnesses. They have learned to reach out and value what they can learn from the Esopus healers, healing ways passed down through the generations.

* * *

Using the Tanum Underworld Posture (Fig. 2.6) on 12/30/15, I connect with the Esopus family I lived with as a young child many years earlier:

I am Jannetje when an Indian woman finds me in my garden weeding and thinning the carrots. It takes a few moments, but I soon recognize her, Kisux, meaning Moon. She is the young girl I played with when held captive by the Esopus maybe 15 years before. When we were young, she would point to herself and then the moon to tell me that was her name. She now has a papoose on her back, a baby girl. Her husband is nearby. They came into town with a bundle of beaver skins to trade and had been to the store in Wiltwyck, where they traded for a hoe for their garden and some ammunition for his gun used for hunting. When I recognize Kisux, we hug. She now has learned some Dutch so we can talk together and share stories. I am also married and have a young boy, Teunis, two years old, who is playing in the yard where I can watch him.

As we talk, I pick a couple of carrots and start down to the stream to wash them. Kisux reaches out and tugs at my arm, takes a pinch of tobacco from her pocket, and offers it to the Great Mother in thanks for the carrots. Kisux is shocked and feels a sense of fear in not thanking the Great Mother. I understand and thank her for the offering and then I too give thanks to the Great Mother for the carrots. I share with her some stories of healing with the herbs I learned from my mother, who learned them from Kisux's mother.

On New Year's Eve, 12/31/15, while using the Priestess of Malta Middle World Posture (Fig. 2.7), I return to the history of Wiltwyck:

In May 1658, after drinking too much brandy, a 10-gallon keg, the Esopus kill Harmen Jacobsen and burn the home of Jacob Adrijansen. The Dutch call upon Governor Stuyvesant for help. When he arrives and evaluates the situation, he recommends that rather than living on separate farms, that the nine families move and live together in a stockaded village. The village is first called Esopus and then becomes Wiltwyck before it becomes Kingston. All nine families sign a peace treaty made with the Esopus. The Esopus blame the problem on drinking and youth, but the conflict continues. Lambert Brink arrives later and builds a home in 1661 outside the stockade at the edge of the new village, Nieuw Dorp, that is now Hurley.

In this experience, it again becomes apparent that the continued conflict is at least partly because of a conflict of religious beliefs. The Esopus see the stockade being built around the village, with the Dutch not paying respect to the trees used to build the stockade. Venerating all life of Earth is central to their religious beliefs. Some trees came down from Fort Orange (Albany). Also, building the stockade sends the message that the Dutch do not trust us, an insult to the Esopus. The Second Esopus War of 1663 when the Esopus burned Nieuw Dorp, Hendrickje, and the three children, Huybert (8 years old), Jannetje (6 years old), and Cornelis (3 years old), are captured and held for three months before being released. They were living outside of the village stockade.

On 12/31/15 in the evening, I use the Venus of Galgenberg Upper World Posture (Fig. 2.8) and journey back to when Kisux's brother struggles with what to do:

I am a young Indian man, Kisux's brother, Maxke Walwes, meaning Red Fox. I am laying on the ground looking at the night sky and feeling tiny. The trees near me are huge as they rise above me, but I also feel part of nature. The bear and even some deer are bigger than me, but Mother Earth gives me a deer when I need one. Other times, the deer have much to teach me and I am smaller than the deer. There will be a day when I am to give myself to her, maybe by giving myself to a bear or to a snake, or just to the Earth. We are all part of each other. The bear and the snake are my ancestors. The wolf is the ancestor of our people. Maybe it will be to a wolf that I will give myself. Wolves need to eat, too. Looking at the distant stars and moon that are so far away, farther than the distant mountains, I am so small, but someday the wolf might appreciate me as food like I appreciate the deer, barley, and beans. My friends, who are angry with the white-man, feel big, especially when they drink of the white-man's drink. They want to take back the hunting lands that the white-man has taken. They have traded beaver skins for guns and gunpowder and with a gun, they feel big. They forget that someday they will give themselves back to the Earth and that they are small where the surrounding Earth is so big. It is better to feel small and to appreciate everything that the Great Mother has given us, plants that heal, and food to eat that keep us healthy. And she now has given us the people who come from across the Ocean. They bring us guns and hoes to dig into the Earth, but they show no respect for the Earth. What are we to do? They scare us, but we are not showing Mother Earth that we love her when we kill them and they kill us. What are we to do?

Returning to the history of the two wars on 1/1/16 while using the Freyr Divination Posture (Fig. 2.2), I describe where Hendrickje and the children were taken when captured:

This and several of the previous ecstatic experiences take me between the lines of Augustus Van Buren's history of the two Esopus Wars.[1] Hendrickje and her three children are taken to a Wappinger Indian village and held captive by this Lenape tribe just north of what is now Newburgh, New York, and released in August of 1663 to Lieutenant van Couwenhoven. The captives of the Second Esopus War included 8 women and 26 children from Hurley. When they were at a safe distance from Hurley, the Esopus separated them and took them to different Indian villages in the area. The Wappinger took Hendrickje and her children by canoe down the river about 30 miles to the village where they stayed for the three months of their captivity. The Esopus held several captives for nearly a year, but when released, all had been treated well and were in good health. Though the Dutch painted the Esopus as savages, seeking revenge upon the white man, none of the women or children died or were injured in captivity. The honor of no woman was assailed, and all were returned. A most remarkable fact to reflect upon when forming our estimate of the red man's nature.

In this experience of the new year, the two children who are now adults, Huybert and Jannetje, are talking with Kisux, with whom they played as children when held by the Wappinger. They recall the peacefulness of the village and know how the Esopus sought to live in peace, but the Esopus complained they received no respect from the Dutch, who called them savages. The Dutch continued to hold a few Esopus prisoners, who were sent to the Caribbean Dutch Island of Curacao as slaves. These two children, along with their mother, Hendrickje, also want to live in peace, recognizing how the Esopus live in peace and love the Earth.

On 1/1/16, while using the Olmec Prince Posture (Fig. 2.3), I become Huybert's Ox:

I am in the field with Huybert, plowing with him directing me. He is very somber, thinking of yesterday's conversation with Kisux and recalling the life of the Esopus of the village, of how even at that young age, Kisux and Maxke Walwes would stop when we were helping in the garden and give thanks to the

Great Mother with a pinch of tobacco. With these memories, he feels a special reverence for the Earth he is plowing and for the strength of his ox pulling the plow. He stops and puts his arm around my shoulder, hugging me in thanks. When we finish plowing, he gives me an extra handful of hay that I eat out of his hand, a special time for us together. His farm is quite successful, and it is apparent that his love for what the Earth provides is what makes it successful. Realizing this, he has to thank his young experience with the Esopus, who he has learned to value, feelings that differ greatly from the feelings of the other Dutch living in the area. Yet he realizes he is not alone. There are other boys held by the Esopus back in 1663, and when he has a chance, he will talk to them about their experiences.

On the occasion when the son of Evert Pels comes into town to trade for needed supplies, they will talk. This son of Pels married an Indian girl and remained with her tribe, honored for not deserting his Indian bride and their unborn child, thus redeeming the honor he lost when his father took part in the 1659 murder of an Esopus, a murder that led to the son's captivity.

On 1/2/16, while using the Tlazolteotl Cleansing Posture (A.22), I return to my ancestors of Wiltwyck:

After the Second Esopus War, the Esopus can only come to the military fort, the Redoubt, outside of the stockaded village of Wiltwyck to trade for supplies. After his conversation with his sister, Jannetje and Kisux, Huybert's outward interest in life among the Esopus again becomes alive. He knows that the son of Evert Pels occasionally comes to the Redoubt to trade skins for needed supplies, thus he watches for the younger Pels, wanting to talk to him about his life and about his religious beliefs. When they finally get together and talk, Pels invites Huybert to visit him at his Esopus village. In this conversation and in their following meetings, Huybert learns Pels continues to pray to God, but his feelings about what the church preaches are quite different. He now sees stewardship for the Earth as much more central to his belief and that having dominion over the Earth no longer means he should take all that he can from the Earth, but that in his wisdom he needs to seek how to protect the Earth and all life of the Earth. He thinks of God as being much more aware of all life on Earth, not just human life. Man created in the image of God makes little sense to him because he thinks of God more like the nurturing Earth Mother.

Pels expresses disgust for how the Dutch take from the Earth and try to accumulate wealth and supplies, showing no faith in what the Earth provides. He sees the Esopus know what is available and what they need throughout the year to survive. By following this knowledge, they are never in need, and life is simple and harmonious. What is most amazing is that by giving thanks whenever they take something from the Earth and by not taking more than they need at the time, there is always enough and that the animals are not afraid of the Esopus but make themselves available to them at their time of need. Their relationship with deer, bears, and other hunted animals differs greatly from the Dutch who go on a hunt and bring back as much as possible. He knows that the Dutch seek peace with the Esopus but do not believe that the Esopus want peace. He remembers the language the Dutch use in describing the Esopus as savages, an attitude that disgusts him. He now knows that the Esopus want peace as much as the Dutch, but for there to be peace, mutual respect is necessary. Huybert feels the same from the brief time he spent with the Esopus.

As they talk, Huybert mentions the legend of the daughter of Berent Slecht, who married a young Esopus brave, and that they live nearby. Huybert does not know the entire story, but Pels knows of her and thinks that they should visit her. Pels is eager to reach out and show Huybert the true nature of the Esopus and influence him to show respect to the Esopus, hoping that others might also come to show such respect. Sometimes Jannetje is part of the conversation, but they have not yet brought Cornelis to listen to such thinking. Cornelis and his wife live farther north, and they rarely see him.

As this story unfolds, I think of the many stories of white men marrying Esopus and living among the Esopus, stories that have been told over the following 300 years. It is apparent that many white men found the Esopus respectable and to be appreciated. The Dutch, using wampum beads as a currency in trade, for paying fines, and defining the exchange rate or value of the wampum, shows this needed respect. Their relationship with the Esopus is not all evil.

Using the Priestess of Malta Middle World Posture (Fig. 2.7), on 1/3/16, I return to this exploration of the Dutch respect for the Esopus:

I am walking up the Esopus Kill, or river, above Nieuw Dorp with Jannetje and the son of Pels on our way to visit the village where the daughter of Berent Slecht, who married an Indian brave, lives. As we near the village and the Esopus see us, she runs to hide, fearing that we might want to take her back to Hurley. We talk with the chief of the village and reassure him it is not our purpose. We want to learn from her how she is adjusting to life among the Esopus, and of her thoughts about living with them. We tell the chief that Pels also lives with the Esopus in another village, and he is the one who is doing most of the talking because he has learned their language. She soon comes out from hiding and we sit and talk. Her experience of living in the village is very positive. She and her husband have had a child and the entire village is there to help in caring for the child. She has learned and values how the Esopus live and is especially excited about learning the medicinal qualities of the many plants that grow in the area. She hears from Jannetje what she has been learning about the plants, and a bond forms between the two women.

We talk about and share with her our thought on how to show and convince the Dutch that the Esopus want peace and that we love the Earth as much as the Dutch love their God. We assure her that there are a few of us in Nieuw Dorp and Wiltwyck who trust the Esopus and value their way of living and that she could help in convincing others. She reports that her parents, who have a farm outside of the town, feel the same way about the Esopus, and they support her in her decision to live with them. It is more the people in town who think the Esopus are savages and are not to be trusted.

On 11/6/16, while using the Hallstatt Warrior Posture (Fig. 2.4), I again visit an Esopus Village:

In an earlier time, I am the first white-man to visit an Esopus Indian Village, and I am greeted hospitably. I recall the words of C. A. Weslager, "Regardless of his nationality or skin color, they greet a visitor with warm hospitality. Deeply ingrained in the Delawares' tradition is the obligation they share their food and the comfort of their wigwams with a stranger. It was not uncommon for an Indian host to offer his wife or daughter to a visitor."[2] As I sit by the fire outside of one hut with several Esopus, I am offered food, a wooden bowl of a steaming tasty stew with venison, corn, beans, and squash. I feel their warmth and hospitality, even though my appearance is strange to them and we do not understand each other's language. I carry a musket, but they have seen nothing made of metal. Yet I feel their warm welcome.

I then think of the war parties of the Esopus but realize that it is the white man who saw them as war parties. Before the coming of white man, there may have been some fighting between tribes, but much less than after the coming. The Esopus are a peaceful people and live harmoniously with all life of the Earth. Their religion does not put them above other life of the Earth, as does Christianity. The white man though, feels threatened in this faraway and strange land by the extreme differences they see in the lifeways of the Esopus and their own, even though the Esopus are more defenseless than the white man. The white man are not acting in a "loving Christian manner," and are the ones who broke the peace, forcing the Esopus to defend themselves. Their only weapon before the advent of guns is the bow and arrow. The white man sees the Esopus living in the Stone Age. Imagine how life on this continent could have been different if we would have shown the Indians respect and understood their harmonious relationship with the Earth, if we hadn't attempted to force our God upon them, if we would have shown them the same hospitality that they showed us. We probably wouldn't now be trying to force ourselves on the many other nations of the world as we are doing, and the global climate catastrophe would not be threatening our survival. We have much to learn from the Esopus and, in their great patience, they are now open to teaching us their ways.

Standing in the Tlazeoteotl Cleansing Posture (Fig. A.22) on 1/7/16, I again identify as a white woman who lives with an Indian brave:

Standing in this cleansing posture, I feel myself being cleansed of fear and the anger that results from fear. I am in the Esopus village in what is now Marbletown as the Dutch woman who is living with the Esopus. Weslanger[3] mentions that white women taken captive by the Delaware (Lenape) Esopus in warfare often refused to be rescued after they had become members of the Indian community. "They didn't want to return to the subordination accorded them in colonial society." I feel the freedom of letting go of my fear. I let go of this fear when I feel the respect of the community for what I offer as a woman. As time goes on and I see how they lived with the knowledge of all life around them and what the Earth offered them, I feel their confidence in their simple lifestyle growing within me. We will healthily survive through all the seasons.

This fear began 10,000 years ago in the human attempt to control the Earth, first through agriculture and the domestication of animals, and then through the attempts to control other humans, including women. A need to gain and maintain control generates the fear of the loss of control. Until then, in the hunter-gatherer society, humans did not put themselves above other life and experienced a sense of oneness with everything around them that provided a sense of security without fear. They venerated the Great Creator Spirit, and one with this spirit are the spirits of all life and of all features of nature. The Lenape prayed and continue to pray to these spirits, *maytscheetschank,* and feel secure in the belief that the Earth will provide for them. After being thrown out of the Garden of Eden, learning through the evolution of the knowledge of good and evil, Christians, including the Dutch, attempt to control the Earth, feeling that life on Earth is full of suffering and doubt. Only through salvation would they upon death enter heaven, where they would find peace and harmony.

As this woman who lives with the Esopus, I feel the security in the Indian community, with my husband, an Indian brave, and in their way of life. Through my dreams and visions, the world of the spirits of Earth comes alive and shows me the way to this security. The only insecurity and fear I feel come from the Dutch colonialists who are a threat to the Esopus, but because I am living with the Esopus, they seemed to not be a threat to my village but came to it in curiosity and wonder, not understanding why I would prefer to live this primitive way of life. Yet, when the Dutch, English, French, and other settlers see that some of them find a sense of peace and harmony in the Indian way of life, it only adds to their fear and sense of threat from the Esopus. They could not understand that we do not fear burning in hell as they do.

On 1/10/16, using the Freyr Divination Posture (Fig. 2.2), I join an Esopus chief in the sweat lodge:

I am in a sweat lodge with the chief of the Esopus village. He is struggling with several problems and does not know what to do. He decides he must bring together the other chiefs in the area. The problem confronting him is that the younger men of the village want more and more of the things the white man brings, especially the brandy which is causing so many problems. These young men are trapping more and more of the beaver and other animals because the white man wants all they can get. He sees the beavers will soon go extinct because the younger men are taking them all, even the pregnant females and the young that would provide us with beavers in the future. This scares the elder/chief. He does not understand the white man, why he wants all the furs he can get. Also, he does not understand why they do not want us to hunt and fish around their villages. He does not understand the white man's ownership of land. Land belongs to everyone, including the animals and fauna of the Earth. He feels very confused. He welcomes the white man as he would anyone visiting, but the white man is taking everything of theirs. The chief wants to live in peace, but his people are being killed and they are killing the white man when they have had too much brandy.

Then I am an observer of the meeting of chiefs, six of them. We are all again cleansed in the sweat lodge, cleansing our minds so we can think clearly. One thing we know is that we need to work together and decide together. Though we speak the same language, we have lived separately and independently of each other. In this way, we have lived in peace. We have not tried to take the land from the neighboring tribes of Esopus, though sometimes they attack us and try to take our land. We need to stand together to defend our land, especially from the white man. We need to convince the younger men of our people to not drink white man's brandy, though we have been trying to convince them but have failed. Before the white man came, we were happy without their iron axes and hoes, their colored cloth, iron kettles, and guns. The brightly colored cloth makes it hard to hunt because the deer see us coming dressed as a white man. These things make life easier, but no longer peaceful. We are not living in harmony with the spirits of the Earth. It is sad.

The chief of each village returns home and calls a meeting of all the people of the village to tell them how they see what is happening and try to convince them of how important it is to return to the old ways. Some men know that they have to go farther and farther away to trap beavers, but they do not know what would happen if they did not have beaver hides for the white man. We have to go to the hunting grounds of other villages and even the hunting grounds of other tribes, and we are making enemies of these other tribes. We need to trade for guns, gunpowder, and lead, so we can defend ourselves in fighting these other tribes. The white man may go on the warpath. We just don't know what to do. The wives of the men have tried to get their husbands to stop drinking brandy, but they don't stop. They say they cannot stop. They want it so badly. They don't know what to do.

On 1/11/16, while using the Olmec Prince Posture (Fig. 2.3), I become a beaver, a story that brings this series of experiences to an end:

I become a beaver, maybe the last one in the pond. The Indian elder is beside the pond, talking with the others of the village. I feel the old feeling of trust towards the people, something that I have not felt for some time. He is saying, "Have you forgotten your ancestors. The beaver is your ancestor and the old stories tell of how we venerated, how we respected him. It is because of this respect that we live a healthy and good life. We need the beaver to give himself to us. Now we are taking him without a word of thanks. We have become greedy.

"Remember the story of our journey to this land and how the land provided for us. We knew every animal and every plant. They are all our ancestors and we showed them respect. Then (2,000 to 2,500 years ago) we started planting corn, and then beans and squash. These plants gave themselves to us and we were thankful, but we have changed. We worked hard to grow these plants and forget that they are our ancestors. We take them for granted. Sometimes they do not grow well, and we sometimes feel hunger. We would move to a new place where the Earth is good and would again grow our food. Now we give our corn and the beavers to the white man and we again feel hungry. We have forgotten how the plants of the Earth give themselves to us and we have forgotten where to find them. We have given almost all the beavers to the white man and soon there will be none left. Things are changing and if we forget the old ways, we may disappear like the beaver. We can't forget our ancestors. We have lived in peace and harmony with our neighbors. Now our neighbors have become our enemy because we are fighting over their hunting grounds. Because we give the hides of the animals to the white man, there is no longer enough for all of us in our hunting grounds."

The elder grandfather turns towards the pond and sees me, a beaver, watching them. A couple of men reach for their spears. "See, he might be the last beaver in this pond. Some of you are ready to throw your spears at him and then there will be no beavers in this pond. We used to make sure that the beaver we took was the old one and would not have babies. We would make sure that we left the young because we knew that they would have babies for the next year. Now we no longer care. We have forgotten that they are our brothers and sisters."

As we know from history, the Lenape had to move. They moved to Oklahoma, Wisconsin, and Canada, and we have not seen a beaver around here for many years. Though 400 years later, I now occasionally see a beaver.

CHAPTER 9

Living in Oneness with the Sami Reindeer, Finland

For the next eleven days, I will travel with my daughter, her husband, and grandson around the Baltic Sea before venturing south to Berlin. We will begin in Stockholm before taking a seagoing ferry to Tallinn, Estonia. From there, we will take another day trip by ferry to Helsinki, Finland. We will then take a short flight to Riga, Latvia, from where we will fly to Berlin. Finally, we will return to Stockholm before flying home. This trip takes me to the lands of my very distant ancestors. A genome study revealed that I have the U5 gene configuration that over 50% of the Sami reindeer herders of the far north have, a people who migrated northward into the Finnish artic from the eastern shore of the Baltic Sea before the ice age some 30,000 years ago.

In the early morning of 11/26/14, while in Stockholm, I stood in the Priestess of Malta Posture (Fig. 2.7) while going into ecstatic trance:

We are staying near the palace in Stockholm on Gamla Stan Island at the Urban Hostel. From near there, I go back to an earlier agricultural time when the size of one's herd of sheep and cattle is a sign of prestige and wealth. I sense that there is a wolf with me, a threat to the herd. A man's wealth used to attract a wife was the size of his herd. Upon marriage, the wife would go to live with her husband. With the patrilocal marriage, veneration of the nurturing Great Earth Mother ended, and competition for wealth to attract a wife became important. Later, the richest kings would have many servants and the lives of his wives became plush. In earlier times, with the worship of the great provider Mother Earth, the man would go live with the band of his wife. With this change in how people lived, wives suffered leaving their families. The people worshiped Odin, a masculine warrior god, and deification and worship of the king became prominent. People lived longer in the times of the nurturing Mother Earth Goddess when they worked together in cooperation as they hunted and gathered what they ate. They wandered their territory as they followed the herds of animals they hunted and knew well the flora with its nutritional and medicinal benefits.

On the evening of 11/26/14, we begin our sea journey to Estonia. I stand in the ferry's stern in the Feathered Serpent Posture (Fig. 2.9):

I pray to Surt for warmth, wondered why this giant of the south is an evil threat. Surt is a threat to the people of the colder climate of the north. I feel the cold of the Baltic experienced by the Viking seamen while standing at the stern of the ferry. I feel the strength and stamina of these ancient seamen as they deal with the elements of the earth, a challenge to their stamina in conquering the Earth rather than appreciating the nurturance of the Great Mother and the warmth of her fire. Their gods provide these seamen with tests of strength. A blast from a fog horn brings me back to standing in the middle of the stern with the water being churned up by the motors of the ferry. I see some lights in the distance shining through the fog from another ferry going in the reverse direction or a fishing boat as we travel throughout the night from Stockholm to Tallinn.

As the people worship the warrior gods, Odin and Thor, leaving behind the Great Mother, they seek to be competitive in winning wives by flexing their muscles. Some, with exceptional strength, will become warriors for their local chieftain, thus leaving the village of their parents. This tears asunder families which used to be the center of life. Now the chieftain becomes central while the men stay in the chieftain's hall and their wives stay in the hall of the women who raise the children of the kingdom.

Then on the morning of 11/27/14, while standing at the stern of the ferry in the Hallstatt Warrior Posture (Fig. 2.4), I return to Viking times:

The Jarl, a Scandinavian nobleman, travels the region to collect tribute for his chieftain, tribute he takes in exchange for protecting the land from raiders and other chieftains who seek to expand their domain. The size of the Jarl's goat herd, which is cared for by slaves, determines his wealth. I find myself as the son of the Jarl, and I am expected to become a retainer of his chieftain, who worships the strength of Odin and Thor. If I become his retainer, I need to show my youthful strength to be respected by the chieftain and to attract women.

Yet, I remember the stories of Baldr as told to me by my mother, and I want to be gentle. As she tells the story of Baldr's death, it instills within me the absurdity of power over being gentle and compassionate. I am named Baldrson by my mother because she loves the stories she told me as I was growing up. Baldr is the poet and storytelling god of the Nordic people. My mother remembers the stories of when a wife would stay home in the domain of her parents and bring her new husband to live with her. Then it was a matriarchal time when people venerated the Great Mother Earth Goddess.

Returning to the herd of goats, goats first came from the south, brought north by traveling merchants, first domesticated by hunters when they would kill wild mother goats and take the young ones home to nurture and tame. A wealthy man may have from 100 to 200 goats, but in payment for protection during these violent times, a chieftain takes what he needs, likely half, to feed his retainers, hopefully leaving the goat herder with enough goats to keep up the herd population for future years.

My mother still clings to the Mother Goddess and does not feel much reverence for the warrior gods, Odin and Thor. She has a special place in our hut with an image of Freyja, the goddess of fertility and childbirth, the granddaughter of the Great Mother Goddess. My mother blames the death of her first son on the worship of the warrior gods and resents them. They make little sense to her when she hears the stories and sees the nurturing and compassion of the gods and goddesses of the Vanir. Being my father's son, I feel confused.

The evening of 11/27/14, I find a special spot in Tallinn in a garden and stand in the Mayan Oracle Posture (Fig. A.14):

The spirit of Baldrson again comes to me. I feel my mother's pain at having lost a son who had become a retainer of the chieftain, and I am happy watching over my father's goats. I watch the flora growing on the hillside and learn from what I see. Where the goats graze and eat the flowers of the plants, they do not grow back thick like where flowers bloom and are not eaten. There are many flowers and the goats like certain ones better than others. But what they like most does not come back strongly the next year. I learn that when the flowers bloom, I need to move the goats to a different place until the end of the blooms. The goats like tender plants before they bloom. There is always something to learn. During the day, my sister comes and takes a goat, one at a time, to milk. Occasionally, we butcher a goat for its meat. They provide for us and we protect them from wolves and other predators. This life is compassionate and nurturing.

My father, the Jarl, sometimes expresses disappointment that I do not seem interested in becoming a warrior of the chieftain, but he is not at home much because of his duties of visiting the families of the chieftain's domain to collect the tribute they owe the chieftain, so his disappointment does not cause me to suffer. He knows his wife would prefer that I stay home and care for the goats. She does not talk with him about the gods and goddesses.

The next morning, 11/28/14, I lay back on a bench in a garden in the Tanum Underworld Posture (Fig. 2.6):

I am swimming in the Baltic on my way to Finland and then back to Uppsala, where I meet young warriors practicing, hoping they will become the strongest with the strength of Beowulf. As I hear the stories of the strength of Beowulf in his swim from Denmark around the tip of Sweden and onto Finland, competing with a warrior who challenged him to this race, I feel the excitement of the adventure. Beowulf's competitor made it only to the tip of Sweden, a story that is recorded in the ancient poem of Beowulf. I am familiar with this feeling of excitement in seeking strength and power, though it is a feeling I seek to reject with an intellectual preference for nurturance and cooperation.

Then, while in the Estonian capital city of Tallinn I find myself in trance some distance to the east of the city in the forested countryside, sitting and watching the animals that dwell there, deer, bear, wolves, and other animals, some stalking others, and some with ingenious ways of avoiding their enemy, a fine balance of life in nature. This balance is the way the Earth provides for all life, the way I value and prefer. The competitiveness of the warrior works against and destroys this balance. Yet, I am part of a world of competition, and to survive, I play its game. The Old City of Tallinn is peaceful, beautiful, and artistic, with a large central crafts market. The artisans need to be competitive in producing quality crafts, but they are materialistic and removed from the world of nature that I find for myself in that distant spot to the east of the city. Some artisans are making reindeer hide hats with fur ear flaps that are the best in keeping one's head warm, but I am afraid that they do not respect or show appreciation for the reindeer that sacrifices itself to the artisan. They most likely purchase the hide and do not meet the living reindeer itself.

I stand in the Nyborg Man Posture (Fig. A.15), a Nordic Feathered Serpent Posture. It is the evening of 11/28/14 while I am still in Tallinn:

I go back in time to become a warrior of the chieftain, as my father dreamed I would become, a warrior who soon dies in fighting for the chieftain. I visit my brother on the hillside and feel his sense of peace and nurturance in watching the goats graze on the grass. He has moved beyond the era of the hunter-gatherers in his herding of domesticated animals, animals that have given up their independence and ability to survive on their own, yet in herding, he finds peace and contentment. I want to let go of my testosteronic energy and find peace. It is where I feel at home, at home in our gardens.

Traveling in these cities, I feel a more competitive strength. Even at home, I push myself rather than slowing down to relish the Earth and what I plant in the garden. Can I work in the garden with a feeling of caring for Mother Earth? I so quickly feel a sense of strength and competitiveness while in the garden as I struggle to develop it into a permaculture, a garden that can take care of itself. I seldom find peace and enjoyment at the moment, but am looking forward to what the garden could be. Though the wildness of nature is not available to us for foraging as it was for the hunter-gatherers, a permaculture can bring us closer to that world of gathering. With the hybrid plants developed over the years by agriculturists, a permaculture can be exceptionally productive and seems to be the best hope for our survival.

* * *

Then on 11/29/14 I sit in the Lady of Cholula Posture (Fig. A.11) while on the ferry trip to Helsinki:

Again, I am the brother to the herder of goats, the brother who dies in battle, a youth on a youthful adventure to seek fame and fortune. Before I die, I survive by raiding and pillaging defenseless villages. I feel the power of this life. I will return to find a wife once I find my fortune, a fortune to impress her. Being on the Baltic brings this feeling alive within me. A nurturing son or husband would be at home on land with Mother Earth, and not need to face the misery of the cold to show strength. On the other hand, I could be a merchant who brings people things they don't have, things that they lived without when they were hunter-gatherers. Now they want these things to show their wealth while supporting the new life of consumerism, fame, and fortune.

In seeking fame and fortune, in seeking to become a great warrior of the chieftain, I need to put the thought of a wife out of my mind. I need to be one-minded in practicing and strengthening my skills as a warrior. Love cannot distract me. Such distraction can leave me vulnerable and if I should die because of such a distraction, I would be doomed to Hel's domain rather than Valhalla, the place where a hero goes after death.

As we return to Tallinn from Helsinki on the evening of 11/29/14, I sit in the Shekmet Initiation Posture (Fig. A.17):

I am tired and repeatedly fall asleep, but then I wake and find myself on a fishing boat. I know my fish and baits and I am successful as a fisherman. Again, I am living a life of proving my strength in facing the Earthly elements of being on the sea. Again, my testosterone rages to prove my manliness. Each day I go aboard my boat and go out onto the sea to face Jormungand, the sea serpent that dwells in the sea and surrounds the Earth such that it can hold its tail in its mouth. As it lets go of its tail and thrashes, huge waves rock the boat, a terrifying challenge for fishermen.

I see Thor out fishing with the giant Hymir. Thor hooks Jormungand using as bait an ox's head. He pulls it aboard, much to the horror of Hymir. As Thor reaches for his Mjollnir, his great hammer, to dispatch the Midgard serpent, Hymir cuts Thor's line. Jormungand sinks to the bottom of the sea where it finds safety.

As a fisherman, I stay within sight of the shore where I feel safe. I then see my wife's cousin, who is a fisherman off the coast of the southern tip of Sweden. He has caught an eel that he smokes and offers me a piece. It is delicious. With the birth of a new era of Baltic fishermen, I can see their boats, boats that offer them greater comfort. I can see their lights in the distance on this dark night. Fishermen now have weather reports that tell them when it is safe to go out on the sea, so now they can avoid the thrashing tail of Jormungand.

The 36,000-year-old Venus of Galgenberg posture (Fig. 2.8) takes me into the heavens early in the morning of 11/30/14:

As I fly around the earth, I see luminous fibers stream upwards to me. I follow them down back to the Earth. At the other end of the fibers, I see people in trance practicing altered states of consciousness, some dreaming in sleep and others sharing their dreams with others of their community. A handful are using the Cuyamungue Method of ecstatic trance and sharing their experiences of harmony and personal growth. From past times and the present, in the era of time-free consciousness, from the islands of Micronesia and many other parts of the world, people share their dreams and trance experiences. They experience peace and harmony as they learn and grow from these experiences. I first travel inland to Germany. There I am with Janna and Ki as they practice ecstatic trance, then I flow down along the Danube where the Venus was found. So much positive energy opens itself with the power of trance.

On this trip with my daughter and her family, as we venture around the Baltic Sea, my ecstatic trance experiences take me to the ancient people of the area, the Ynglings. And then, as we travel south towards Berlin, I find myself in the world of Brünhilde, Sigurd, and Gunnar, people of the Nibelung. This journey brings alive within me *The Saga of the Volsungs*.[1]

Brünhilde resents the Great Mother and the women of her age, who flaunt their weakness in their submission to men. She drinks the urine of a male horse, Grani, to give her hair on her body and the strength of a man. Other women drink the urine of a pregnant mare to receive the power of seduction. Sigurd and Gunnar of the Nibelung, who worship the old gods, struggle for the love of Brünhilde, who has lost her precious ring in the river. As a fish, I find her ring, which brings me to better understand her. This story examines other dimensions of the Nibelung, the story of the Ring.

On the afternoon of 12/1/14, while at the Riga Airport on the way to Berlin, I sit in the Lady of Cholula Divination Posture (Fig. A.11):

I go to the Hallstatt cave in Germany. I call upon Odin to help on the hunt for Brünhilde's ring. Odin turns me into a fish with his power of shape-shifting, and I swim the Rhine River. I see the glitter of gold of a ring at the bottom of the river and dive, take it in my mouth, and swallow it. A fisherman on the bank of the river catches me, and when he cuts me open, he finds the ring. He takes the ring to his wife, who is greatly pleased with this ancient treasure, a ring that gives her the power of a woman over men in seducing them. The ring, tempered with the urine of a pregnant mare, brings her the power to seduce men, but also the weakness of love. This creates a problem for this fisherman because other men find her attractive in her seductiveness, and he becomes jealous.

Then on 12/1/14, while in Berlin, I lay in the Sami Underworld Posture (Fig. A.16):
I meet Brünhilde, who is angry at the Great Mother for not standing up to the men of Odin to show them her strength. Brünhilde eats of the golden apple of Idunn and drinks the urine of a male horse, Grani, an ancestor of Sleipnir, Odin's eight-legged horse, to stay strong while growing hair on her legs and chin. She joins the men in controlling the earth and gives up the magic of the Great Mother. She builds a wall of fire around her domain to protect herself from men. One man, Sigurd, can with his great strength and with the strength of his horse Grani, jump the wall of fire. Gunnar, who is sworn in brotherhood to Sigurd, seeks the love of Brünhilde, but he cannot break through the wall of fire to reach her, so he beseeches Sigurd for help. With the power of shape-shifting, he changes his shape to that of Sigurd and breaches the flames, riding Sigurd's horse, Grani. Believing in Gunnar's strength, Brünhilde marries him.

Then, on 12/2/14, while sitting in the Olmec Prince Posture (Fig. 2.3) along the Spree River in Berlin, I had the following experience:
I become a bird flying along the Spree River that is just outside our apartment window in Berlin. Then I become a fish swimming in the Rhine River. As the fish, I again find a ring and swallow it. I then return to being a bird and see two women arguing as one throws a ring into the river. The man who had given it to her was unfaithful. He took back the ring he first gave her to give to his best friend for his friend to give to his new wife, but he gives Brünhilde another ancient ring to replace it. He thinks

she should be pleased with the new ring that was also part of the hoard of gold that Sigurd found in the cave of Fafnir, the dragon that he slew.

The ring, Andvaranaut, that Sigurd first gave to Brünhilde, holds a curse of death. When Gunnar, in the shape of Sigurd, travels through the wall of fire to gain the hand of Brünhilde, he carries another ring given him by Sigurd to give to her. While in bed, he takes the ring Andvaranaut from her and gives her the new ring. Upon leaving the domain of Brünhilde, he returns Andvaranaut to Sigurd, who then gives it to his wife, Gudrun, the sister of Gunnar. The next day while Gudrun and Brünhilde are bathing in the river Rhine, Brünhilde sees the ring, recognizes it, and realizes that Gunnar has been unfaithful to her. Another piece of the story that needs to be told is that when Sigurd is visiting the family of Gunnar, Gudrun, and all of her brothers. Their mother, Grimild, a sorceress, seeks Sigurd as a son-in-law. They give him a drink of forgetfulness so that he forgets his love for Brünhilde.

The story continues on 12/3/14 while using the Mayan Oracle Posture (Fig. A.14):

I ask the Mayan Oracle, "What gave Brünhilde her strength and the ring, the curse of death?" I first see Slepnir in his barn and an old hag taking him hay. She sleeps in the barn near him on hay that smells like urine. She was born and grows up in the hay of Sleipnir. As a young girl, Sleipnir's urine gave her the strength to take care of the powerful horse. I then find myself in Brünhilde's hall behind the wall of fire and see her drinking a steaming liquid from her horn. One of her servants mixes herbs into the steaming liquid that he just brought from the barn, a liquid that gives her the strength of a man.

I then find myself in the cave of the dark elves, who are smelting gold into a ring, mixing the gold with the urine of a pregnant mare that they collected at night, and using it to temper the gold. I then see Gudrun. She is in a horse stall with a pregnant mare drinking urine, feeling weak and soft. The tempering of the ring makes the owner seductive in winning men, but soft and weak, a weakness that leads to her death.

On 12/5/14, we have returned to Stockholm and I use the Tanum Underworld Posture (Fig. 2.6):

Because of Sigurd's marriage to Gudrun, Brünhilde despises her husband, Gunnar, and refuses to get out of bed or eat. She is feeling the weakness of love and the curse that the ring Andvaranaut put on her. Gunnar seeks to make her happy, and she tells him it might help if he would kill Sigurd, but he has sworn allegiance to Sigurd and cannot kill him. So he and his brothers arrange with their youngest brother to kill him, a brother who has not sworn allegiance to him. This brother finds Sigurd in bed with Gudrun, his sister, and runs his sword through him. Sigurd awakens and before he dies and throws his sword at the brother, killing him. As is tradition, Gunnar builds a high funeral pyre upon which both Sigurd and Gunnar's brother are placed. As it burns, Brünhilde joins them on the pyre and dies, thus the curse of Andvaranaut continues and leaves Gudrun without a husband. Gudrun eventually marries King Atli of the Ynglings as prophesied. Some recent researchers believe that Atli is Atilla the Hun.

Now I find myself as Atli, who is getting old and with little self-confidence, fat, and with no powerful sons. I have strong retainers, but wonder why they stay with me. I am not benevolent and give them little other than sufficient food and drink and a warm place to stay. I am uncertain that my wives are faithful, and one had a healthy son that I want to believe is mine. I still have the power and authority to claim him as my son even though he does not look like me but looks more like my strongest retainer, who seems to have a lot of interest in him. Others think I am in denial, but I know better and use my authority to get what I want. I know I am obese. To the end, I put my hope in my so-called son. I respect his father and I have no one else to take my place. I really can't trust my wives and especially my newest wife, Gudrun. I don't trust her brothers and don't know who she is loyal to. I'm not dumb. Some of my retainers have left me because of my greed, but number one will stay because his son is to become the next king.

On 12/5/14, while over Greenland on my way home, I sit in the Shekmet Initiation Posture (Fig. A.17):

Atli dies. He was a Hun and had conquered the Yngling to become their king. Most of his original men have died or have converted to the Yngling beliefs. His most powerful warrior is a Yngling. The Ynglings individually were stronger warriors than the Huns, though the Huns were greater in number. His retainers put Atli on a funeral pyre, but they do not know what is going to happen to him since he is a Hun. His wife, Gudrun, and the lover to his number one retainer, remembers the old ways and seeks to teach their son the magic of the old ways, though the son follows his father, who follows Odin and Thor. This balance leads him to understand the need to be a benevolent king. They, the Ynglings, rule northern Sweden and the Skjǫldung to the south. Since the Ynglings and Skjoldung are allies, together they rule Sweden.

Now, sometime after my return home, I return to the Baltic to explore again my Scandinavian roots. While in Helsinki, I spent considerable time in the museum examining the artifacts and displays of the Sami reindeer herders. On 2/28/16, while using the Sami Underworld Posture (Fig. A.16), I had the following experience:

I am pulled headfirst through water into the underworld. The flow of water moves faster and faster as it carries me downhill into a cave and eventually the flow levels off in the underworld. As I lay on the ground, I see people walking upside down on the ceiling. A fire is burning from the ceiling with the flames flaming downwards, but the smoke rises. Above the ground, people are walking with their feet connecting to the feet of their upside-down ancestors in the underworld. Above ground, they are calling to the spirits of their ancestors from the underworld by walking through the trance-inducing labyrinth. As they walk the labyrinth and reach the center, they lay down as the village drummer drums, and from below the center is the fire from where the spirits rise in the smoke to commune with the person above.

The spirits below know the Sami are a directed people with great commitment to where their lives are going, but when they walk the labyrinth, the direction seems aimless, with no direction. This concerns the spirits of the lower world, so they rise to see what is going on and if they can be of help.

Being drawn to the Sami is a known connection to my ancestry since I possess a gene configuration that over half of the Sami reindeer herders possess. On 3/18/16, I return to this heritage while using the Hallstatt Warrior Posture (Fig. 2.4):

I find myself somewhere in eastern-central Europe, in what is now Hungary. It is probably from 30,000 to 40,000 years ago, before the ice age. I am part of a small hunter-gatherer band of five or six families. Winter is approaching and we are moving north towards what is now Poland. We are following a herd of aurochs that is roaming the river's edge. When we reach the river, we set up camp, each family building a shelter using the hides of the aurochs. A couple of the more domesticated aurochs carry what each family needs on their backs, including a ceramic bowl of embers to start their fire upon moving. The fire burns, heating a rock that is placed in the bowl of water to heat it. We each carry a few pieces of smoked and dried meat, a piece of which is placed in the bowl of heating water along with some collected herbs to make a soup or stew. The herd we follow with which we are very familiar is browsing along the river where there is plenty to eat. Now, being at the river's edge, fish are plentiful. The mountain from which we came will soon be snow-covered and there the herd will find little to eat. The herd had one elderly bull which we will eventually kill, but for the present, we have all that we need as we settled in the camp.

After we complete putting together our shelters, the men sit around the fire talking of the animals as they knap flint spear points. Close to where we camp is a good supply of flint, something that is not readily available during the summer on the mountain. Though one herd is nearby, other herds are not far away, so along with fish, there is plenty to eat during the summer. Other bands are also setting up camp in the area. Each chooses a spot to camp where they had camped the previous year. All is pleasant and peaceful. The bands cooperate with each other with the renewal of old acquaintances from those bands whose summer camps in the mountains were not close by. With the coming spring, the young people will be courting, with frequent intermarriages between the people of the nearby summer camps. So often the people of the nearby summer camps are related, brothers and sisters, aunts and uncles, cousins, and parents. These times are matriarchal and the man would usually join the band of his wife. We worship the great Mother Earth Goddess who provides for us. Families carry with them an image of the Mother Goddess with her enormous belly and breasts, bringing nurturance to the family hut.

This journey with the Sami continues on 3/19/16 as I sit in the Olmec Prince Posture (Fig. 2.3):

In this shape-shifting posture, I quickly became an aurochs, browsing along a river in what will be in the distant future Poland, not too far from where the river flows into the Baltic Sea. The river will eventually become known as the Vistual River. As an aurochs, I am hunting for particular plants that I especially like, plants that grow below the edges of glaciers, tender green plants, but I am not finding many and gradually work my way northward towards the colder climate. Though I am not thinking about this, it seems warmer and the cooler weather to the north is more pleasant. I have moved, migrated considerably farther north over the last couple of centuries. The ever-present humans who follow us camp nearby.

As a human, I wake up one morning to realize that it is about time to move again from our campsite because the aurochs have moved a considerable distance to the north. It is towards the middle of the summer. Our ancestors tell us that in the past we did not need to move this time of year. We pack, taking everything from our aurochs-hide tent, wrap what we are taking in the furs we use for bedding, dried meat, the bowls we cook in and eat from, our flint pointed spears, the sinew thread we use in sewing, bone needles, softened hides we make into clothing, and whatever else we need and load it onto our backs. We carry it some distance beyond where the aurochs are grazing, knowing that they will continue to move to the north during the summer to better grazing pasture.

As we pass by the aurochs, they look up at us unconcerned and quickly return to their grazing. We seek a sheltered spot at the forest edge in which we set up the camp, sheltered from the cooling climate and somewhat sheltered from the rain. When it rains, we need to close the rain flap over the smoke hole of the tent, but the rain continues to seep in and everything becomes damp. The shelter of the forested area of our new camp provides us with a renewed supply of provisions, including the plants we gather to eat and to spice our meat stews. The young people are out gathering grass used to soften our beds and the floor of the tent to make it more comfortable. This new matting makes the tent smell fresh and good. Mother is busy in the kitchen area of the tent at the edge of the fire, preparing an aurochs stew for our evening meal. Aurochs meat, as well as other meats and fish, are a big part of our diet. So the peaceful and harmonious life provided us by Mother Earth resumes after a strenuous day of moving.

Again, using Sami Underworld Posture (Fig. A.16) on 3/20/16, I delve deeper into my Sami roots:

I am lying on the ground in the Sami Underworld Posture with a drummer drumming at my side. I am the elder of our *siida*, a small group of families, who is of an age no longer able to do the strenuous work of the younger men. The people of our siida have been asking why the aurochs keep moving north, meaning that we now have to move several times during the summer to follow them. I am journeying to ask this question of our ancestors. Lying face down with my arms outstretched, I slide into the soft earth before me and down into the underworld. When my head pops through and then my body, I am upside down or suspended from the ceiling of this domain of the ancestors. I see the ancestors around me walking on the ceiling as I am walking.

These spirits look at me with curiosity, and I ask them the question of why are the aurochs moving north. The answer I receive is that the aurochs are wise, and we are to follow their lead. They know where they need to go for the best food and the right temperature. They are going into an uncharted land of the north, the lands where humans have not lived, a place that we will find undisturbed and safe. The aurochs listen to the Mother Goddess of nature, who tells them what is best for them, and we need to follow. When I return to the encampment and report what

I learned to the people, satisfied with the answer, they prepare for the next move up through the land that in later years will be Lithuania, up along the eastern coast of the Baltic Sea.

Because of his knowledge, the people often turn to the siida's elder shaman and respect him for what he offers. Following the aurochs is a spiritual experience that continually brings them to oneness with the Earth. They depend upon the aurochs for so much: meat, clothing, and the tents they use in the nomadic ways. Because of the respect these people show the aurochs and the safety they provide them by keeping away the wolves and other potential predators, the aurochs trust the Sami, stay near their encampments, and are occasionally willing to sacrifice one of their own to these people. These people also hunt other animals and in their respect for the aurochs, they take only what the herd offers them, an elderly bull or cow who can no longer keep up with the herd. The aurochs feel this respect coming from the humans when they dance and seasonally celebrate the aurochs.

But things are about to change. With the approach of winter, the aurochs turn and move to the south. At this time the Sami find themselves among herds of reindeer that continue to move north. The land to the north is undisturbed and the plants and wildlife are abundant. It feels natural to continue moving north. To the south, it is turning much colder. Some of the siida turn south to follow the aurochs, but many continue north with the reindeer. Soon they will be in Finland, as it will be known in future years, in the artic that remained warmer during the ice age. The waters of the artic will provide abundant fish, while waters around the Baltic will be frozen in thick ice.

I use the Calling the Spirits posture (Fig. 2.10) on 3/21/16 to continue this journey to the north:

I stand atop a hill somewhere up the eastern coast of the Baltic Sea, probably what in later years is Russia. I am standing in the

Calling the Spirits Posture with my head thrown back and my mouth howling. Down below, I hear the bellow of reindeer and I bellow to them. I look out into the forest of pine and birch and strongly feel Mother Earth, who provides for us. In later years, we will give her the name *Maadteraahka*. The *aahka* ending to the name means *woman*. I thank her for everything that is around me and see that what there is for the reindeer to eat is plentiful. She provides for all life.

After a while, after I get my fill of the fresh mountain air and the blue sky on this beautiful morning, I return to the siida to greet the people of the encampment with the message to never forget *Maadteraahka*. A constant reminder is her daughter, *Oksaahka*, who protects the doorway to their tent, their *goahte*, making the doorway sacred. Beneath the hearth of the goahte in the underworld lives a second daughter of *Maadteraahka*, *Saaraahka*. She brings sacredness to the hearth. Walking through the doorway and standing at the hearth are sacred experiences not to be forgotten. I, as the elder of the siida, the reindeer herders' encampment, do not need to remind the people of these goddesses who protect them. Their spirits are very alive throughout the day. The mother goddess's third daughter is *Joeksaahka*. *Joeksaahka* is the protector of animals and the hunt, and for these people, she is the protector of the reindeer that have become their life. As I follow the herd, I seek *Joeksaahka*, who protects them from wolves and other predators. The hunting and gathering Sami are a people of the Earth and followers of their Earth Mother goddess and her three daughters. Life would lose its meaning and sacredness if the goddesses were forgotten.

To make their tents comfortable they use as a floor covering twigs of the birch, and when that is not available, pine boughs that bring a scent of freshness to the tents and soften the Earth under their fur robes and bedding upon which they sleep and find warmth. Again, the Sami continually thank the trees for what they offer in providing this comfort and warmth when burned. The goddesses cannot be forgotten when the Earth is so much part of their life. As they move on throughout the year and the seasons, following the wisdom of the reindeer, the goddesses move with them to the north. The bellowing of the reindeer provides the people with a great sense of reassurance. I throw my head back and bellow to feel this reassurance.

Then, on 3/22/16, this journey with the Sami continues with the Freyr Divination Posture (Fig. 2.2):

I again am with the reindeer herd followers as the herd slowly moves north. This time I am with a hunting party. We see a large doe struggling along behind the rest of the herd of about 50 reindeer, a situation that left the doe vulnerable to wolves or us hunters. It is apparent that *Joeksaahka* is offering her to us and we oblige by taking her with our spears. But, there is one energetic young hunter with his spear who uses it on a nearby younger doe with one newly born daughter. Whether he is just confused when our leader tells us to take the older doe as to which doe he points, or if in his young enthusiasm wants to impress others with the skillful throw of his spear, in either case, he is strongly reprimanded and is made to clean it and drag it home by himself, with the young one crying at her mother's side.

Another of the younger hunters picks up the young fawn and carries it back to his goahte. The young children of the *siida* quickly gathered around the hunter and the fawn, all wanting to hold and cuddle it, feeling its softness. What a natural act of young children. Soon they wonder what to feed it, knowing that it would usually nurse off her mother. A couple of young mothers of the siida come to the rescue in curiosity, wondering what it would be like nursing a young fawn and they find it an acceptable experience. Thus, the Sami are on their way to domesticating the reindeer, a move towards controlling nature, separating them from our Great Earth Mother.

But these people stay with the herd and this fawn lives in two worlds, in the encampment of the Sami and with her herd. At first, the children keep the fawn in the family's tent, but quickly the family builds a small tent next to theirs to protect the fawn from the winter elements, though the children of the siida often spend the night in this small tent with the fawn. As it grows larger, the children know she should start eating grass and bring her grass to nibble on. When she starts to seek and eat grass on her own, she soon starts running with the herd. At first, the herd ignores her and sometimes tries to push her away, so she runs back to the siida, where she is still very comfortable. But she is persistent and soon the herd accepts her. In this way, the people do what they need to in giving her back to the herd they follow and to the Earth by rescuing the fawn in reciprocity for all the herd has given them.

This was inevitable with how close the Sami lived with the reindeer. As the years go by, the people rescue the newly born when the mother, for some reason, dies, thus the herd and the people became more and more intertwined.

While using the Priestess of Malta Middle World Posture (Fig. 2.7) on 3/23/16, the Sami learn to milk the reindeer:

I am again in the siida, the encampment of the Sami as they follow the herd of reindeer as it slowly migrates northward, this time near what in later years would be known as Finland. There is some excitement. Several men came carrying a weakened reindeer doe who has just given birth to a stillborn and had great difficulty. She is one of the reindeer raised in the siida and is quite comfortable being around humans. She is bawling because of her full udder and the women know she needs to be milked to relieve the pressure. For the first time, they pass around a cup of reindeer milk for all to taste, and its flavor is appreciated. Thus, another step is taken in domesticating the reindeer. After that the people watch for opportunities to find does in milk without young ones to drink from them, milk that is appreciated by the Sami, and an improvement in diversifying their diet. The bonds of the Sami and reindeer continued to grow closer and closer.

I have been writing about how agriculture and the domestication of animals, activities of controlling the Earth to the advantage of humans, have led to our separation from the Earth as part of the interdependence of all life and to the destruction of life on Earth, yet the Sami's domestication or semidomestication of the reindeer bring them into a closer bond with these herds, herds that continue to run wild, led by the wildest buck of the herd. This bond demonstrates a close interdependence with reciprocity that continues to support both reindeer and humans. Is this an exception of how domestication has led to the demise of the Earth? I think the Sami have crossed the line as we will see in the next steps of domestication in my experience of 3/24/16 while using the Olmec Prince Posture (Fig. 2.3):

Again, I become a reindeer, one raised by the Sami. We are moving up through what in later years will be known as Finland. I have a strap across my back and at either end is a bundle of the things the people are having me carry to their new encampment. The load is heavy, and I am tired, but I continue trudging forward anyway. It is not long before we stop, and they take the pack off my back. I can return to run with the herd. I run in circles around the corral they have us penned in. Life has lost its freedom. Tomorrow, they will let us out of the corral and lead us up the mountain where we can find something to eat, but they circle around us with their dogs to keep us together and do not let us wander off. Wandering off is not safe because of other wild animals in the area, such as wolves.

Who am I? What have I become? Some of us refuse to carry anything on our back or let them milk us, but those who refuse still move with the herd and go into the corral at night for protection from wolves. They have learned from us where we like to go at different times of the year, and they are kind enough to take us to those places, but we no longer can decide for ourselves when and where we go. We have become domesticated; we do what the people want and go where they want us to go. This is no longer the way of nature. We no longer can sacrifice ourselves to the wolves and other predatory animals. We have become the food for only the humans. Life becomes harder for the wolves and other predatory animals. They throw ropes around us, throw us to the ground, and cut marks in our ears so that they know who we belong to, who owns us. We are no longer free but now owned. We are slaves and they do with us what they want.

Something is missing in life. We no longer feel part of the world around us, the world of nature. Before we listened to the wind, the rivers, the trees, the grass, the wolves, the bears, and we were part of all of them. Now all of this around us seems meaningless. They herded us across the rivers, through the forests, past the surrounding wildlife, and we pay no attention to it. The wind blows, the snow falls and we don't notice it. We move through life, but we are not part of life. We are numb.

Finally, on 3/25/16, this journey ends while using the Feathered Serpent posture (Fig. 2.9):

I am back in the siida. Our hut, our goahte, used to have only one door, a sacred door guarded by *Oksaahka*. Now it has two doors, the one guarded by *Oksaahka*, through which is carried the meat of the sacred wild bear, or the wild moose. It is the back door. The other door, the front door, is not sacred, and through it, we carry the meat of the domesticated reindeer or cow. Life is changing. Whereas before the blood of the animal was smeared on the jamb of the door in thanks to the animal that was killed in the hunt. We paid respect for its life. It was wild and had a life of its own. It had a place in the interdependence of all life, the interdependence we respected. We learned about all that is of the Earth by watching to see the relationship of all life. We respected the bear, the reindeer, and all life, as our ancestors. We came from this life, from the Earth, from our Great Earth Mother. We believed in giving back to the Earth as much as we took from her.

At first, in rescuing a newborn reindeer, or relieving the pain from milk of a doe who lost her newborn gave back to the herd by relieving its suffering, but now we control and just take from the herd. We have placed ourselves above, superior to the reindeer and have forgotten how much they taught us and took care of us. We now bring the meat from the reindeer into our goahte through the front door, the door that is not sacred. We no longer think of the reindeer as our ancestors because our ancestors were independent and able to follow their own free will. The reindeer is not independent.

Our world used to be one, one with the Earth, the Great Mother Earth. Now it is divided, it is two, the sacred and the profane. It has two doors, the sacred and the profane. It is fearful to think that soon even the sacred door, the sacred Mother Earth, will be forgotten and our tent will again have only one door that anything can enter.

This experience of the Sami's transitioning into the new, modern world is felt with disappointment, the disappointment of the loss of the sacredness felt towards our Great Earth Mother.

CHAPTER 10

Seeking Peace of the Community Garden Terraces, Peru

In August and September 2015, my wife and I traveled to Peru with a group of people with Overseas Adventure Travel. Again, I used ecstatic trance twice a day to bring this adventure to a deeper, more spiritual level by communing with the spirits of the land.

To begin this journey on our first evening at our hotel in Lima, I found a quiet place to stand in the Calling the Spirits Posture (Fig. 2.10). Upon arriving in Lima that afternoon, we drove along the coast of Lima with its high bluffs.

In this ecstatic trance experience, I see a Spanish ship come ashore with its men wading the last few feet onto the beach. They climb the bluff to be greeted by the indigenous and hospitable people of the land. Then I see waves of people coming from the distant north at a much earlier time, the time of Monte Verde. I also see people coming from across the ocean, maybe along the Antarctic coast. I see waves of people coming from different places and at different times to what is now Peru.

This experience provoked many questions, e.g. what happened in the southern hemisphere during the ice age? Boris, our tour guide, could answer some. The hunter-gatherer era in the Andes ended around 9000 BC. Monte Verde, the oldest archeological remains estimated from 14,900 to 33,000 years ago, was a small semi-permanent settlement. The ice age in the north began melting 13,000 years ago. People came from the north after the ice age, about 11,500 years ago. The domestication of animals begin about 7,000 years ago, and the mining and use of gold and copper began about 1500 BC. These estimates answered most of my questions regarding what happened when.

The next morning, August 25, 2015, our first day in Lima, I sat in the Lady of Cholula Divination Posture (Fig. A.11):

I am at the Huaca Pucllana ruins in Lima. There is a celebration at the top of the pyramid led by the leaders and priests. There are people are at the bottom and I am working with them in their gardens. The priests are seeking to be closer to the gods by going to the top of the pyramid. There was a closeness to the gods, the Earth spirits, during the hunter-gatherer age, but as people became agriculturists and lived in cities, they sought to control their environment rather than listen to Mother Earth and lost their power of seeing and hearing. Atop the pyramid, they think they are closer to the gods, and when in ecstatic trance, they can again hear the gods. We, at the bottom of the pyramid and close to the Earth, experience the spirits of the Earth.

That evening, August 25, I sat in the Chalchihuitlique Metamorphosis Posture (Fig. A.2), a figure I saw today in the museum, sitting cross-legged while grasping her knees:

I see the three animals, the condor of the heavens, the puma of earth, and the serpent of the underworld. I become a stalking puma and find a tapir to kill. I am a hunter. There are agriculturists living in a former village next to the pyramid. They are growing corn, potatoes, beans, pumpkins, sweet potatoes, peanuts, and fruit, and have domesticated ducks, guinea pigs, and llamas. They still hunt deer. There may have been warriors in this village next to the pyramid, but I am a farmer tending my gardens, hoeing around the potato plants, and feeling close to Mother Earth. I know that part of what I am growing will go to the emperor who looks to the condor, while the warriors who live in the rooms of the pyramid look to the puma, but they will leave me enough for my use and for my family because they need me to be strong as the puma in gardening and providing them with food.

On August 26th, we leave Lima very early for our flight to Cusco and the ride to and through the Sacred Valley to Urubamba. On the way to Urubamba, we visited the Piscq Ruins at the south end of the Sacred Valley. That evening, I stand in the Hallstatt Warrior Posture (Fig. 2.4) in the hotel's garden:

I am at the Piscq Ruins at the edge of the terraces. Above the terraces are the Inca ruins. Beyond the ruins, across the ravine, are many holes in the mountain's side, ancient graves, some with stone retaining walls in front of them. I am on the hillside watching the activity of the people in colorful clothing working on their garden terraces. The retaining walls of the terraces are about 12 feet high. Both the men and the women are cultivating around the potato plants. I see smoke rising from the cooking fires of the village below with the wonderful smells of what is being cooked. The fires are on the patio in front of the adobe brick homes with thatched roofs. A man carries an offering of potatoes to the ancestral spirits at a grave across the ravine, honoring the spirits and the Earth. On the hillside with the graves are some narrow terraces where barley is growing. He takes his offering to the entrance of a grave in the hillside and leaves it on the ground. He stands for a few moments with his arms raised to the heavens towards the setting sun before he turns and returns across the ravine back to the village and his family where he sits and begins eating his meal. He and the other families continue venerating the Earth with the offerings to the Earth and to their ancestral spirits, offerings of what they grow. Their life is harmonious and peaceful, even when the warriors come down to collect their share of what the garden produces. They are not greedy and leave what the family needs to survive in a healthy manner, though it takes the farming family more work than it did in earlier times to provide for themselves and the emperor, priests, and warriors.

In the hotel garden in Urubamba, on the morning of August 27, I sit in the Lady of Cholula Divination Posture (Fig. A.11):

Again I am at the Piscq ruins. A young boy greets me and takes me through the garden, telling me about the three sections of the garden, one for the emperor, one for the community, and one for his family. He takes an ear of corn from the community section, and we go up to a burial site on the hillside to leave an offering to the ancestors. He offers it first to the four directions, then to the three worlds, the upper world, the earthly realm and the underworld, the worlds of the condor, puma, and the snake. He takes me back to his adobe brick home where his mother is spinning wool from the alpaca. There is a loom nearby where she weaves colorful pieces of fabric, but now she is preparing the wool to be used in the weaving. At one end of the room is an altar where he places some kernels of corn that lie among bits of the other harvested produce from their garden, offering the corn in thanks to the god of prosperity, Ekeko. His father is out on the garden terrace, turning the soil to plant corn.

At the ruins at Ollantaytambo, on August 28th I stand in the Calling the Spirits Posture (Fig. 2.10):

I am at the Ollantaytambo ruins, walking through the peasant village below the ruins and terraced gardens. A man comes out and motions for me to follow him to the fields where he is hoeing a row of corn. As I sit watching out over the valley, I know that a third of the corn goes to the emperor and feeds the warriors who get their strength from the fanged deity, the puma. The warriors become the fighters like the puma, the middle world deity. They pay little attention to venerating the condor of the upper world or the serpent of the underworld, the other two spheres. The puma is of the Earth, and its power is masculine.

The peasants venerate the fertility and strength of the female puma and all life and substances of the Great Earth Mother. In the fortress on the hill, the Inca priests and warriors, with their idols/deities in the niches on the walls, venerate these deities, the condor, puma, and snake, with offerings of foods, and gold and silver objects of beauty. They sometimes sacrifice a young girl in special times of need. The peasants venerate the Mother Goddess with gifts of corn, cornmeal, and other foodstuffs.

While in Ollantaytambo, we visited a traditional Inca home with its altar in one large room. Different foods and grains hung from the arms of a figure of Ekeko, the god of abundance. In the wall above the altar is a hole holding three human skulls, the skulls of ancestors. Guinea pigs run free around the room, eating from a pile of green barley stalks. Hanging on the wall are several dead, dried animals. There are two beds and a ladder to a loft. In ecstatic trance, these experiences become more real within me and I become part of them.

On the train to Machu Picchu, we passed cornfields that are plowed using oxen. I see a pit, maybe 10 feet deep and 20 feet in diameter, housing three cows. A dug cave is at one end with thatching above it. We also see stone-lined aqueducts flowing with water from the glaciers way above the fields. We are traveling along the Vilcanota River in the Sacred Inca Valley.

On August 28th in the afternoon at Machu Picchu, I use the Calling the Spirits Posture (Fig. 2.10) while standing on the steps next to the 8th terrace near the temple of the condor. In the Southern Hemisphere, I call the spirits in the reversed direction, since the seasons are reversed, calling for the spirits of the summer from the north and the spirits of winter from the south:

The emperor, other leaders, and warriors worship the sun god as represented by the condor in the condor temple, the milky-way in the temple of the three mirrors, and the sun in the sun temple. The puma, the fanged deity with its stalking strength of the middle world, is not represented at Machu Picchu but worshipped by the peasants and workers of the land, the weavers, and potters. The seers, healers, and shaman venerate the serpent on their home altars. Along the Vilcanota River of the Sacred Inka Valley, there is peace.

Then, on the morning of August 29th, while walking back down from the Sun Gate of Machu Picchu, I use the Olmec Prince Metamorphosis Posture (Fig. 2.3). I sit in this posture just before reaching the agricultural terraces of Machu Picchu. I stop at a grassy area to the left of the Inka trail for this ecstatic trance experience:

I become both the Puma and a peasant in the time of the Inka. I have a difficult time relating to the time of Machu Picchu, so go further back in time to the hunter-gatherers. There, I can feel myself stalking like the puma on the hunt. As the peasant in my hut, I have on my altar the image of a puma where I leave foodstuff, pieces of meat, while I give thanks. It feels right. Then I move forward in time to when, as a peasant, I feel intimidated by the emperor who no longer venerates the puma but instead the condor of the heavens, the upper world. I still venerate the puma because it is the earthly animal of strength and I need strength to labor for the emperor. One of my labors is as a runner of messages and I run along the Inka trail to Machu Picchu. I do not have a place for an altar to my ancestor, the puma, and feel somewhat lost in how to live in this new world of the powerful emperor, the Inka.

While using the Chalchihuitlique Metamorphosis Posture (Fig. A.2) on the evening of August 29th, I find myself as the Inka:

I am the Inka, above everything. I am the sun, the milky way, the condor. I control the Earth, the puma, and the snake of the underworld. The puma sits at my side, as do all the people of my domain. I reside on the mountain top close to the heavens. I am carried on a litter, not touching the profane ground of the Earth.

Earlier, the deities of the Earth were the puma and serpent. The people of the Earth still get their strength from the puma and the seers/diviners from the serpent. There was a time when everyone venerated all three worlds, the heavens, the middle world, and the underworld, and they were one with the Earth. Now the Inka controls everything and has powerful armies. All serve him and protect him from his enemies. Everything of the Earth is his, which will lead eventually to the destruction of the Earth.

The new conquistadors from Spain seek the same other world power in the name of their god and subjugate the people, eventually killing the Inka.

The morning of the next day, the 30th, we visit the ruins at Tipon with its aqueducts. On the way to the Tipon ruins, we stop at the edge of the village of Tipon, where an indigenous family is plowing a field with two oxen, a field in which they are going to plant potatoes. They let me take the oxen pulled plow for a circuit of the field. Before I start and at the end of the circle, the farmer pours beer on the ground from a cup as an offering to Mother Earth, the Sun God, and the four directions. They still are or have returned to venerating the Earth as I do in ecstatic trance.

* * *

While at Tipon, I sit in the Jama Coaque Diviner Posture next to the falling water of an irrigation channel that has flown for likely 700 to 800 years from the beginning of the Inka times, demonstrating the incredible hydro-engineering of the time. The falling water is flowing from one garden terrace down to the next.

Sitting in trance, I become the farmer with the oxen and can feel the strength he gains in his veneration of the Earth.

Again, I feel the strength of the people of the time in building this incredible irrigation system that has never failed in all these centuries, the strength of the puma. As the puma, I am with these people now and in ancient times, showing that the people continue to venerate the Earth, although the Inka ruler/deity has turned his attention to the condor and the sun. When the Inka reign ends, the veneration of a heavenly god continues with the continued destruction of the Earth by the Spaniards. The Spaniards, as do most people of today, see everything of the Earth as a commodity by which they greedily profit, forgetting that everything is interdependent with each substance/species of the Earth of equal importance for our survival, no better than anything else, even the Homo sapiens. This problem continues today with the predicted end of the human species. The ancestor of the indigenous people, the puma, and the serpent are every bit as important as the condor. These people venerate even the flowing water, flowing to all the fields of the valley from the glaciers high in the Andes. Water is necessary for all life and not to be a commodity for profit.

Yesterday, we visited the ruins of the fortress of Sacsayhuaman. This morning, the 30th, while sitting in the Chalchihuitlique Metamorphosis Posture (Fig. A.2), I return to Sacsayhuaman:

I am at Sacsayhuaman, watching the warriors of the Inka practice with their spears, clubs, and slingshots. Some men have carried the Inka on his litter from his primary palace in Cusco to this fortress outside of the city to speak to his troops who are there to protect his domain. In speaking to them, the Inka calls them the furious head of the puma. Sacsayhuaman is the head of the puma, while Cusco is its spine and body. The Inka is the condor, the bird of the heavens, sun, and milky-way, but he also venerates the puma, the strength of his warriors, litter carriers, stonemasons, and engineers who built the fortress, his palace, and his retreat at Machu Picchu. When he visits Machu Picchu, some warriors accompany him. Machu Picchu, by its location at the head of the Sacred Valley, is considered safe. Cusco is the heart and soul of the Inka. The sacred temple of Cusco is dedicated to the sun, Coricancha.

On the morning of September 1st, I stand in the Feathered Serpent Initiation Posture (Fig. 2.9) and become a warrior of the Inka:

The land of the sacred valley is community-owned and parceled out to the families to farm. When the husband leaves to be a warrior or worker for the Inka, which is about 300 days of the year, the community pitches in to provide security to the family. In this experience, I become a warrior. My uncle and his children help with the farming when I go to Sacsayhuaman where I am trained as a warrior before I go on patrol, journeying around the empire to enforce the rule of m'itra, of giving a third of everything produced to the Inka and a third to the community. The empire is quite peaceful and people are cooperative in providing for the Inka and his warriors. The peasants save seeds from the community's third of the harvest for next year. This new system works well. With the fertile soil, we have enough to live on comfortably, and we feel secure.

* * *

On this second morning of September, I stand in the Hallstatt Warrior Posture (Fig. 2.4):

I visit an ancient Peruvian farm village. The community is responsible for the land and allots sections to each family to farm. A large army of Inka arrive in the village and tell the villagers about m'itra, the new system, that all men above the age of 15 years need to spend part of each year working for the Inka as a warrior or in construction while a third of their farm produce or their crafts such as pottery and weaving go to the Inka. If the villagers don't agree, the warriors will escort them to the edge of the empire and send them away. The people are frightened but have nothing else they can do, so the empire remains in peace. The army is of farmers using any weapon they can bring from the farm. My wife could have come with me when I joined the army, but she had to stay home to care for the two children. She gets considerable help from the community. I will be in the Army for about 300 days of the year since it takes only about 65 days of farming to provide for the family.

On the afternoon of September 2nd, I sit in the Jama Coaque Metamorphosis Posture (Fig. A.9):

I become the puma, the ancestor of the indigenous people. Do the people still recognize me? The farmer continues as he did in the past to venerate the Earth as represented by the puma. The Spaniards do not interfere with this practice. They continue to accept a third of the produce, thus they allow the farmers to continue in their rituals. After the decimation of the Inka, how do the Spaniards treat the people? Because the Spanish invaders are primarily men, they have interbred with the native women with little genocide. The priests' position is to educate and convert the natives to Christianity. Tobacco is sacred to South America and not used for smoking as used now, but used for smudging to cleanse a person's aura. Much of the people of Peru are of mixed blood.

That afternoon I stand in the Hallstatt Realm of the Dead Posture (Fig. 2.4). We are on the road down the valley to Titikaka:

I am a farmer with a herd of alpaca. I have been shearing them for the wool with the plan of getting it to market. As I shear, I give thanks to our Earth Mother, giving her a cup of beer in reciprocity. She offers an abundance of barley upon which the alpaca graze. It is spring and their coats are heavy. I stack the wool I shear along with the wool from several other herders of alpacas and sheep. I have spent much of the winter sitting at the side of our field watching/herding the animals. As I shear them, I can tell that the females are pregnant. I believe that our Great Earth Mother has been good to us. I wait for the truck of the middleman who comes by to buy the wool that he will take to the market.

I then use the Tlazeoteotl Cleansing Posture (Fig. A.22) on the next morning, the 3rd.

I stand in the hotel garden overlooking Lake Titikaka. What comes to me are several things I saw yesterday on the ride from Cusco. I saw many herders watching their cattle, about a dozen in each herd. Without fencing, the cattle are free to roam but watched by the herder, though some farms have stone wall fencing for their animals. There are also herds of sheep and alpaca. I feel the connection between the herder and his animals, contentment and trust of the herder feeling at one with the animals, which are so much part of his or her life. This is the way life should be, recognizing the interdependency of all things, with our life depending on the cattle, sheep, and alpacas, bringing us into a relationship with the animals, experiencing them as equal to us. The illness of our culture that needs to be healed is the manner in which we put ourselves superior to all else and see everything as a commodity from which to profit, but to the indigenous people of Peru, the animals are to sustain their lives, not to make them rich with huge commercial herds. Their relationship with their Great Earth Mother is sacred. Three scenes I appreciate are of the people bringing in their cattle for the evening, one with the cattle following a young girl with a dog behind herding them. The other is of a man following his herd, carrying a switch to keep them together. The last scene is of a man standing near his herd before bringing it in, sprinkling some herb ritualistically on the ground, showing thanks to our mother, the Earth. It is so good and inspiring to see people still remembering the Earth.

We stopped at the ruins of Raqchi. There we talked with one woman carrying a large bundle of corn stalks, walking with it some distance home to feed her cattle, alpacas, and Guinea pigs, enough corn stalks to last two days. Earlier, as we visited a market, we saw a woman selling bundles of barley for one solis each as feed for the animals. Earlier we entered a home with Guinea pigs scampering around the room with barley on the floor as feed for them. This evening I stand in the Tlazeoteotl Healing Posture (Fig. A.22) as the word of the 9th Inka came to me, words that I heard spoken today.

What I learn each day has a big influence on my ecstatic experience. Today I learned of the three words of wisdom of the 9th Inka. First, he said that what is good for the bee is good for the honeycomb. That suggests he understood the importance of the interdependence of all things. Second, he commented that love, work, and teaching are most important. The third was reciprocity, i.e. we need to offer something in return for what we take from the Earth. In standing in the Tlazeoteotl posture beside

Lake Titikaka, Mama Quocha, the Goddess of Water, becomes important, showing that we are composed of and dependent upon water. These words of wisdom show a deep understanding of the veneration for our Great Earth Mother, of venerating everything of the Earth. I see how the people of the Inka learn and remember these things despite the Catholic Church. While visiting a farming community, I see they continue to demonstrate these values. My ecstatic experience is to review and incorporate within me these teachings that need to be part of our everyday life in order for the Earth to continue sustaining us.

After having visited the Uros people on their floating reed islands on the lake, on September 4th I use the Lady of Cholula Divination Posture (Fig. A.11):

I am on a boat on Lake Titikaka. We just visited the Uros people who live on floating islands made of totora reeds. The island we visited was about an acre in size. I find myself on the island watching Jamie call together the wild ibis that seem very comfortable with the humans in this small place, again reflecting the oneness with the Earth with their simple life. As I learn, they do not eat the ibis except for the blood, which cures epilepsy. They fish through a hole in the reed island and from their reed boats. The men collect reeds to keep the island and their reed-thatched homes in good repair. On the island, there are 6 families with 23 people and in total there are 90 islands with about 2,000 people all living together in peace. These people know how to sustain themselves on these reed islands. They interact with modern culture by making and selling their crafts. They don't pay taxes, but they can vote in Peruvian elections. They speak a separate language, Aymara.

This ecstatic experience brings the experience of visiting the reed island to a much deeper level and more alive within me. Jamie, a man with a wife and four children, shows me around the island and explains things. Originally, in ancient times, the people lived on the totora-reed boats and they would bring them together at night as a community. Then they learned to cut sections of the roots of the totora reeds and tie them together, anchoring the island in place and covering it with reeds. It takes about a year to build one island and their reed-thatched houses on the island. The island's homes and boats needed to be repaired continually with the totora reeds. They live by fishing, eating bird eggs, and the totora reeds. They make craft items which they use, along with fish, to trade for grains, other vegetables, and craft materials. They live a peaceful life and feel secure on their island, which they can move if threatened. Lake Titikaka is sacred to the Inca, and from this lake, the first Inka rose in its mist. The Inka did not threaten the Uros people, and they continued to live independently from and in peace with the Inka. As Jamie shows me, the island he is on is most friendly and his family lives in peace with the five other families. I feel he is living in harmony with everything around him. His simple way of living reflects a oneness with the Earth. I see two of their younger children fishing through a hole cut in the island for fishing. Some men are out fishing from their reed boats while others are out cutting totora reeds, which they continually use for food and repairs. The women lay on the reeds their weaving, embroidered hangings, model boats, and other crafts to sell in their more modern community. They have several solar panels on the island which provide them with radios and an electric light for which they need the money from selling their crafts and fish. Someone is just returning from shopping on the mainland for foods they couldn't raise and for craft supplies. Thus, the money from selling fish and their crafts to visiting tourists from the mainland allowed them to pay for these things. Their way of life is very sustainable in their veneration of our Great Earth Mother, Pachamama, and the water mother, Mama Qocha. The embroidered wall hanging

I bought shows they also venerated the sun god, Apu-punchau, and the condor, puma, and snake representing the three worlds. They offer a great example of how people can live peacefully and sustainably with the Earth.

That same day we also visited the Island of Taquile, so on the afternoon of the 4th the Olmec Prince Metamorphosis Posture (Fig. 2.3) takes me to Taquile:

After visiting the Uros people, we went on to a second island, Taquile, with about 3,000 people. The island has no motorized vehicles and the town square is at the top of the island's mountain, so there is much labor in carrying things to the top. The people's fame is for their weavings, using sheep's wool from the island's herds. A family may have one cow, but there are no other large animals. There is no electricity except for batteries and a few solar panels, so they use candles and flashlights. The people work together as I see today with the men redoing the stonework of the town square.

In this experience, I become a young boy of ten years. I walk across the square and up the stairs to where my father is working with other men weaving colorful fabrics. My mother sends me to get him because she wants him to come home for lunch. After lunch, both mother and father go to the square and join in with the weaving coop. They want me to go to our garden plot and turn over the earth to prepare it for planting potatoes. I have a friend working on the terrace below ours so we can talk, shouting to each other as we prepare the field to plant in spring, in about three weeks. We work hard and my father is teaching me many things about how to live as I grow up. We have a loving and peaceful family and community. After I finish one row in turning the soil, I go back to watch and learn how father weaves. He has me carding wool, cleaning it before the women spin it. We sell what we weave on the mainland or to visitors who come to the island. Life again is simple, peaceful, and sustainable as we work hard together in our community.

On the 5th, I stand in the Hallstatt Warrior Realm of the Dead Posture (Fig. 2.4) in the hotel garden overlooking the Lake:

I again became the boy on Taquile. He is talking to his great grandfather about life and work, talking to him at his graveside in the field below our house. The great grandfather was a weaver too. As a boy, he helped tend the sheep and the garden. Life then was very harmonious. They did not have solar panels or flashlights but used fat from the sheep for candles. They did not have motorboats but used wooden rafts. There has been progress, but the people still look to the wisdom of their ancestors to give direction to their lives. I am struggling with the thought of moving to the city, thinking that life would be better there, but I hear about the crime in the city and believe that life on Taquile is more harmonious. Yet dividing the land into smaller and smaller parcels with the growing number of children makes it harder to produce what a family needs, including the need for fields to pasture the sheep. Yet the people work together and always seem to find a way. As I think about it, I decide it is best to stay on the island but to have only two children. That way will slow the growth in the number of people on the island, though it may be difficult to control the number of children I may have.

On the evening of the 5th, I stand in the Feathered Serpent Initiation Posture (Fig. 2.9) at the center of an Inka cross that is laid out in the hotel garden on the shore of Lake Titikaka:

I am again the boy on Taquile Island, age 13-years and old for his age in his thinking. I am working hard to become a good weaver to support my eventual family. Other youths have left the island for a life in the city, but I know my decision to stay on the island is the best way to live, to live in a community of loving people. I know that my decision is the best.

Our journey to Peru has ended, and we have returned home. I see that the people of the various communities we have visited live simple lives in harmony with all that is of the Earth; the families living in the sacred valley, the families in the outlying areas of Cusco, the families of the islands of Lake Titikaka and the families who live below the sacred site of Sillustani, a pre-Inka burial ground on the hill above Lake Mayo near Puno. I have learned a lot to take back to our valley in Pennsylvania of experiencing the feeling of harmony in living a simple and sustainable life in harmony with all that is of the Earth.

Now, in January, after returning home, 1/13/16, I return to Peru with the Lady of Cholula Posture (Fig. A.11). The Lady will take me to a spot in Peru most spiritual to me:

I ask the diviner, where do I go now? I go to Peru, first plowing my field with oxen, then to the ancient terrace where I cultivate the soil with a wooden branch hoe, to plant potatoes and corn. The terrace soil is built up with compost, vegetative materials, and fertilizer from the animals carefully cared for by the people. The flow of water to the terraces is controlled to not allow erosion. On the steep mountainsides, the eroded soil had to be built up with care. The people understand the value of rich soil.

Then I go back in time to Europe where the soil was rich but then abused, so the people had to move on to the West to find new fields of rich soil. Then I go to Iceland and Greenland where the early settlers took the few available trees for building and heat. The erosion and lack of compost from the fallen leaves of the trees quickly depleted the soil of nutrients.

I then returned to Peru, where the people care for and venerate the soil, and enjoy working on a terrace. My terrace is where I grow a third for myself, a third for the empire, and a third for the community. I work and see the value of my productivity. I can be proud of what I produce.

It is important for me to return sometime later to where I have traveled using ecstatic trance, to deepen the experience of my journeys. On January 14th I use the Mayan Oracle Divination Posture (Fig. A.14) and return to the Piscq ruins in the Sacred Valley of Peru:

I return to Peru and Piscq, where I become the young boy walking along the hillside with the healer of their village. In returning to my experiences in Peru, I feel a special pull to return to Piscq. I realize that the great Inka, with the invasion of the Spanish Conquistadors, struggled with the need to venerate the icons of the three worlds, the serpent, puma, and condor, and not just the condor. Yet, his life is separate from the Earth in his greed to control everything of the Earth surrounding him. Something is missing that he tries to regain through worshiping the three icons.

As I walk along a path along the hillside across from our terraced fields, the shaman points out the paw prints of a stalking puma. As we turn to the East, the terrain opens up and we see in a clearing ahead of us a condor feeding upon the remains of a llama that the puma had feasted upon. The Earthly puma feeds the condor of the upper world. They are both alive and their spirits are within me, not outside of me, represented by an icon. As we walk, we see a hole in the hillside, the entrance to the domain of the serpent, the snake that feeds upon the rodents that do damage to our gardens. We thank the snake for helping in protecting our gardens by leaving a pinch of cornmeal in front of the entrance to its home. As we return, we leave a pinch of cornmeal at the remains of the llama, thanking it for sacrificing itself to feed the condor and the puma. We venerate this balance and interdependence in nature with our gift of cornmeal in reciprocity.

I feel my connection to the Earth is alive when I return to the garden, where I can feel the soil sifting through my fingers as I dig in it to plant a potato. When we nurture the potato plants by weeding and loosening the soil to cover them, we offer thanks and receive the gift of saving the weeds to decompose as compost. When we harvest the potatoes again, we offer thanks with a gift of compost that we have saved to keep the soil fertile. The compost is from last year's potato plants and other leftover vegetation. When we then dig in the soil to prepare for our subsequent planting, we offer the Earth other gifts such as cornmeal or tobacco in thanks. We cannot forget to give thanks, as has been forgotten by the Inka in his separation from the Earth. The healer/shaman of our community is there continually to remind us of our interdependence with everything of the Earth.

On January 15th, I continue on this journey of renewing my experiences of Peru with the Olmec Prince Posture for Metamorphosis (Fig. 2.3):

I become a snake in a den next to the wall of the terrace in which the young boy is working. I crawl out and up into the garden. The soil is loose and a perfect place for rodents to nest, rodents that I seek to eat. Life is easy and comfortable here. Then I again become the boy who is again with the shaman as they watch the snake with a bulge partway down its body, a bulge of a rodent he had eaten. The shaman is explaining how the snake from the underworld promotes transformation as it transforms itself when it sheds its skin, a transformation that is needed for our society to survive. The men/farmers as warriors in the army of the Inka spend a good part of the year away from the farm and are forgetting this sense of oneness with the Earth as they patrol the land of the Inka, watching for the enemy and expelling those who do not support the Inka. Their food comes from the Inka, forgetting that before that it comes from the Earth.

The shaman explains that the snake from the underworld is from the world of our ancestors and the spirits of the ancestors, spirits that teach us and remind us of how we are supposed to live, spirits that go way back to when we used to be the animals of the Earth, animals that, as our ancestors, have so much to teach us and remind us how to live. We depend upon these animals and the life of the Earth to survive and we need to thank them continually for what they give us and teach us. Though we keep guinea pigs in our homes to eat and we raise them like we do alpaca and llamas, they still have their own life, and we need to honor them as we do the condor, the puma, and the snake. They are all our ancestors and we cannot forget what they give us. We need to listen to these spirits and live as they show us how to live.

I listen to the shaman and am familiar with many of these spirits. In the garden, I feel and see their presence. As I hoe and pull weeds as I harvest what we have planted, my dreaming mind can see these spirits rising from the Earth. I can see the puma stalking the llama, and I can see the condor eating from the carcass of the llama. I can see the snake stalking the hole of the rat, slithering into the hole, and cornering the rat. I can see the snake returning to its den in the rocks near the terrace wall to feed its young. I can see how all this life depends upon each other and how I depend upon them. I can feel part of all life on Earth, and I have stories to tell my father when he returns from his duty of being a warrior for the Inka, stories that are important of which he needs to be reminded. I am thankful to the shaman/healer to remind me of these stories.

* * *

On 1/16/16, the Hallstatt Warrior (Fig. 2.4) leads me on this journey:

I am again back with the young boy, maybe 10 or 11 years old, in his terrace garden. The community shaman passes by the terrace on his way to the place of the ancestors across the ravine. When I see him, he motions for me to follow. He is carrying his drum on his shoulder along with a sack of the other things he uses as he practices his worship of the ancestors. We cross the split log bridge and walk up the path to the first cave in the hillside. There we stand, facing the cave in the same posture in which I am standing, the Hallstatt Warrior. As the young boy, I have learned how to journey in this way by quieting my mind as I move my attention to my center of harmony. My attentiveness pleases the shaman, for he is always open to teaching and is drawn to those who are ready to learn.

As we stand there with the shaman beating on his drum, I soon find myself back a couple of hundred years on the bank of a river, the Vilcanota or Urubamba River. Near me, in front of his adobe hut, stands a middle-aged man, my great, great or great, great, great grandfather. He is standing with a hoe stick in his hand, looking out into the garden between his hut and the river. There he has planted corn and potatoes. On the hill, above his hut, is a small village near where Ollantaytambo is now found. We see smoke rising from some huts in the village. There, people are making pottery and weaving fabric. My ancestral grandfather also weaves when he has time, primarily in the evening. They are self-sufficient. My grandfather grows extra corn and potatoes for the community, especially those who are elderly and the poor, who do not have the means to grow potatoes for themselves. He also has a small plot for tomatoes and peppers that he grows to share with the people of the community.

My ancestral grandmother, along with her daughter, are nearby watching the four alpaca that they have for the wool they use in spinning and weaving. She lets her daughter watch the animals for a while as she ventures off next to a wooded area to collect other herbs and wild plants, fruits, and roots that she uses in cooking. Their life is pleasant and peaceful as they live as part of their community. This is before the coming of the powerful Inkas and the need to give a portion of what they grow to the Inka and his warriors. It is peaceful in this river valley high in the Andes.

We continue on this journey on January 17th using the Priestess of Malta Middle World Posture (Fig. 2.7):

I return to the riverside farm near Ollantaytambo. The farmer's family is preparing to walk up to the village on the hill above them. They have prepared a sack of potatoes and corn that they are carrying. The villagers welcome them. Each day, farmers from the outlying area go to the village with something to contribute to a community meal and today is this family's turn.

The women of the village, including the farmer's wife's mother and an uncle, have a fire burning with a large pot hanging over it. They throw some of the corn into the pot. But some of the corn is also ground into cornmeal and placed in a pot of water with ashes from the fire, where it soaks for a while before it is taken out and placing it on hot rocks to dry. Then it is ground into flour. They then add water to make it into dough and spread it on hot rocks to bake into a type of bread. The women have also dug a hole and lined it with rocks in which they put the potatoes along with rocks from the fire, covering the hole to allow the potatoes to bake. Another farmer has brought some peppers to mix in to spice the soup. It is not long before the community meal is ready and about thirty people gather to eat, sitting on the ground with bowls of food that they eat with their fingers, dipping their fingers into the bowl of soup that they hold close to their mouth. They also place some of the cooked food on the bread/tortillas that they roll up and eat again with their fingers.

At the close of the meal, the villagers give a gift of pottery to the farm family, knowing that though they spin and weave wool that they do not make pottery. The farmer's uncle is one of the village potters. His son is married and his children enjoy playing with the farmer's daughter, their cousin. They appreciate the gift as they prepare to return home, looking forward to the next visit to the village in a few days. After a round of hugs, they walk back down the hill to their hut near the river, again a very pleasant and peaceful day in the sacred valley of Peru.

I journey into the upper world as a condor, using the Venus of Galgenberg Posture (Fig. 2.8) on the morning of the 18th:

I fly over the Sacred Valley. I look beside me and see my large wings. I am a condor. As I look down, I see small clusters of homes of the people of the valley. They are near the river, the Urubamba River. At the edge of these small villages, I see a pile of refuse, of vegetative wastes and animal bone and entrails, just what I seek to eat. I fly down to one of these piles to feast on what I can before a villager comes out to the pile. These people are hunter and gatherers and one thing that they have been digging in their gathering is the tubers that we now know as potatoes. As the potatoes sit in a basket near a hut, the eyes of the potatoes begin to grow, and when the wife/mother brings in these potatoes, she cuts out the eyes before cooking them and the eyes find their way out to the garbage pile. On these trips to the garbage pile, someone notices how the potato eyes have grown into potato plants, and as he digs in the garbage, he finds new potatoes. With this discovery, he takes some potato eyes to plant, but the only good soil is down near the river. So he takes the eyes down to the river edge to plant them.

He knows that the soil near the river is rich from the spring flooding of the water running off the mountains. The good topsoil washed away leaves the ground gravelly like above the village, where it is very hard to dig. These people have built their adobe huts up above the river where it does not flood. He knows that there is good soil at the bottom of the refuse pile where the garbage has rotted, so he tries something new. He takes the soil from the garbage pile and builds a stone wall around it so it will not wash away from the water coming off the mountain and in this soil he plants the potato eyes in a garden close to the village.

As I fly above the villages and as time passes, I see the beginning of the long wall of a terrace and behind the wall, the people are now putting their garbage and also the leaves and other plant debris from under the trees in the nearby jungle. They see that the soil under the jungle trees is thick and rich from the leaves that have fallen there. They carry the leaves and some of the soil down to put behind the wall where they now plant their potatoes. As time goes by, the rock wall gets higher and higher and the garden behind it grows wider and wider. They eventually realize that the wall is high enough and the garden wide enough to where they build a second wall at the far edge of the garden where it ends against the poor rocky soil.

During this time the people notice that when they throw a small ear of corn in the garbage pile, it too grows into a cornstalk and produces corn, thus they learn also to plant corn, and eventually other plants such as peppers from the seeds of the pepper. Thus, the garden terraces of the Sacred Valley grow, but it takes many generations and the growing population for the terraces to grow. Eventually, in the time of the Inka, the Inka will bring many men together to build the walls and make great gardens to feed his warriors and the people of the Valley.

* * *

Finally, I bring this journey to Peru to an end on January 19th, 2016, with the Feathered Serpent Initiation Posture (Fig. 2.9):

Again, I return to the young boy at Piscq and the shaman as they walk and talk of honoring their ancestors. I have many questions that the boy and the shaman may not have answers to or even have thought of, but I ask them through the boy. In communing with the ancestors, we go back to the time of the hunter-gatherer as if they had the answers, and there is considerable evidence that they lived longer than during this era of the Inka. As the hunter-gatherer moves into the era of the farmer, the people learn much about the production of food. What was wrong with this change in the way of life?

The shaman recognizes he spends much of his time gathering herbs for healing because of the many ailments of the people of the community, and that the people are not always healthy. Since they are dying earlier, they must not be as healthy as they were when they hunted and gathered. Now, in planting gardens, the variety of food we consume is much less. We now eat only a few dozen different foods at most while the hunter-gatherers ate several hundred. This is something I heard from a researcher about the diet of the Indians of the northwest coast. This researcher believes that this greater diversity in diet made the people of the time healthier.

In other parts of the world, the evolution from hunter-gatherer to farmer and domesticator of animals led to the depletion of the soil. Among the Inka and other indigenous peoples who continue to value the soil and who value reciprocity, of giving back to the Earth, they recognize and know how to maintain the soil's richness.

Another important factor that was lost in this transition to the era of the agriculturist is the value or attitude of cooperation that was lost to the attitude of control, control of the Earth that has led to conflict, war, and greater community stress and tension, of people striving for personal wealth and power versus working together for the health of the community. The boy and the shaman did not have this broader perspective that some now have in watching our destruction of humanity. Though it may be impossible to return to being hunter and gatherers, we can move in that direction in caring for the land and all life of the Earth, of venerating the interdependence of all things and reciprocity in maintaining this interdependence, of increasing the diversity of our diet, and of seeking to work together cooperatively.

CHAPTER 11

Learning the Power of Ecstatic Trance, New Mexico

This next to the last chapter is of the time I have spent in the sacred space of the kiva at the Cuyamungue Institute on the Pojoaque Pueblo north of Santa Fe, New Mexico. As I learned and experienced the power of ecstatic trance, these prior experiences of personal growth and healing freed me from some personal issues and enabled me to go beyond myself to face what we are doing to destroy the Earth. In moving towards healing the Earth, I needed to let go of the feeling of self-importance that I have experienced in my writing to learn and feel the power of being one with all life, with Gaia. Some of the following experiences are from my previous books, but in rereading them now, several years later, I find deeper understanding, first of letting go of the attitude of self-importance in order to experience effectively and teach ecstatic trance. Another early issue was the strength ecstatic trance offered me in dealing with prostate cancer. Here I see the relationship between these issues, the issues of self-importance, teaching, writing, and cancer. As a teacher, I needed to let go of feeling important, but coming from deep feelings of inadequacy, the new feeling of self-importance has felt good.

With a piece of my genetic heritage coming from the Sami Reindeer Herders, I have been reading about these people of Lappland. Regarding self-importance, Emilie Demant Hatt's foreword to the book by Johan Turi, himself a hunting and gathering Lapplander, tells of his wish to tell others of nomadic life, but... "the Finns and Lapps mocked him for working at anything so useless as writing. They looked upon it as a waste of time, as a thing that could produce no daily bread."[1] To Turi, writing was not an issue of feeling important but an issue of bridging the gap between the life of the nomadic people and the lack of understanding of others in the area who resented them. I think my writing is to offer a greater understanding of ecstatic trance in demonstrating its power to those who lack this understanding.

Soul Retrieval Workshop

The first sequence of experiences occurred in 2010 when I took part in the institute workshop led by Ki Salmen on Soul Retrieval. We experienced two or three ecstatic trance sessions each day.

On our first evening of 8/26/10, we used the Tlazolteotl Cleansing Posture (Fig. A.22):

The sound of Ki's rattle divides. I hear a deeper sound as if the wall of the kiva behind her was saying, "Tell me, tell me..." over and over. Tlazolteotl wants me to reveal something. I was sweating profusely for the entire 15 minutes until the end.

I think what I was supposed to face will become evident in two days when the Olmec Prince posture shows me I was ignoring my mouse spirit while taking myself too seriously. This next Calling the Spirits experience along with Tlazolteotl and the next three experiences leading up to the Olmec Prince experience led me to connect again with the innocent mouse spirit that became an important spirit guide to me many years ago.

This next experience was on the morning of 8/27/10 when we used the Calling the Spirits Posture (Fig. 2.10):

I join the coyote that I heard howling during the night. I become him and howled to/with the other coyotes. He is the trickster, the contrary. "What is he saying to me? What am I saying to me?"

What will eventually become clear from his trickster ways is to show me with laughter the ineffectiveness of feeling important.

On the afternoon of 8/27/10, we used the Mayan Oracle Divination Posture (Fig. A.14):

I find the Mayan Oracle sitting under a tree. She, with the motion of her head, beckons for me to sit down beside her. This tells me I can do the journey for myself. I look to her with the question of how many parts of me am I seeking. By putting her right hand behind her ear, she indicates for me to listen. As I listen, a coyote yips and howls. Then a second coyote yips and howls. Then a third one yips with no howl. I look to her questioningly, and she just shrugs her shoulders. This tells me that the coyote is to be my spirit guide, though I yet do not understand the issues or parts of myself that need to change.

On the afternoon of 8/28/10, we use the Jivaro South American Posture (Fig. A.10), an underworld posture:

I slide out the top of my head and along the ground outside of the kiva. As I glide along the ground on my back, a coyote paws at me. To get away from its paw, I float up onto a tree branch. There I see I am in a native village with huts of grass arranged in a circle. I float down to lie on the ground with the native dancers dancing around me. I am not the only one. All nine of us in the kiva are there lying with our feet towards the center. Smoke is rising from small geysers between us here and there, rising from the ground. Several coyotes are jumping around from geyser to geyser, pawing at them as if trying to stop them, but when the coyotes leave my geysers of smoke, I can breathe them in, the two or three that are next to me. They feel cool, a cool breeze, but they smell of smoke. Then I find myself back in my body with the cool breeze.

These geysers of smoke I later realize are cleansing the two or three parts or spirits I need to face, one of which is the mouse.

The next morning, on 8/29/10, we use the Olmec Prince Metamorphosis Posture (Fig. 2.3):

I can't hold the corn goddess posture, so I switch to the Olmec Prince. At both of my power spots, one across the ravine from the dormitory and the other beside the road on the way up to where we greet the morning sun, I am the mouse looking up at me. I can feel my nose twitching as I call, "Don't ignore me," over and over, "don't ignore me as you have done for so many years." Then I/we notice a coyote to my right with the mouse to my left. The coyote first puts his face right against mine, then he turns his back to me, repeating this over and over. This action tells me to not take myself so seriously.

Instructor Training Workshop

Then, a week later, I am part of Belinda Gore's initial instructor training workshop. On the morning of 10/5/10, we use the Lady of Cholula Divination Posture (Fig. A.11). The question I ask of the diviner is, "What do I offer to provide direction for myself, our group at home, and the Institute?"

I walk up the dirt road on my way to where we greet the sun and come to a woman, the Lady of Cholula, sitting on the stump of a tree beside the road. She motions for me to come and sit on a stump near her as she stands and straightens her skirt before she again sits on her stump facing me. I can feel lines of energy flowing from her entire body to mine and I feel the warmth. With this energy is the thought/message of doing what you have already been doing. I know what that is, but I want validation for what it is, teaching and writing. She says nothing, but my energy of these two concerns flows to her and her energy comes back saying, "Yes." She nods to me and I get up and continue walking along the dirt road.

That same afternoon we use the Calling the Spirits Posture (Fig. 2.10):

The airflow of my breathing catches a bee in it. The bee asks me to hold my breath for a moment so that it can escape to bring me the spirits I'm calling. I do and it leaves and soon returns, followed by a bear, another of my power animals. The bear wants me to feed it by gathering some honey. This places me in a bind as a beekeeper who has successfully kept bears from my hives.

My coyote guide is standing to one side laughing and though the bear is not laughing outwardly, inside he is. He has put me on the spot and I feel it. Though the bear is nurturing and strong, I still give him an electric shock instead of honey. He wants me to appreciate him.

Again, I see that I have put importance before oneness, of putting the collection of honey above the nurturance and strength of the bear.

On the morning of 10/6/10, we use the Bear Spirit, a healing posture (Fig. 2.1):

I become very hot. My breathing goes down to my groin. The sound of the rattle becomes bursts of sparks in my groin, more global than before when the spirits directed the sparks to the cancer cells in my prostate, healing and doing what they need to keep me healthy.

I initially wonder why the issue of my prostate cancer returns at this point. Now I realize that like cancer, the issue of self-importance was still eating at me. In the afternoon, we use the Olmec Prince Metamorphosis Posture (Fig. 2.3), and I am the rattler for the session. I ask the Olmec Prince what he offers me and whatever I become in this posture, what does it have to teach me.

I do not have much of an experience other than being a rattlesnake. I'm just coiled, with my rattle held up at the center of the coil. I am not especially threatening or threatened, just rattling. Near the end, I crawl towards the kiva door, waiting for it to open so I can leave. At first, I think this is humorous and I am not being serious but just trying to be funny, but then as the snake, I'm just being me, not trying to change the world, telling me I am okay with just being nothing special.

The next morning on 10/7/10, we use the Chiltan Spirits (Fig. A.3), another healing posture:

The time went quickly. First, I notice my enlarged breasts that have developed since I have been on a testosterone blocker. Then I feel very hot and this energy goes to Deborah, who I am facing in the group, sending my healing energy to her. Then I experience the spirits in a circle around me. At first, there are maybe 10 or 12 of them, but then there are at least 41, packed together shoulder to shoulder. As I inhale, they move in closer, blending into each other, and as I exhale, they step or drift back so they are not so tightly packed. They keep up this dance for a while, then those in front of me move in and pass through me before connecting with those behind me. They divide into two circles, one to my left and one to my right, like cell division. I am at the point between them where the two circles of spirits touch. Then the two groups divide similarly into four before they again connect at the point where the four circles touch. Then they break apart and move back again into one circle. This dance then repeats several times with the spirits passing through me. I am being healed. The cell division stops, and the divided cells join in a healthy healing circle dancing around me.

Later that day, we use the Lady of Thessaly Posture (Fig. A.12), an initiation posture:

I am sitting on a rock somewhere along the coast of Greece, watching the water. I roll and lurch forward, stretching out my arms as I dive into the water with my arms forward. I glide through the water and can breathe underwater. I see a shipwreck and glide through a window or hole in the wreckage and along the deck. I notice I have fins and a tail fin. I head towards a cave and go in. The light is flowing into the cave from a hole in its ceiling. There is a beach in the cave and I glide up onto it. As I leave the water, I again become human. I climb a ladder out of the cave and find myself in the bright sun. I lie down in the sun when the drumming ends.

The message is that I am reborn in the sun's light after I glide through and leave the wreckage behind.

The next day on 10/8/10, we use the Singing Shaman Posture (Fig. A.19):

I see the drones of many bagpipes, then the pipes or spires of Shiprock. I am walking from the north towards Shiprock. I see spirits flying or floating around and in between the pipes, spires, or masts of the rock. As I approach the scree of the rock and start climbing it, I find at the top a medicine man with his head back, facing east, calling the spirits of the east. As I approach him, he turns to me and welcomes me. He smudges me and beckons me to join him in calling the spirits. As we do this, I feel exhilarated. When we finish together, we climb off the scree. At the bottom, he motions for me to continue north as he returns to his place at the base of Shiprock. I saunter to the north.

This experience is another validation that I am going in the right direction with my life, walking north, the direction of my elder years and spiritual self.

Masked Trance Dance Workshop

The following year, I return to Cuyamungue for the advanced training workshop to become an instructor of Ecstatic Trance, the Masked Trance Dance Workshop, again led by Belinda Gore. Our sessions begin on 7/18/11 using the Bear Spirit Posture (Fig. 2.1):

As I stand, I see waves or clouds of energy rising from the rattle, warm energy that settles over me from my head and slowly settling or drifting down through my body like clouds, wave after wave of strengthening energy. As the waves settle, I feel myself being slowly pulled to the ground, my knees touching the ground, and then my hands. I crawl forward and after a few strides, I realize I am a bear, lumbering along towards my cave. I find another bear, a nurturing female, in the cave, the one on whose lap I have sat before and off of whose tits I have nursed. This time I sit next to her, feeling strong and comfortable. We are equals. I sit there for a while, then I stand and walk to the entrance of the cave, tip my head back, open my mouth, and roar. The drumming ended.

This experience and the workshop take me beyond healing and into the realm of becoming one with the Earth, of becoming one with or equal to the bear, not superior to the bear.

* * *

The next morning on 7/19/11 we use the Olmec Prince metamorphosis posture (Fig. 2.3):

I see two hind feet of something kicking, pushing dirt out of a hole at the rhythm of the drum. I become that something, maybe a groundhog. It is too dark underground to see, but I am in a den with roots that I can smell coming down from the roof. I nibble on one and it tastes like sassafras. Then I dig along in the tunnel and come to other roots. Most of them I cannot identify. Then I come to a beech root. I know the flavor of beech. I soon come up out of a hole and can see I am near our pond. I wander over and take a drink. It feels refreshing.

Again, I am identifying with and becoming one with the Earth by becoming a groundhog.

Later that day, on 7/19/11, we use the Chiltan Spirits Healing Posture (Fig. A.3):

I feel myself opening up. I see the spirits as wisps of smoke drifting around the room. They come to me, filing into my chest, filing in order of how they were called, beginning with the spirits of the east. All are sedate except for the spirits of the south who are dancing around and have a lot of playful energy. After a while, I see all the spirits dancing in a circle. The spirits of the south continue to dance with a lot of energy. The spirits then stop dancing and are just milling around except for those of the south who come and face me. This time they come with more seriousness as if they are trying to tell me something.

Returning to this experience several years later, I see they are telling me of the magical energy of childhood, an energy that is usually suppressed by rationality but now needs to be remembered and recovered in order to be part of all life on Earth.

* * *

On 7/20/11, we use the Sami Underworld Posture (Fig. A.16):

The time went quickly, even though I had a cramp in my arm while drumming. Where I am standing, I sink into the Earth, down, down. Soon my legs are hanging from the roof of a cave, kicking around looking for a foothold, but none is to be found. Soon, as I sink further, I just drop a few feet to the ground. I feel exhausted and lie down. There is a bear robe/rug on the ground that I lay on. The next thing I know is that a bear is lying next to me. I am a bear and we are embracing. It feels like we are a comfortable old married couple. She then rolls over on her back with her four legs up in the air. I get up and wander out of the cave, lumbering along slowly, just watching and looking at the world. I come to a rotting tree and start digging or scrapping for bugs. The drumming then ends.

Again, I am experiencing a sense of oneness with the bear.

That afternoon we use the Jama Coaque Diviner Posture (Fig. A.8):

I go into a pavilion in the jungle where Jama Coaque sits. The pavilion has open sides and a banana-frond roof. I sit down before the diviner and ask him for the message of my current journey. He jumps up quickly and dances lively, like the spirits of the south. I continue to sit and look up at him. He then motions for me to get up and follow. He goes down the several steps to the village square and motions for one villager to drum and others to dance, with the youth dancing with great energy. The shaman's wife then comes out and they dance together more sedately. I also find the energy to dance, but my wife is not there.

Again, the message I receive is to carry the ecstatic trance experience to the youth who are most able to experience it fully.

* * *

The next day, on 7/21/11, we use the Bear Spirit Healing Posture (Fig. 2.1). The day before, we start to make paper-mache masks of our power animal, and mine is the bear. At breakfast, Richard of the group reports to me that during the night a mouse had eaten off one ear of my mask.

During this experience, I first hear the bear say, Ouch! The mouse is biting off my ear. The word sacrifice comes to mind. The bear does not resist being chewed on, but what is the sacrifice or benefit of the sacrifice? Then my hearing aid plays its little tune in my left ear, saying the battery has gone dead, the same ear that the mouse chewed off. Then I hear growling. My first thought is that the sound is from a motorcycle, but then I realize it sounds more like a bear.

In the talking circle, Sue, who is leading us in the Bear Spirit ceremony, suggests that losing the bear's ear has something to do with my deafness? Then someone in the group squeals, pointing to a bear mask hanging on the Kiva wall above me. A mouse pops out from behind the mask and scurries out the door. This causes considerable laughter.

Later that day, we use the Tlazoteotl Cleansing Posture (Fig. A.22):

As several times before, I enter a small chapel, adobe, with a low rectangular altar, behind which I see a priestess of Tlazoteotl sitting on a cushion. Each previous time, I have an offering for her. This time, as I stand in front of her I become incredibly hot and melt like wax into a puddle on the floor. There is a low door to her left that on previous occasions I go through to meet spirits dancing around me with various messages. This time the spirits come out of the south and become mice running playfully all over me, sitting on my shoulders, and scampering up and down my body. I become the bear who now embraces or gives freedom to the mice to run over him. He honors each of them. I realize the bear from the west opens himself to valuing the playful childlike spirits of the south. It brings unity to the west and south. With this, I decide I am going to paint mice all over my bear costume.

On 7/22/11, we use the Tennessee Man divination posture (A.21):

I remember little. I remember walking slowly uphill to the south and the mice scamper over me. I take one at a time in my right hand and honor it by offering it to the six directions and then letting it go as I offer it to Mother Earth.

Since I have ignored my mouse spirit guide for several years, I now realize that I need to honor it and show it respect.

Later that day, on 7/22/11, we use the Cernavoda Healing Postures (Fig. A.1):

I go into the woods and first I see a wild boar rooting with its nose in the ground to find roots. I am then rooting as a boar. He asks me a question. I don't remember what, but I answer "Keep on going." I continue rooting, come to a wall, turn to the left, and root along the wall. I keep on going and never find the end of the wall.

The answer I get from this experience is that there is no end to my search for spiritual growth. There is always more to learn.

For our last session on 7/23/11, before we choreograph and perform the Masked Trance Dance, choreographed from all of our experiences, we use the Feathered Serpent Initiation Posture (Fig. 2.9):

I am standing in front of a Mayan Pyramid and an enormous snake, covering about a third of the steps of the pyramid, is crawling down the steps. Then I am at the top of the pyramid, standing over a hole that I presume is where the snake came from. I go down the hole and am lowered down into the pyramid where I find a large well-lit room with an altar, a large table-like altar with a large bowl with smoke or steam coming from it. I get up and lay on the altar. Somehow, I know I am supposed to do this. First, someone cuts off my head and then cuts me open and takes out my heart. They then hold it in the smoke coming from the bowl, smoke for cleansing. Then they put my heart back inside me and sew my head back on. I go over to the bowl and cleanse myself in the smoke. I leave the temple; go down the steps and across the open area of the village to the edge of the jungle. I know I don't want to walk into the jungle as a person, so get down on all fours and become a jaguar. I walk through the jungle to a river where I get a drink and then I sit on the riverbank, cleansing and licking my fur.

This typical death-rebirth experience offers me a cleansing experience that brings me into the natural world of the jungle.

Soul Retrieval Workshop

The following year, in August 2012, I organize and lead a workshop at the Institute on Soul Retrieval. On 7/26/12, in the morning, in preparing myself for leading the workshop, sitting alone in the kiva below the causa, I use the Chiltan Spirit Posture (Fig. A.3).

I am standing with the sun hitting my right cheek. The spirits are coming in on the sunbeam. They flow around me and focus their energy on my left arm, which is doing the rattling. I become incredibly hot from their presence and feel them entering me, opening yet draining my energy at the same time, i.e., I feel myself standing taller yet melting.

In melting, I feel I am sacrificing something of myself to the group, my self-importance, as I stand tall.

*   *   *

That afternoon, as the group first convenes, we use the Bear Spirit Healing Posture (Fig. 2.1):

At first, my body feels out of sync with the rattling. I want to slow the rattling to let my body catch up to it, but I know that would disrupt others. So I let my body bounce and feel the spirit of Richard within me. I have been in several workshops with Richard and while in trance, he frequently bounces with the rattling as he stands. This brings me in sync with the rattle. Though I think I stop bouncing, at one point I open my eyes and realize that I am still bouncing. Each bounce hammers down the energy coming into my body, and I become extremely hot. With this growing energy, I feel alive in trance through to the end. I forgot I am rattling and once or twice I feel myself slowing down, which brings me briefly out of trance.

Later that day, with Marsha drumming, we use the Lady of Cholula Divination Posture (Fig. A.11):

I go quickly into a deep trance and forget what my first two images are. Then I am in Millheim, parallel parking my car (a black car) in front of the Green Drake. I then am in the coffee shop talking to a friend, asking him a question, but I forget about what. I feel as if I am in a very deep trance.

This friend is very much into sustainable living and has studied the ways of the hunter-gatherers. I frequently turn to him with questions of living in oneness with the Earth.

We begin the next day, 7/27/12, using the Hallstatt Warrior Initiation Posture (Fig. 2.4):

I am back in Germany around 5000 BC. This time my ancestor, who previously got me to lead the men on a hunt, takes me to meet his family. In their hut, situated against a rock cliff, I meet his wife; a young daughter, about 10 years old; and a son, about 8 years old. The wife and daughter are busy around a central fire with a large pot hanging over it. The son takes a liking to me and grabs me by the hand, pulling me outdoors. He wants to show me how he can throw his spear. After a while, his mother calls and we go in for lunch, a stew with meat and vegetables. It is very tasty with a somewhat sweet flavor. We eat quickly, but then I am asked what I am thinking about, and I answer I am wondering about the sweetness of the stew and pull out a small berry. I ask what it is. The daughter says it is a lingonberry. After a while, she too pulls me outside and takes me to show me where she picks the lingonberries. I want to stay with them longer, but I had to end the rattling.

I feel very close to the people in this experience, my hunting and gathering ancestors, from whom I have learned a lot of the ways of the hunter-gatherers.

As the workshop continues on the next day, 7/28/12, we use the Sami Underworld Posture (Fig. A.16):

I go into a cave with beautiful stalactites and stalagmites, with light shining from a hole at the top. I'm in a boat in this water cave. Going a little farther into the cave, I'm in total darkness, then I come out into a small lake and can see fish, birds, and other animals. I go into the forest and it is beautiful and spiritual. I am at the shore, which is also beautiful and spiritual, then it becomes the beautiful and spiritual desert. I then find myself in the far north, where I find beautiful and spiritual glaciers. I feel myself rise above all the crap of the world, finding beauty and spirituality everywhere. I then go to my garden, where I can work spiritually, freeing myself from the crap of the world. Yet I know this is easier said than done.

In both this and the previous experience, I find beauty in life, in oneness with the Earth, finding what life should be like.

* * *

Later that day, we use the Feathered Serpent Initiation Posture (Fig. 2.9):

We are all sitting around an evening fire in a wooded grove. I notice something rising from me, little flakes of something that drift towards the fire and rise in the rising air. They catch fire with the glowing ash rising higher. Someone gets up and starts chasing the glowing ashes, catching them and putting them in a jar, laughing all the time. He then brings me the jar, saying "you lost something." I say good riddance and throw the jar into the fire. We all continue to celebrate and enjoy each other and the fire while the clown who caught the ashes continues to dance around, laughing. At one point or at first, I think it is my grandson catching and collecting fireflies, then instead I see him as a Heyoehkah rising above it all.

A necessary part of oneness with the Earth is to not feel the weight of an unnecessary sense of seriousness. The Earth is to be enjoyed as it knows what we need and nurtures us. Can I say good riddance to the heaviness that I carry much of the time in my feelings of disgust for the greed and destruction I see around me?

The next morning we use the Venus of Galgenberg upper world posture (Fig. 2.8):

I rise and fly over our garden where my wife is working. I then go beyond the garden to the quarry and see the enormous hole in the ground. I continue north to where drilling derricks are drilling for gas and then to the west where the pipeline is being laid. From high up, I can see large urban areas and the polluting glow of night lights. As I rise higher and higher, the glow of artificial light disappears and I see the beautiful glow of Mother Earth.

Also, while flying between the quarry, the gas wells, the

pipeline, and the glow of cities, I see beautiful mountains, bodies of water, forests, and open green places.

My struggle with letting go of the disgust I feel towards what is happening to the Earth continues, and the reminder of the beauty of the Earth is fleeting.

We continue with the Olmec Prince Metamorphosis Posture (Fig. 2.3) on 7/29/12:

While drumming, I hear a flapping sound and see a bird, then birds, flying, darting back and forth while they catch insects in flight. They are barn swallows. They return to their mud nests high in the rafters of the barn to feed their young. I become one of them, dart to eat insects, and return to the rafters, realizing that I spend my time high up and rarely, if ever, do I go down to Earth. This brings me as a human a feeling of sadness of not connecting with the Earth, yet I am of the Earth as the swallow feeding its young.

I am experiencing oneness with the Earth, this time as a barn swallow. The metamorphosis brings alive within me the experience of the swallow.

The Men's Conclave at Cuyamungue

The following year, I return to the Institute in the fall to attend the first men's conclave. On 10/3/13, the group of men begins with the Chiltan Spirits Healing Posture (Fig. A.3):

As I inhale, I pull the vibrating spirits towards me. As I exhale, they stop coming towards me but vibrate more and grow bigger. This continues for quite a while. Eventually, as I inhale, they flow into me, and as more and more of them enter me, I vibrate as they are doing. As I vibrate more and more, my body disintegrates, flows out of the kiva and in all directions. I become one with the junipers around the kiva. I, as the juniper, vibrate and the vibrating energy flows through the branches to the berries. The berries vibrate and grow bigger. Then a coyote comes to the juniper and eats the berries. I become the coyote. He soon stops outside the kiva and howls for a while before coming in. He is one within me as I stand in the kiva, howling. Soon my body quiets and the spirits are again outside of but around me as the drumming ends. I feel the circle of interdependency, the circle with the juniper and the coyote brings alive our oneness with the Earth.

The next morning, 10/4/13, we use the Sami Warrior Underworld Posture (Fig. A.16):

I slide or slither into a hole as a snake and follow it down to a den where I have room to curl or coil up with another snake among the roots of a tree. The den is dark and comfortable. I feel some moisture around the roots that trickle near me and from which I drink. Then I have no memory, must have fallen asleep.

These experiences of oneness with the Earth bring me a vivid sense of harmony and lightness in living.

The next day, we experimented with a new posture that I previously had determined to be a middle-world posture, the Højby Posture (Fig. A.7) I found in a book from Denmark:

I fly over the hill to the river gorge. On the other side of the gorge, I see a stalking mountain lion moving along the wall of the gorge seemingly aware of the colors and finding a good match to his own color in the wall where he then stands motionless and watches. A short distance from him is a hole in the wall. It is afternoon, and a coyote comes out with several pups. The mountain lion remains motionless for a long time. Near the end, one little one ventures a little farther from the den beyond his mother, and the lion leaps for it, gets it and carries it off.

Again, I experience the interdependency of life on Earth, of Gaia, and feel the sacrifice the coyote made to the mountain lion as part of this interdependency.

Later that same day, we used the Venus of Galgenberg Upper World Posture (Fig. 2.8):

I first see spirits rising out of me, but I stay on the land. Eventually, I see the Earth before me, but it still feels as if I am on the land. I then see the left portion of the Earth in the sunlight and the right in darkness as I peer down at the Earth. I notice a tall building in a city, NYC, the Empire State Building, and then I see on the other side a tall sequoia. I find myself fascinated by these two towering things, comparing them as if I am supposed to choose. The Empire State Building has an orangish-red aura, as if I see it through a thermo-lens, seeing it as it gives off heat. The aura around the sequoia is bluish-green. Then I am a raven building a nest near the top of the sequoia, flying freely to get sticks and twigs and back to the nest. It feels free to fly. The drum missed a beat, and I find myself as a raven perched on top of the fence next to me, cocking my head back and forth, listening to the drumming. When the drumming again evens out, I fly north towards a stand of ponderosa pines, then I am back on the land as me with an energy line waving with the beat of the drum, pulling me upwards towards the sun as in one of the Nordic upper world images, feeling the wave waving me up.

I had no hesitancy in deciding to choose the sequoia. The heat of the Empire State Building left me cold.

The men's conclave ends on 10/6/13 with the Bear Spirit Healing Posture (Fig. 2.1):

I see the kiva full of fireflies and as I inhale, the light from the fireflies streams towards me and enters me through my nose. As I exhale, the fireflies' light grows brighter. As I inhale, the fireflies rise with their light shining. As they reach the top, the light dims, and as I exhale, they drop to recover their light.

These five sequences of experiences at the Cuyamungue Institute show the change that has occurred within me over the four years of experiencing ecstatic trance at the institute. Initially, I had personal issues I needed to resolve before I could let go of my self-centeredness to experience a sense of oneness with the Earth. As Thomas Berry says, "to save the Earth from the destruction we are imposing on it, we need to feel again a part of all life on Earth and not superior to it. To gain this sense of harmony, we need to reconnect with our ancient ancestors, the ways of the hunter-gatherers and their shamanic ways, ways of power that flow from being part of all life on Earth."[2]

CHAPTER 12

Epilogue

Where has my journey across three continents taken me? At each stop on this journey, I have visited both ancient spirits and contemporary spirits of the land. In almost every case the ancient spirits of the hunting and gathering era have something of great importance to tell me, of how peaceful their life was while venerating the Great Earth Mother, of being one with everything of the Earth, both alive and inanimate, of not putting themselves superior to other life, and of not attempting to control the life and Earth around them for their personal benefit. Greed was rare. The hunter-gatherers were givers, giving whatever they had to the community and its visitors. Celebrations often were to give away all that they had.

Why was this message to me from the spirits so consistent? The message was an answer to the question I have held for a few years: How can we survive the global climate catastrophe, how can we survive the impending demise of our way of life and the impending doom of our species?

Some messages I receive from these ancestral spirits show me the transition from the hunter and gatherer's Garden of Eden into the world of the agriculturist and the domesticator of animals, the world when humans left behind their beautiful garden in their attempt to do better than what the Great Earth Mother had provided them for many thousands of years. Some might consider this evolution from hunting and gathering to the planting of gardens and domesticating animals as progress, but in hindsight, it has led only to the destruction of the Earth's resources, the extinction of a huge number of the species of life that have lived upon the Earth for many millennia, and now the impending decimation of the human species.

To again live the life of the hunter-gatherer would be impossible because of the environment and species we have destroyed and because our numbers have become too great. But a significant decrease in the Earth's human population seems inevitable, whether because of disease, starvation, war, or natural or manmade disasters. Over the last ten thousand years, we have learned a lot from agriculture. Much of what we have learned is what we have done wrong, but also what we have gained from this knowledge is how to farm in a more natural and sustainable way, by giving back to the Earth through such techniques as composting and mulching, ways that now allows us to end the use of chemical fertilizers. We also learn that we can end the use of pesticides and herbicides by what we plant with what. Cities seem much less sustainable, but even their rooftop gardens are a beginning. The diversity of what we eat is much less than what the hunter-gatherers ate, and this lack of diversity has had a negative impact on our health. As our population decreases, and the great quantities of food are no longer shipped to us over great distances, we will again explore what else around us is available to eat. There is much for us to learn, and asking the spirits of our ancient ancestors, as did our ancestors who lived in harmony with the Earth, can lead us in the right direction.

This message relates to our survival and the survival of our children and grandchildren. The time has come when our lives and the lives of future generations are in great jeopardy. Yet the foolishness of greed and the hoarding financial wealth by taking from the Earth continues for many. These hoarders are fearful of the future and too afraid to listen to this message. They react with anger and even violence in their corrupt ways to gain more money, money that provides no actual security for the future. They react in conniving ways to control what they believe can be their future, a future that is quickly coming to an end.

The message of how, for thousands of years, people knew how to live in oneness with the Earth and all life on Earth needs to be heard. This ancient life was a nurturing life of compassion and cooperation. Though interpersonal conflicts occasionally arose, it was a life of peace. What the Earth provided them sustained them, a life maintained by giving back to the Earth as much, if not more, than they took, of venerating the Earth and all life on Earth.

APPENDIX
The Ecstatic Postures

Figure A.1. Couple from Cernavoda
Healing Posture

Figure A.2. Chalchihuitlique
Metamorphosis Posture

Figure A.3. Chiltan Spirits
Healing Posture

Figure A.4. Danish Realm of the Dead Posture

Figure A.5. Feathered Serpent Initiation Posture of Odin

Figure A.6. Freyja Initiation Posture

Figure A.7. Højby Middle World Posture

APPENDIX: THE ECSTATIC POSTURES 271

Figure A.8. Jama-Coaque Diviner Posture

Figure A.9. Jama-Coaque Metamorphosis Posture

Figure A.10. Jivaro Underworld Posture

Figure A.11. Lady of Cholula Divination Posture

Figure A.12. Lady of Thessaly Initiation Posture

Figure A.13. Lascaux Cave Upper World Posture

Figure A.14. Mayan Oracle Divination Posture

Figure A.15. Nyborg Man Feathered Serpent Initiation Posture

APPENDIX: THE ECSTATIC POSTURES 273

Figure A.16. Sami Underworld Posture

Figure A.17. Sekhmet Initiation Posture

Figure A.18. Shawabty Initiation Posture

Figure A.19. Singing Shaman Posture

Figure A.20. Tandragee Idol Healing Posture

Figure A.21. Tennessee Man Divination Posture

APPENDIX: THE ECSTATIC POSTURES 275

Figure A.22. Tlazolteotl Healing Posture

Notes

Chapter 1: The Spirits
1. Gebser, *Ever-Present Origin*, 45-60.
2. De Quincey, *Radical Nature*, 101.
3. Gebser, *Ever-Present Origin*, 61-73.
4. Ibid., 73-97.
5. *The Economist*, "What is Spooky Action at a Distance?" March 16, 2017.
6. Sheldrake, *The Presence of the Past*.
7. Laszlo, *The Akashic Experience*.
8. Braden, *The Divine Matrix*.
9. Laszlo, *The Akashic Experience*, 250.
10. Waggoner, *Lucid Dreaming*, 78-79.
11. Castaneda, *The Eagle's Gift*.
12. Chambers, *Beowulf*, 16.
13. Laszlo, *The Akashic Experience*, 248.
14. Eisler, *The Chalice and the Blade*, 71.
15. Gimbutas, *The Goddesses and Gods of Old Europe*.
16. Sahlins, *Stone Age Economics*, 33.
17. Goodman, *Ecstasy, Ritual, and Alternate Reality*, 17-18.
18. Clow, *The Mayan Code*, 115.

Chapter 2: Ecstatic Trance
1. Gore, *Ecstatic Body Postures*, 6-8.
2. Ibid., 12.

3. Ibid., 32-35.
4. Ibid.
5. Gore, *The Ecstatic Experience*.
6. Goodman, *Where the Spirits Ride the Wind*, 156-157.
7. Coles, *Shadows of a Northern Past*, 136-137.
8. Ibid.
9. Ibid.

Chapter 3: Living in Peace with the Goddess: The Ynglings of Sweden

1. Coles, *Shadows of a Northern Past*, 136-137.
2. Ibid.
3. Ibid.
4. Ibid.
5. Ibid.
6. Ibid.

Chapter 5: Learning the Ways of the Chumash Shaman of California

1. Gamble, *The Chumash World at European Contact*, 31.
2. Ibid., 78.

Chapter 7: Venerating the De Dannan's Circle of Light, Ireland

1. Gregory, *Gods and Fighting Men*.
2. Malone, *Discovering Ancient Ireland*, 16.
3. Kinsella, *The Tain*.

Chapter 8: Learning the Esopus Way of Oneness with the Earth, New York

1. Van Buren, *A History of Ulster County Under the Dominion of the Dutch*, 79.
2. Weslager, *The Delaware Indians*, 51.
3. Ibid., 62.

Chapter 9: Living in Oneness with the Sami Reindeer, Finland

1. Byock, *Saga of the Volsungs.*

Chapter 11: Learning the Power of Ecstatic Trance, New Mexico

1. Turi, *Turi's Book of Lappland,* 12.
2. Berry, *The Dream of the Earth,* 211.

Glossary

Nordic Words

Alfdene: The young boy who listens to the village shaman and learns about the dwelling place of peace, Griðbustaðr, after death, knowledge that he shares with his friend.

Asgard: The domain of the Æsir in the Sky World.

Astrid: The Earthly wife of Sclyd Scefing, a marriage encouraged by Gefjon. She raises Beow, the son of Gefjon and Sclyd, who is to become the second king of Denmark.

Baldr: The most beautiful and gentle son of Odin and Frigg, who dreams of his own death, a death caused by the trickery of Loki. He returns after Ragnarǫk to become the god of gods.

Bastu: Sauna.

berserkers: Warriors who work themselves up into a frenzy before battle and are thought to be invulnerable.

Beow: The son of Scyld Scefing, who became the second great king of Denmark.

Bragi: A son of Odin and the god of poetry, the husband of Idunn.

Eikþyrnir: The stag that lives on the roof of the great hall at Valhalla and provides the warriors with an endless supply of water that drips from his antlers.

Freyja: The sister of Freyr and daughter of Njord. She is one of the fertility goddesses of the Vanir who goes with her father to live among the Æsir.

Freyr: The brother of Freyja and the son of Njord. He is one of the fertility gods of the Vanir who goes with his father to live among the Æsir.

Gefjon: The fertility goddess who plows the land from Sweden to form the Danish island of Zealand. She is the wife of Scyld Scefing, the first king of Denmark, and the caretaker of those women who die as virgins.

Gratabjǫð: Literally, "weeping fields." The fields of the goddess Gefjon that are along Harmagil, "the gorge of sorrow," where those women who died as virgins reside and can see across the gorge the warriors who died in their first battle.

Griðbustaðr: Literally, "the dwelling place of peace," the place where those who understand and practice the compassionate magic of the Vanir reside after death.

Gylfi: The king of Sweden who makes a deal with Gefjon that gives her the land that she plows out to sea that becomes part of Denmark.

Harmagil: Literally, "the gorge of sorrow." From this gorge rises the smell of sulfur from Niflheim. It separates Gratabjǫð, "weeping fields" from "the cliff of lucklessness."

Heiðrun: The goat that resides atop the hall in Valhalla that provides an endless supply of mead to Odin's warriors.

Heimdallr: The Vanir god who lives among the Æsir, and who is given the position of guarding Bifröst, the rainbow bridge, because of his acute hearing. He could hear the grass growing.

Hel: The daughter of Loki and Angrboða whom Odin throws into the underworld to care for those who died not honorably in battle, but of illness and old age. Hel (sometimes called Helheim) is also the name of the underworld ruled by Hel.

Hliðskjálf: Odin's high seat from which he can see over the nine worlds.

Hrethel: The son of Gylfi.

Hrungnir: The giant who injures Thor in battle.

Hygelac: King of the Geats and the son of Hrethel.

Hygd: Wife of Hygelac, queen of the Geats.

Idunn: The Vanir goddess who keeps the gods young by giving them the golden apples from a tree in her garden and who teaches the healing powers of plants and trees. Her husband is Bragi, god of poetry.

Ivaldi: The father of the dwarfs who make Freyr's magical ship.

Jötunheimr: The domain in Midgard that is the realm of the giants.

Kavsir: The wisest of the gods who first brews mead from the spittle of the gods. The god who recognizes the purpose of the burned net that the gods found in the hiding place of Loki.

Loki: The trickster god skilled in shape-shifting and the father of Jörmungandr, Fenrir, and Hel. His confrontations with the gods because of their hypocrisy leads to his restraint until Ragnarǫk, the final battle that brings an end to the world. He causes earthquakes.

Midgard: The Middle world; our world as we know it.

Mjölnir: The hammer of Thor that causes lightning when thrown by Thor. When thrown, it returns to his hand.

Moðir: The mother of the Vanir, of Njord and grandmother of Freyja and Freyr, and Great Earth Mother.

Nanna: Baldr's wife and one of the Vanir.

Njord: A god of the Vanir and father of Freyr and Freyja. The god of the wind and sea who marries the giantess Skaðr.

Oðr: Freyja's wandering husband.

Odin: The god of gods, the Allfather, and the father of Thor and Baldr.

Ragnarǫk: The final battle between the gods and their adversaries that brings an end to the world as we know it and the rebirth of Baldr.

Sæmingr: The king of Norway at the time of Gylfi

Scyld Scefing: The first King of Denmark and husband of the goddess Gefjon.

seiðr: The magic of the Vanir.

Sigyn: Loki's wife who remains faithful to him until the end. When Loki is restrained with a poisonous snake hanging over his head, Sigyn catches the dripping poison in a bowl.

Skjǫld: The first king of the Skjǫldung whose son is Scyld.

Skjǫldung: One of the major ancient tribes of Nordic people of Denmark and Southern Sweden, centered on what is now Gammel

Lejre, Denmark.

Skaði: The daughter of the giant Thiazi and the wife of Njord.

Skiðblaðnir: The ship of Freyr that always has wind for its sails but can be folded small enough to be carried in his pocket.

tack: Thank you.

Thiazi: The giant who kidnaps Idunn, who afterwards is returned to the gods by the shape-shifting powers of Loki. Thiazi is killed in a fire in Asgard.

Thor: The son of Odin whose mother is Fjorgyn. He is the husband of Sif. This warrior god brings lightning and thunder with the throw of his hammer.

Thorgil: Thorsteen's older brother who is a retainer to King Gylfi.

Thorstain: Thorsteen's father.

Thorsteen: Geat warrior to King Gylfi, who was killed by a Norwegian warrior because of being distracted from fighting by his love for Vigdis, as illustrated in the petroglyph at Tanum.

Ullr: The Vanir god of archery and skiing, the creative son of Njord and Sif, and the grandson of Moðir.

Valhalla: The realm in the Sky World that is the home to those who die valiantly in battle and is presided over by Odin.

Vanir: The race of fertility gods and goddesses that predates the Æsir. Because of their magical powers, their battles with the physically powerful Æsir end in stalemates.

Var: The goddess of oaths and marriage.

vejde: The plant woad that produces a blue dye.

Vigdis: Daughter of the Geat farmer Vivil who followed the ways of Freyja but fell in love with and married the warrior Thorsteen who soon after the marriage died not as a hero in battle and is mourned by Vigdis as shown in the petroglyph at Tanum.

Vilborg: Vigdis's mother.

Vitar: Vigdis's brother, who is a retainer to the king.

Vivil: Vigdis's father.

volva: A seeress or shamaness and practitioner of seiðr.
Ynglings: One of the major ancient tribes of Nordic people of Sweden based in what is now Gammel Uppsala, Sweden.

Words of the Chumash

antap: A society of the wealthy class of Chumash.
paxa: The village leader of the dance celebrations, second to the chief.
tomols: The large plank canoes of the Chumash.

Gaelic Words

Beltaine: The celebration of the coming of Spring, May Day.
carrick: rock.
Dagda: The son of Danu, sometimes thought of as the father of Danu.
Danu: The mother goddess, the Great Mother, of the De Danaan.
De Danaan: The early hunting and gathering inhabitants of Ireland who, upon the arrival of the Gael, went into hiding in the otherworld, the Sidhe.
dun: A fortress of the otherworld. A fortress.
Gael: The later invaders of Ireland.
Lugh: An ancient Irish deity, the master of all skills.
Lughmasadh: The celebration of the harvest and the coming of autumn.
Mananna: A trickster of the otherworld who entices the Gael to come to the otherworld.
Mebd: The Queen of Connacht who organized the cattle raid of Cooley.
Tadg: The Gael who was kidnapped and when he went looking for his home was blown out to sea where he comes to an island of the De Danaan and meets Mananna.
sidhe: The otherworld, the world of the De Danaan.

Germanic Words

Andvaranaut: Golden ring of Brünhilde tempered in urine of mare, giving the wearer seductive power over men.
Atli: A hun, invader of Sweden who became king of the Yngling.
Brünhilde: Amazon warrior. Drank the urine of Grani to grow hair on body to gain the strength of a man. Fire around her domain kept men away except for the powerful warrior, Sigurd, whose powerful horse, Grani, could breach the fire.
Grani: Powerful horse, ancestor to Sleipnr, who could jump the fire surrounding Brünhilde's domain.
Grimild: Sorceress and mother of Gudrun.
Gudrun: Sigurd's and Atli's wife.
Gunnar: The sworn friend to Sigurd, who shifted shape to look like Sigurd to marry Brünhilde.
Nibelung: The ancient tribe of Germany.
Sigurd: Struggled for the love of Brünhilde, husband of Gudrun, and friend of Gunnar. The strongest of warriors.
Skjǫldung: The ancient tribe of Southern Sweden and Denmark.
Sleipnir: Odin's eight-legged horse.
Yngling: The ancient tribe of Eastern Sweden.

Esopus Lenape Words

Maytscheetschank: spirit

Sami Words

aahka: woman.
goahte: The tent dwelling in which the Sami live.

Joeksaahka: Third daughter of Maadteraahka, who protects the animals and the hunt, especially the reindeer.

Maadteraahka: The Earth Mother.

Okaahka: The daughter of Maadteraahka who protects the doorway to the goahte.

Saaraahka: The second daughter of Maadteraahka who brings sacredness to the hearth.

siida: Sami encampment of several families.

Words of the Inka

Apu-punchau: The Sun God
Coricancha: The Sun
Ekeko: The God of Prosperity
Mama Quocha: The Goddess of Water
M'itra: The policy of the Inka that a third of all that is produced goes to the Inka and warriors, a third goes to the community, and a third is for the family. It is also the requirement that each boy over the age of 15 years will spend part of each year working for the Inka.
Pachamama: Great Earth Mother

Bibliography

Berry, Thomas. *The Dream of the Earth*. Berkeley, CA: Counterpoint, 2006.

Braden, Gregg. *The Divine Matrix: Bridging Time, Space, Miracles, and Belief*. Carlsbad, CA.: Hay House, 2007.

Brink, Nicholas. *The Power of Ecstatic Trance: Practices for Healing, Spiritual Growth, and Accessing the Universal Mind*. Rochester, VT: Bear & Co., 2012.

———. *Baldr's Magic: The Power of Norse Shamanism and Ecstatic Trance*, Rochester, VT: Bear & Co., 2013.

———. *Beowulf's Ecstatic Trance Magic: Accessing the Archaic Powers of the Universal Mind*. Rochester, VT: Bear & Co., 2016.

———. *Trance Journeys of the Hunter-Gatherers: Ecstatic Practices to Reconnect with the Great Mother and Heal the Earth*. Rochester, VT: Bear & Co., 2016.

Broadbent, Noel D. *Lapps and Labyrinths: Sami Prehistory, Colonization and Culture Resilience*. Washington DC: Arctic Studies Center, 2010.

Byock, Jesse (translator). *Saga of the Volsungs: The Norse Epic of Sigurd the Dragon Slayer*. Berkeley, CA: University of California Press, 1990.

Castaneda, Carlos. *The Eagle's Gift*. New York: Washington Square Press, 1991.

Chambers, R. W. *Beowulf: An Introduction to the Study of the Poem*. New York, NY: Cambridge University Press, 1959.

Clow, Barbara Hand. *The Mayan Code: Time Acceleration and Awakening the World Mind*. Rochester, VT: Bear & Co., 2007.

———. *The Mind Chronicles: A Visionary Guide into Past Lives.* Rochester, VT: Bear & Co., 2006.

Coles, John. *Shadows of A Northern Past: Rock Carvings of Bohuslän and Østfold.* Oxford, UK: Oxbow Books, 2005.

De Quincey, Christian. *Radical Nature: The Soul of Matter.* Rochester, VT: Park Street Press, 2002.

Eisler, Riane. *The Chalice and the Blade.* San Francisco: Harper San Francisco, 1988.

Emerson, V. F., "Can Belief Systems Influence Behavior? Some Implications of Research on Meditation," *Newsletter Review,* R. M. Bucke Memorial Society, 5:20-32.

Gamble, Lynn. *The Chumash World at European Contact: Power, Trade and Feasting Among Complex Hunter-Gatherers.* Berkeley, CA: University of California Press, 2011.

Gebser, J. *The Ever-Present Origin.* Athens, OH: Ohio University Press, 1985.

Gimbutas, Marija. *The Goddesses and Gods of Old Europe: Myths and Cult Images.* Berkeley, CA: University of California Press, 1982.

Goodman, Felicitas. *Ecstasy, Ritual, and Alternate Reality: Religion in a Pluralistic World.* Bloomington, IN: Indiana University Press, 1990.

———. *Where the Spirits Ride the Wind: Trance Journeys and Other Ecstatic Experiences.* Bloomington, IN: Indiana University Press, 1990.

Gore, Belinda. *Ecstatic Body Postures: An Alternate Reality Workbook.* Rochester, VT: Bear & Co., 1995.

———. *The Ecstatic Experience: Healing Postures for Spirit Journeys,* Rochester, VT: Bear & Co., 2009.

Gregory, Lady. *Gods and Fighting Men.* Buckinghamshire, UK: Colin Smythe Ltd., 1979.

Kinsella, Thomas (translator). *The Tain.* Oxford, UK: Oxford University Press, 1990.

Laszlo, Ervin. *The Akashic Experience: Science and the Cosmic Memory Field.* Rochester, VT: Inner Traditions, 2009.

Laszlo, Ervin and A. Combs, eds. *Thomas Berry: Dreamer of the Earth: The Spiritual Ecology of the Father of Environmentalism.* Rochester, VT: Inner Traditions, 2011.

Malone, Kelli Ann. *Discovering Ancient Ireland.* Dublin, Ireland: History Press Ireland, 1988.

Margolin, Malcolm. *The Ohlone Way: Indian Life in the San Francisco-Monterey Bay Area.* Berkeley, CA: Heyday Books, 1978.

Sahlins, Marshall. *Stone Age Economics.* New York: Routledge Press, 1974.

Sheldrake, Rupert. *The Presence of the Past: Morphic Resonance and the Habits of Nature.* Rochester, VT: Park Street Press, 1995.

The Economist Magazine. "What is Spooky Action at a Distance?" March 16, 2017.

Turi, Johan. *Turi's Book of Lappland.* Costerhout, The Netherlands: Anthropological Publications, 1931.

Van Buren, Augustus. *A History of Ulster County Under Dominion of the Dutch.* Astoria, NY: J. C. & A. L. Fawcett, Inc, 1989.

Waggoner, Robert. *Lucid Dreaming: Gateway to the Inner Self.* Needham, MA: Moment Point Press, 2009.

Weslager, C. A. *The Delaware Indians: A History.* New Brunswick, NJ: Rutgers University Press, 1990.

www.ingramcontent.com/pod-product-compliance
Lightning Source LLC
Chambersburg PA
CBHW030135170426
43199CB00008B/76